Law and Visual Jurisprudence

Volume 2

The Series Law and Visual Jurisprudence seeks to harness the diverse and innovative work within and across the boundaries of law, jurisprudence, and the visual in various contexts and manifestations. It seeks to bring together a range of diverse and at the same time cumulative research traditions related to these fields to identify fertile avenues for interdisciplinary research.

In our everyday lives, we experience law as a system of signs. Representations of legality are visually manifested in the materiality of things we see and spatially experience. Methodologically, aesthetic texts of legality semiotically emerge as examples of visual jurisprudence and illustrate the constitutive waltz between social governance, formal law, and materiality.

In its tangled relationship to regulation, the visual complexity of law is semiotically articulated as an ongoing process of meaning imbued with symbolism, memory, and cultural markers. Through a legal semiotics framework of symbolic articulation and analysis, the examination of law that happens in conjunction with the visual expands understandings of how law is crafted and takes root. Additionally, such an inquiry challenges the positivist view of law based within the courtroom as disciplinary spatial practices, the observation of everyday phenomenon, and the visible tethering of regulation to cultural understandings of legality generate a framework of visual jurisprudence. The Series seeks to enliven such frameworks as those in which law happens precisely without formal institutions of law and through which a visual-based methodology of law is crafted through everyday instances of ordinariness that contextualize the relationship between law, culture, and banality.

The Series welcomes proposals – be they edited collections or single-authored monographs – emphasizing the contingency and fluidity of legal concepts, stressing the existence of overlapping, competing and coexisting legal discourses, proposing critical approaches to law and the visual, identifying and discussing issues, proposing solutions to problems, offering analyses in areas such as legal semiotics, jurisprudence, and visual approaches to law.

Keywords: Legal Visual Studies, Popular Culture, Everyday Law, Spatiality, Legal Semiotics, Legal Geography, Legal Materiality, Legal Transplant, Bioethics, Cyber Law, Communication, Heritage and Territory, Design, Marketing, Packaging, Digitalization, Arts.

More information about this series at http://www.springer.com/series/16413

Eduardo C. B. Bittar

Semiotics, Law & Art

Between Theory of Justice and Theory of Law

Springer

Eduardo C. B. Bittar
Faculty of Law
University of São Paulo
São Paulo, Brazil

ISSN 2662-4532 ISSN 2662-4540 (electronic)
Law and Visual Jurisprudence
ISBN 978-3-030-58879-3 ISBN 978-3-030-58880-9 (eBook)
https://doi.org/10.1007/978-3-030-58880-9

This Springer imprint is published by the registered company Springer Nature Switzerland AG.
The registered company address is: Gewerbestrasse 11, 6330 Cham, Switzerland

"In the domain of relations between Semiotics and Art, but also between Art and Law, the Author is dedicated to an innovative enterprise"
("Dans le domaine des relations entre la Sémiotique et l'Art, mais aussi entre l'Art et le Droit, l'Auteur est dédié à une entreprise innovante")

—**François Ost**, Professeur Émérite invité à l'Université Saint-louis, Bruxelles, Bélgique

"Western iconography and the symbolic character of Law are explored in this judicious, innovative and reflective publication"
("L'iconographie occidentale et le caractère symbolique du Droit sont explorés dans cet ouvrage judicieux, novateur et réfléchi")

—**Antoine Garapon**, Magistrat, Secrétaire Général de l'Institut des Hautes Études sur la Justice, France, Paris

"Semiotics, Law and Art is a jus-philosophical work that talks about other works, the works of art, invoking poetic and sensitive language, doing justice to this interface between the Theory of Law and the Theory of Justice"
("A reinvenção plausível de um internal point of view, autonomamente comprometido com as exigências específicas do Direito, não é hoje sustentável sem a assimilação lograda das possibilidades e dos recursos de um contexto materialmente situado, inscrito por inteiro na realidade histórico-social e assim mesmo co-determinado por factores naturais, institucionais e culturais. É o exercício in progress desta dialéctica interno/externo (com as perspectivas externas a trazerem-nos por um lado os recursos da semiótica narrativa de Greimas e por outro lado a inter-relação constitutiva com as experiências estéticas da pintura, da arquitectura, do teatro e da literatura) que confere a Semiótica, Direito e Arte de Eduardo Bittar um significado precioso, tanto mais precioso de resto quanto preocupado com a exigência de construir uma ponte (reciprocamente produtiva) entre os universos da Teoria do Direito e da(s) Teoria(s)da Justiça...")

—**José Manuel Aroso Linhares**, Full Professor of the Faculty of Law of the University of Coimbra, Coimbra, Portugal

Part I
General Part

Chapter 1
Semiotics, Law and Art

1.1 Introduction: Between Art and Law

A new horizon of research has opened up in recent years considering the input of the relation between *(law & art)*. There are many was of approaching the theme of *art* in its correlation with *law*. The many ways of approaching this correlation allowing fields of connection between *art* and *law* very different from one another, which are: (i) *art* as an *object of the protection* of law which treats the creations of culture, art, literature and sciences, and, therefore, as an object of the *Law of the Author*;[1] (ii) *art* as the main protagonist, and as an object of *Right to Culture*;[2] (iii) *art* as an object of protection, considered as historical-cultural patrimony, and, in this regard, an object of investigation of the *Law of artistic, historical and cultural patrimony*; (iv) *Law* as an object of art, *art* being a *way of representation* of the historical forms of Law, especially through the statuary of justice, symbols of justice, paintings of justice, liturgy of justice, architecture of the palaces of justice,[3] making up the so-called *Legal Symbolism*;[4] (v) *art* as a *cultural document*, and thus, as memory and a concrete way to the access and knowledge of the history of justice;[5] (vi) *art* as a *tool* of diffusion and education of citizenship and justice, especially considering the various forms of violence, oppression injustice and the absence of recognition.[6]

---

[1] *Vide* Bittar (2015a).

[2] *Vide Institute of Art & Law* (http://www.ial.uk.com, Accessed 11.03.2020).

[3] *Cf.* Radbruch (1997), p. 225.

[4] *Cf.* Filho and Toscano (2011), p. 24.

[5] *Cf.* da Cunha (2010), p. 220.

[6] *Cf.* Gorsdorf (2014), p. 60.

E. C. B. Bittar, *Semiotics, Law & Art*, Law and Visual Jurisprudence 2,
https://doi.org/10.1007/978-3-030-58880-9_1

There are, therefore, at the very least six great lines of work, which allow you to connect *art* and *law*,[7] given that the potential contained in each of these lines clearly defines what can be understood and conceived as a delimitation of possible concrete approaches. It must be highlighted, however, that the relation between art and law whether as science, or as a discipline of study, is not recent.[8] This means that the relation between art and law was not established today, but on the other hand, one cannot deny the opening of current times for the close studies in this field.[9]

Consequently, one can see that there are deep and interesting ways of connection between *art* and *law,* and each of these ways of exchange between *art* and *law* opens the field to a border of different work, being four main trends of approximation,[10] that go from *Copyright* to *Right to Culture,* from *History of Law* to the *History of Justice*, from *Law of Artistic and Cultural Patrimony* to *Environmental Law,* from *Methodology of Teaching of Human Rights* to the *Human Rights Education,* and of these further studies of *Law and Literature, Law and Cinema, Law and Architecture.* Considered as 'epistemological walls', 'conceptual barriers, 'theorist obstacles, between areas of knowing as 'distant', and, at the same time, as 'close', wanting to revitalise the strangeness caused by proximity so noticeable, yet invisible, to place itself in the field of study of *significant meaning* for the *experience of Law and Justice.*

That field of work in which it focuses, properly, this research intends to define the concern of creating bridges between *Justice* and *Aesthetics,*[11] and, to this precise extent, the relation between *art* and *law* slides to the field of the relation between two great areas of philosophical knowledge, which are, the *Philosophy of Law* and *Aesthetic Philosophy.*[12] Indeed, this same strangeness caused by the approximation between *Law* and *Art* is the same contained in the word *Aesthetics* itself, which should be estranged and revisited, to be known and understood. So, the title of the example—as Fig. 1.1 shows when one sees the building of the *Supreme Court of Justice*, in Washington D.C. (USA), one notices that there are representations of justice expressed in the architecture of justice, which pose multiple challenges to its decodification and understanding. Here, *Art* and *Aesthetics* are convened to fulfil an important role of giving tangible existence to the idea of Justice. Therefore, among

[7]"Entre le droit et l'esthétique, ou science du beau, les relations sont minces, bien que le droit protege les arts et les lettres, qu'il ne repugne pas nécessairement à user de l'art poétique pour s'exprimer et que d'aucuns s'efforce de dégager des correspondances entre le système juridique et les formes artistiques d'une même civilization où d'une même société globale..." ("Between law and aesthetics, or the science of the beautiful, the relationships are thin, although the law protects the arts and letters, which it does not necessarily shy away from using poetic art to express itself and none strive to find connections between the legal system and the artistic forms of the same civilization or of the same global society ... ", *translation*) (Terré 2015, p. 26).

[8]*Vide* Filho and Toscano (2011), pp. 21–29.

[9]*Cf.* Franca Filho (2016), p. 92.

[10]*Cf.* Filho and Toscano (2011), p. 21.

[11]*Cf.* Hermann (2005), p. 33. *See too* Dewey (2010), pp. 125–126.

[12]*Cf.* da Cunha (2010), p. 219.

Fig. 1.1 Authority of Law, James Earle Fraser, *Supreme Court of Justice*, Right Side, Washington, D.C., United States of America, Personal archive: Photography: © pyo

the various existing and functionally differing professions, the professions of Law are heavily characterised by *symbols*. But, interestingly, these same symbols are, in the majority of cases, unfamiliar by Legal professionals.

The word *Aesthetics*, in its etymological use (*aisthésis,* gr.) evokes, as Lucia Santaella states, the dimension of the sensations.[13] But, the domain of knowing that is formed around the term Aesthetics, evokes something which belongs to modern vocabulary, indicating the creation of the discipline which it dedicates itself to knowing the universe of the sensitive, dating back to Alexander Baumgarten and Imanuel Kant.[14] The most common meaning of the term *Aesthetics* evokes one, consequently, which is commonly known, from modernity, in the last 250 years, as the knowledge of the arts.

But, when one looks to narrow down the analysis, from the concept of *Aesthetics* held in the thinking of French philosopher Jacques Rancière, it is clear that the word *Aesthetics*, however, does not only remit a discipline about the 'beautiful', but takes us to the understanding by *thinking*[15] the *way of being* objects of art.[16] This means the understanding of the *aesthetic regime,*[17] in other words, the understanding of which art is able to lay down a *new world of understandings*, a *universe apart,*

[13] *Cf.* Santaella (2007), p. 254.

[14] *Cf.* Hermann (2005), p. 34. *See too* Rancière (2009a), p. 12.

[15] *Cf.* Rancière (2009a), pp. 12–13.

[16] *Cf.* Rancière (2009b), p. 32.

[17] *Cf.* Rancière (2011), p. 17.

considering the transfusing of the objective universe, about which art functions creatively, forming a new reality from its *languages.* It is, consequently, in the field of *freedom* and of *creation* that it meets the *aesthetic* dimension, free from rules and made up from its own field of meanings.[18] And it is from its own languages that the arts will form the possibility of *doing differently*,[19] which it attributes to the works of art its avant-garde nature and its capacity of transformation, or even, to the works of art its innovative, visionary and/or revolutionary nature.[20]

It is intended here to work on the idea that the power of citizenship can be explored in various ways, and that 'the spheres and the practices of art', as an armoury of concepts, categories and experiences, can represent an important path (*methods*) to the creation, expression, interpretation and evaluation of *concepts, sensitivities* and *fundamental sensations* to express concerns connected to the *fight and conquest of rights,* to the *forms of* injustice, to the *exercise of* citizenship, and to the protest before the *violation of human rights*. In this regard, if it is to stimulate here a boundary which is still recent in the area of Law—moreover, for the world teaching of Law-[21] and, for this reason, it will bring an original contribution not only in the placement of the *purpose of research*, but also in the *methodological way* of its approach and execution, as this is traditionally centred in the reading of texts and the commentaries of legislation and other sources of Law; here, wishing to consider the symbolic *and aesthetic universe* as a source of the spreading of content and of the expression of *feelings* and *perceptions* of great symbolic value for the *social representation* of justice and of injustice.

The way it is conceived, the *purpose of* research being a typical attribution in any traditional area of knowledge in Law, can only be the privileged object of speculation in the open and reflective field of the *Philosophy of Law*,[22] here understood on the path of development of the concerns of a *Social and Critical Philosophy of Law*. The North American semioticist Bernard Jackson wishes to see the *Semiotics of Law* descend from the great stem of the *Philosophy of Law,* in its realist perspective.[23] In the work *Philosophy of* Law, Portuguese jurist Paulo Ferreira da Cunha dedicates Chap. 3 to *Semiotics of Law,* pointing out that his studies can be very fruitful and promising.[24] By means of the *Semiotics of* Law, the signs can be better worked,

[18] *Cf.* Rancière (2009b), p. 34.

[19] *Cf.* Rancière (2009b), p. 17.

[20] *Cf.* Rancière (2009b), p. 23.

[21] "Law schools are already experimenting with incorporating the arts (...)" (Rapoport 2013, p. 104).

[22] *Cf.* Radbruch (1997), p. 222.

[23] "À ces diverses égards, il paraît légitime d´affirmer que la *Sémiotique*, et en particulier la *Sémiotique du Droit*, relève non du courant positiviste mais de la tradition réaliste de la *Philosophie du droit*" ("In these various respects, it seems legitimate to affirm that *Semiotics*, and in particular *Semiotics of Law*, does not come from the positivist current but from the realistic tradition of the *Philosophy of Law - translation*") (Jackson 1988, p. 64).

[24] *Cf.* da Cunha (2013), p. 209.

understood and the meanings can be better unveiled.[25] Depending on this vision, it is not possible, in any way, to disregard the analytical-social power contained in each *aesthetic* text, and the capacity that each *aesthetic work* owns to anchor the diagnostics of time and the perceptions of reality—to judge it, for example, for the value found in the philosophy of Axel Honneth—leading to content of social change even before the systemisation of empirical data or of the closure of strict analytical frameworks.[26] For this reason, in this choice, decisive contribution is already given, which the perspective of the theoretical-methodological analysis of the *Critical Theory of Society* (*Frankfurt Schüle*) completes by providing the *modus* of conceiving the purpose, being essentially interdisciplinary.

The methodological cutting here implied makes this approach a 'territory of encounters', a 'fertile field of crossings', and considers the borders and scientific boundaries as temporariness of specialised reflection, indispensable resources for scientific precision, but no limits on the task of 'thinking at the border', considering the input of *Semiotics*, of *Philosophy*, of *History*, of *Anthropology*, of *Sociology* to think of art, therefore, for the field of *Aesthetics*. For this reason, the 'thinking at the border' helps to form an *ensemble* of approaches, removing the relation between *Law and Art* from the impoverishment of its approximation, noting in the body of this problematic relation more than the *pastiche* as a way of work, but more the *dignity of art* as a *rebellious-object*[27] to its theoretic limits. This is because, in order to move closer to Art, Law cannot violate it, but it should be moved with all the sensitivity that the matter requires.

1.2 Semiotics, Law and Art

The jurist is always grappling with *signs*, *symbols* and *interpretations*. So, the question of language is of utmost importance for the jurist. To this extent, a *Semiotic Theory* undertakes an important task in the capacity of serving as a style, in the great field of investigations of the *Philosophy of Law*,[28] for the approach of the relation between Law and Art. Since the previous study, entitled Legal Language: semiotics, discourse and law (2015, 6.ed.), resulting from the *Doctorate Thesis* (1999), it could already take into account that, from a Greimasian perspective, *Semiotics* takes care of the *systems of significance*.[29] As Jacques Fontanille identifies,[30] the *texts* (*verbal*; *nonverbal*) have an interest in *Semiotics*, and the *processes of significance* are studied by it. And, here, as François Rastier identifies, in fact, repeating a finding

[25] *Cf.* da Cunha (2013), p. 209.
[26] *Cf.* Honneth (2015).
[27] *See* Rancière (2011), p. 66.
[28] *Cf.* Bittar (2015b), p. 74.
[29] *Cf.* Bittar (2015b), p. 32.
[30] *See* Fontanille (2015a), p. 29.

already accomplished by Louis Hjelmslev,[31] the notion of the *system* is costly to the comprehension of the complex role that the *game between the signs* establishes to form *processes of significance.*[32] This emphasised, in the reading of John Deely, how Semiotics takes into account the *action of signs* in social life.[33]

As far as the *Arts* express themselves on a basis of diverse *artistic languages,*[34] it is clear that the understanding of the study about the connection between *artistic languages* and *legal language* should interest the jurist.[35] This is something that even the studies of the *History of Law* recognise, as does Robert Jacob, in the investigation entitled *Images of Justice*.[36] What should become clear is that the great field of investigations of the *Philosophy of Law* takes into account 'Right' as a problem, and 'Justice' as a question, seeking to treat some aspects here in a more targeted form which affect these big questions of speculation, not being able to devote itself to the *Semiotics of Law*[37] if not the investigation about the field of the *texts* which are relevant to the analysis of 'Law' and of 'Justice'.

It is curious to note that, in the text entitled *Semiotics and Social Sciences* (1976)—of the authorship of Algirdas Julien Greimas, and written in collaboration with Éric Landowski-[38] and, also, in the text entitled *La société réfléchie* (1989)—of the authorship of Éric Landowski-,[39] in the context called *Belle Époque* of *Social-Semiotics,*[40] the French semioticist Eric Landowski evaluates how the *Semiotics of Law* is a field of studies still emerging, made up of its own grammar and dictionary,[41] and how it should structure itself advancing modestly in the face of the field of study of studies which are predecessors to it, and before the magnitude and vastness of questions which are encompassed by its areas of work and investigation.

[31]*Cf.* Hjelmslev (1975a), p. 201.

[32]"Une langue est faite d´un corpus de textes oraux ou écrits et d´un système" ("A language is made up of a corpus of oral or written texts and a system"—*translation*) (Rastier 2017, p. 06).

[33]*Cf.* Deely (1990), p. 41.

[34]*Cf.* Agrest and Gandelsonas (2013), p. 134. See too Landowski: "El objeto de la semiótica, dijimos, es la *significación*" ("The object of semiotics, we said, is *significance*"—*translation*) (Landowski 1993, pp. 76–77).

[35]*Cf.* Greimas and Landowski (1981), p. 75.

[36]*See* Jacob (1994), p. 10.

[37]*Cf.* Bittar (2015b), p. 76.

[38]*Vide* Greimas and Landowski (1981), p. 74 et ss.

[39]"Buscando ubicarse en un nível de generalidade comparable al de la sociologia jurídica, de la fenomenologia jurídica o incluso de la filosofia del derecho, la semiótica jurídica, disciplina naciente, no puede sino mostrar una grand modéstia frente a sus antecesores" ("Seeking to locate itself at a level of generality comparable to that of legal sociology, legal phenomenology, or even the philosophy of law, legal semiotics, a nascent discipline, cannot but show great modesty vis-à-vis its predecessors"—*translation*) (Landowski 1993, p. 75).

[40]"Ce fut un de ces moments-clefs où la 'socio-sémiotique', du moins sous sa première forme, celle qu´aujourd´hui j´appelle de la 'belle époque', commença à prendre ses contours propres" ("It was one of those key moments when 'socio-semiotics', at least in its first form, which I today call 'belle epoque', began to take on its own contours"—*translation*) (Landowski 2017, p. 07).

[41]*Cf.* Greimas and Landowski (1981), p. 76.

Furthermore, apart from a *Semiotics of Law*, a *Semiotics of Art* becomes increasingly accentuated, in the work of Algirdas Julien Greimas,[42] considering the role which *De l'imperfection* (1987)[43] had in the sense of breaking the dichotomy between *feeling* and *thinking*,[44] moreover of breaking through the border between the daily life and the sensitive.[45] And this maturity of the *Semiotics of Law*, and, also, of a *Semiotics of Art*, is what now becomes possible the intersecting of its reciprocal theoretical borders, with the diversified field of Greimasian *Semiotics*.[46]

Following closely by what semioticist Lucia Santaella states, to the contrary of being a field of weakened studies, *Semiotics* had its appearance *boom* in the years 1970–1980,[47] and has now found new niches, new perspectives new unfoldings, continuing a field of fruitful and current studies, research and investigation.[48] In this line, equally, the Greimasian and post-Greimasian semiotic theory went on pluralizing and strengthening itself, since its affirmation, in the decades 1980s and 1990s of the twentieth century, currently leaning towards to renewed perspectives, reacting with dynamism to the difficulties proposed by its own challenges of the new media and formats of communication.[49]

From the view of its objective, the *Semiotics of Law* deals with the *systems of significance* that is relevant to the purposes of *legal discourse*,[50] which mobilise the *legal system* to make changes, adaptations and transformations.[51] However, from this view, in the previous study, it can already move forward in semiotic research concerning the universes of normative discourse, of bureaucratic discourse, of decision-making discourse and of scientific discourse. It is during the project of

---

[42] *Vide* Nöth (2005), p. 145.

[43] "Le domaine du beau ne cesse dès lors de s´étendre à côté du culte de l´artiste et de sa mission, lc spectateur afirme ses droits aux sentiments esthétiques, l´art, dont l´essence semblait enfouie dans les objets créés, penètre la vie qui devient le lieu de rencontres et d´événéments" ("The domain of beauty therefore continues to expand alongside the cult of the artist and his mission, the viewer asserts his rights to aesthetic feelings, art, the essence of which seemed to be buried in the objects created, penetrates life which becomes the place of meetings and events"—*translation*) (Greimas 1987, p. 71).

[44] *Cf.* Landowski (2005), p. 95.

[45] "Ainsi, la figurativité n´est pas une simple ornamentation des choses, elle est cet écran du paraître dont la vertu consiste à entr´ouvrir, à laisser, entrevoir, grâce ou à cause de son imperfection, comme une possibilité d´outre-sens" ("Thus, figurativity is not a simple ornamentation of things, it is this screen of the paraitre whose virtue consists of opening, allowing, a glimpse, thanks to or because of its imperfection, as a possibility of other- meanings"—*translation*) (Greimas 1987, p. 78).

[46] *Cf.* Pietroforte (2016), p. 12.

[47] *Cf.* Santaella (2016a), p. 23.

[48] *Cf.* Santaella (2016b), p. 32.

[49] *Vide* Landowski (2005), pp. 93–106; Landowski (2017), pp. 01–20, epublications.unilim.fr, Accessed 11/03/2020.

[50] *Cf.* Bittar (2015b), p. 62.

[51] *Cf.* Greimas and Landowski (1981), p. 79.

continuity and *deepening* of the *Semiotics of Law*, whose objective is specific,[52] towards the analysis of discourse, that it becomes possible, now, through this work, to proceed to an analysis of the field of *aesthetic discourses* about *justice* and *injustice*. Here, it will dedicate more attention to the *nonverbal signs*, than to *verbal signs*, these that previously have already been sufficiently addressed and discussed.[53]

This study is established here where culture was shifted towards expressing the *sign* about the *just* and the *unjust,*[54] understanding that the field of work *Law and Art,* either in *law's art* or in *art's law*, the example of reflections established by Costas Douzinas, in *Law and the Image,*[55] are projects which possess their ground-breaking studies, as well as innovations by Authors, in very distinct theoretical streams divided in Brazil mainly between Peircean and Greimasian lines,[56] but equally valuable when it comes to adding some contribution to the pertaining speculation of *nonverbal signs*, appreciating the study of the paintings, of the architecture, of the sculptures, of cinema, of theatre and its connections to the world of meaning, of significance and of narration[57] about the *just* and the *unjust.*

1.3 Semiotics, Languages and Art

If the contemporary semiotic studies are divided between multiple streams and theoretical perspectives, they also spread to diverse theoretical fields, among which it qualifies as a recent field, the *Semiotics of Art*. This is a clear finding, of which the fields of studies of *Semiotics*—as Jacques Fontanille observes[58]—are expanded, creating connections and inspiring and founding mixings of new analysis for the diverse areas of study. It is in this respect that a *Semiotics of Law* should be concerned with the acquisitions brought and developed by the field of studies of the *Semiotics of Art,*[59] towards the more precise understanding of *nonverbal signs*—also

[52]*Cf.* Greimas and Landowski (1981), p. 80.

[53]*Cf.* Bittar (2015b), p. 83 and ss.

[54]*Cf.* Leonardi Filho (2006), p. 70.

[55]"The relationship between law and art can be analytically distinguished into two components: law´s art, the ways in which political and legal systems have shaped, used, and regulated images and art, and art´s law, the representation of law, justice, and other legal themes in art" (Douzinas and Nead 1999, p. 11).

[56]*Cf.* Santaella (2016b), p. 27.

[57]*Cf.* Courtés (1979), p. 41.

[58]*Cf.* Fontanille (2015a), p. 22.

[59]"C´est dire qu´elle serait plutôt une sémiotique discursive ou textuelle qui a été *appliquée* à l´art; et qu´on manquerait cruellement d´une Sémiotique proprement artistique, impliquée éventuellement dans des discours ou dans des textes, ou dans d´autres choses encore, qu´on définira plus loin ici" ("This means that it is rather a discursive or textual semiotics which has been applied to art; and that we would be sorely lacking in a properly artistic Semiotics, possibly involved in

called *artistic languages*-[60] by which *content* relevant to the debate about 'Law' and 'Justice' is expressed.

This implies an attitude of *epistemological counter-effort* of surpassing traditional *logocentrism,* which was established in the culture of Law, as Bernard Jackson points out.[61] Therefore, it can be concluded that two branches of new knowledge, as semioticists Lucia Santaella and Winffried Nöth note,[62] are built into its borders, the *Semiotics of Law* and the *Semiotics of Art*, in an interdisciplinary way—given that both dimensions of *Semiotics* open themselves broadly towards the future—[63] replacing itself with this task to improve the quality of the approach of the study of the *nonverbal signs* in the area of 'Law'.

Here, the idea of *text* is key for the whole of *Semiotics,*[64] and, consequently, the main focus of semioticists, as Jacques Fontanille observes.[65] It could not be any different, when it comes to the *Semiotics of art*, considering otherwise that *aesthetic text* is the *unit of meaning* that takes a look at the possibility of the development of the analysis undertaken here. If the idea of text is key to a *Semiotics of Art,* it becomes, of as much fundamental importance affirming that the arts work through *syncretic texts*[66] (an opera, in music; a staged play, in the theatre; a film, in the cinema; a work of art, in painting; a palace, in architecture), where *complex performances* stand out,[67] here making use of terminology extracted from the *Semiotics* of Algirdas Julien Greimas.[68] This is, indeed, one of the most important

speeches or texts, or in other things, which we will define further here"—*translation*) (Tore 2011, p. 01).

[60]*Cf.* Calabrese (2015), p. 33.

[61]*See* Jackson (1988), p. 63.

[62]*Vide* Santaella and Nöth (1998), p. 97.

[63]"Plus qu´une recherche en sémiotique de l´art, les pages qui précèdent n´ont pu qu´indiquer un terrain exceptionnellement vaste, destiné à des études de venir" ("More than a research in semiotics of art, the preceding pages could only indicate an exceptionally large field, intended for future studies"—*translation*) (Tore 2011, p. 07).

[64]"Si le *morphème est l´unité linguistique élémentaire,* le *texte* est l´unité *minimale* d´analyse, car le global determine le local" ("If the morpheme is the elementary linguistic unit, the text is the minimal unit of analysis, because the global determines the local"—*translation*) (Rastier 2017, p. 06).

[65]*Cf.* Fontanille (2015b), p. 85.

[66]"Dans ce cas la *sémiotique textuelle* ne se distingue pas en principe de la sémiotique discursive. Les deux termes – texte et discours – peuvent être indifféremment appliqués pour designer l´axe syntagmatique des sémiotiques non linguistiques: un rituel, un ballet peuvent être considerés comme texte ou comme discours" "In this case textual semiotics is not distinguished in principle from discursive semiotics. ("The two terms - text and speech - can be applied indifferently to designate the syntagmatic axis of non-linguistic semiotics: a ritual, a ballet can be considered as text or as speech"—*translation*) (Greimas and Courtés 1993, pp. 389–390, *Texte*).

[67]"L´objet de la sémiotique n´est pas fait des signes, mais des performances complexes, comme l´ opéra, les rituels, etc."("The object of semiotics is not signs, but complex performances, like opera, rituals, etc."—*translation*) (Rastier 2017, p. 06).

[68]*Vide* Greimas and Courtés (1993), p. 344, *Sémiotique*.

and innovative conquests of the Greimasian semiotic vision.[69] Therefore, it is clear that the *work of art* asserts itself as a *syncretic text*, an object of analysis of the *Semiotics of Art*, from its various viewpoints, pointing to a field full of studies, still emerging, and of great significance for a series of other sciences and knowledge, the example of the relation of possible cooperation established between the *Semiotics of Art* and the *Semiotics of Law*.

Following closely by what François Rastier states, the *semiotic text* strings together, completes and *makes-sense* where it is tied to *social practices.*[70] Also, in the comprehension of Julia Kristeva, there is no *social practice* that is not composed and entangled from the *processes of language*, from religious rituals to artistic practices, from handicrafts to customs, from practices of the advertising of goods to legal rituals.[71] Therefore, further progress could be made to understand that *aesthetic texts* are related to *social practices* determined in time and space, in addition to being connected to *meanings* which are present in the *historical, social, cultural, political* and *economic* environments. Now, what is clear is that there is a huge *semiotic load*, within the western tradition, also pointed out by the *History of Law*, and whose symbolic power can be used by *Semiotics*.

Consequently the importance of moving forwards, in the *Semiotics of Art*, in connection with the *History of Art,*[72] with the *Anthropology of Art,*[73] with the *Sociology of Art*, in order to carry out this reflective exercise in the most appropriate manner possible. Umberto Eco goes on to state that it is impossible to understand the role of Semiotics without associating it directly to a *Cultural Anthropology,*[74] a statement that can be confirmed in diverse studies in the area of *Anthropology.*[75] And what can be seen in this area of investigation is that the collection of *languages* supports all people, cultures, nations, traditions, societies in expressing their ideas and emotions by means of *signs,* making them audible, visible and tactile, as Cliford Geertz determines.[76] It can therefore be said:

> The work of art is a sign that also communicates how it is done.[77]

---

[69] *Cf.* Fiorin (2009), p. 33.

[70] "Le texte isolé n´a pas plus d´existence que le mot ou la phrase isolés: pour être produit et compris, il doit être rapporté à un genre et à un discours, et par là à un type de pratique sociale" ("The isolated text has no more existence than the isolated word or sentence: to be produced and understood, it must be related to a genre and a discourse, and thereby to a type of social practice"—*translation*) (Rastier 2017, p. 08).

[71] *See* Kristeva (1981), p. 35.

[72] "Historians of art often believe that they deal only with objects. In reality, these objects are organized, given life and meaning, by relations. Even though they are frequently unconscious, these involve choices that both history and criticism should require to be elaborated" (Didi-Huberman 1999, p. 71).

[73] *Cf.* Mathias (2016), p. 19.

[74] *Cf.* Eco (1990), p. 169.

[75] *Cf.* Mathias (2016), p. 72.

[76] *Cf.* Geertz (2014), p. 123.

[77] *Cf.* Eco (1990), p. 50.

1.4 Symbolization, Modalities of Signs and Art

The concept of *sign* broadly exhibits the dimension of the semiotic universe.[78] The *sign*—and this Louis Hjelmslev has already pointed out—[79] is the bearer of *meaning,* and, for this reason, it is sustained as a central and fundamental concept for all the development of semiotic research, emphasising the *plane of expression* and the *plane of content.*[80] Furthermore, the concept of *sign* reminds us that *something is in place of something else* (*aliquid stat pro aliquo*),[81] indeed, as Umberto Eco determines.[82] *Being in place of* indicates that the *sign* has an *abstractive function* in social exchanges, being capable of *representing* what is *absent*, elevating everything to the level of languages that can be carried by them, but also points to an *incompleteness* of the sign, as Lucia Santaella analyses well.[83] It is for this reason that Algirdas Julien Greimas can affirm, in *Sémiotique: dicitionnaire raisonné de la thérie du langage,* that the *sign* is "...the unit of the plane of the manifestation, made up by its semiotic function...", between the plane of expression and the plane of content, that makes it express the marked influence of the theoretical conception of the Danish linguist Louis Hjelmslev (expression and content; significant e significance).[84]

At this point, no matter the adoption of the conceptions of Sanders Peirce, of Ferdinand de Saussure or of Algirdas Julien Greimas, the foundation of *Semiology*[85] and of *Semiotics* is connected to the understanding of the diversity of languages[86] in the field of the processes of significance.[87] It is evident that, subsequent to its foundation, these sciences had become distinguished, acquiring very distinct strength and constitution, following more closely the *linguistic* vision from the

[78] *Cf.* Bittar (2015a), p. 35.

[79] *Cf.* Hjelmslev (1975a), p. 201.

[80] *Cf.* Hjelmslev (1975a), pp. 203–204.

[81] *Cf.* Carontini and Peraya (1979), pp. 15–16; *See too* Netto (1980), p. 56.

[82] *Cf.* Eco (1990), p. 26.

[83] *Cf.* Santaella (1992), p. 189.

[84] "Le signe est une unité du plan de la manifestation, constituée par la fonction sémiotique, c´est-à-dire par la relation de présupposition reciproque (ou solidarité) qui s´établit entre deux grandeurs du plan de l´expression (ou signifiant) et du plan du contenu (ou signifié) lors de l´acte de language" ("The sign is a unity of the plane of manifestation, constituted by the semiotic function, that is to say by the relation of reciprocal presupposition (or solidarity) which is established between two magnitudes of the plane of expression (or signifier) and the content plan (or signified) during the speech act"—*translation*) (Greimas and Courtés 1993, p. 349, *Signe*).

[85] *Cf.* Nöth (2005), p. 17.

[86] "Terme de la langue naturelle qu´est le français, langage n´est dégagé définitivément qu´au XIX siècle de sa quase-synonymie avec langue, permettant ainsi d´opposer le langage sémiotique (ou langage au sens general) et la langue naturelle" ("Term of the natural language which is French, language is definitively cleared only in the XIX century of its quase-synonymy with language, thus making it possible to oppose semiotic language (or language in the general sense) and natural language"—*translation*) (Greimas and Courtés 1993, p. 203, *Langage*).

[87] *Cf.* Carontini and Peraya (1979), p. 24.

Saussurean perspective, and the *pan-semiotic* or *multi-semiotic* vision from the Greimasian and Peircean perspectives, the point John Deely makes that *Semiotics* include *Semiology*.[88] For this reason, in the end, for Umberto Eco, *Semiotics* is understood as a *meta-science*, in as far as that it is now spread throughout very broad fields.[89] Finally, *Semiotics* is concerned with the *process of significance*, there is in the idea of *sign* an important point of determination in its field of studies.

This movement achieved, it is important to move forward, in order to understand the specific nature of each the *signs*,[90] as far as they allow the symbolic exchange.[91] It is possible to achieve various forms of classification, all of them instituted and developed by diverse lines of research in *Semiotics*, such as that of Umberto Eco, who differentiates the *signs* into *natural signs* and *artificial signs*.[92] But, for the purpose of this analysis, given that they are divided into *modalities of signs*,[93] they will be presented and identified considering the *symbol*, the *icon* and the *index*,[94] as Roland Barthes points out.[95] All these modalities of signs are used by all the branches of studies of *Semiotics*, including by the *Legal Semiotics*,[96] and by the *Semiotics of Art*. In this way, they can be identified here:

(i) *symbol*: the *symbol* is a modality of sign that represents the object by a relation of *conventional use*, by an arbitrary construction, a socially established comprehension or association.[97] The cross for Christianity, the hammer and sickle for Socialism, the swastika for Nazism, the cross of David for Judaism, the coats of arms for royal families, the icons for secret societies, the flags for the modern nations are examples of *symbols*.[98] It is interesting, however, that Ferdinand de Saussure notes that the *symbol* is not always arbitrary, and stands out precisely as an example of the *symbol of justice*.[99] This is because the *strength of the symbol* does not allow it to be substituted by any other, hence its *persistence*, its *historical constancy*, its role among diverse *cultures, people* and *traditions*, its capacity to cross borders, its *continuity*, as with the *symbol of justice*. Besides having symbolic strength, the symbol has *aesthetic appeal*[100]

---

[88] *Vide* Deely (1990), p. 23. *See too* Netto (1980), p. 18.
[89] *Cf.* Eco (1990), pp. 31–49.
[90] *Cf.* Barthes (1997), p. 50.
[91] *Cf.* Buyssens, (n.d.) p. 82.
[92] *Cf.* Eco (1990), pp. 31–49.
[93] *Cf.* Eco (1990), p. 52.
[94] *Vide* Carontini and Peraya (1979), pp. 19–22.
[95] *Cf.* Barthes (1997), p. 39.
[96] *Cf.* Bittar (2015b), p. 297.
[97] *Cf.* Santaella and Nöth (1998), p. 63.
[98] *Cf.* Eco (1990), p. 48.
[99] *Cf.* Netto (1980), p. 21.
[100] *Cf.* Garapon (1999), p. 43.

and *emotional use*[101] and strong appealing meaning for certain communities;[102]

(ii) *icon*: the *icon* is a modality of sign which *represents* the denoted object by a relation of proximity and similarity.[103] The plant of a house, in relation to the house-object, the painting, in relation to the object represented are examples;

(iii) *index*: the *index* is a modality of sign which *represents* the denoted object by a relation of natural continuity or of the contiguity of the designated object within the existential relations of meaning.[104] They are examples, given by Carontini and Peraya,[105] the smoke that comes out of a chimney as an *index* of fire, the acceleration of the pulse of a patient for the purpose of medical analysis as an *index* of a state of health, the finger that points to a certain object-of-the-world, or even, a photograph in relation to the object photographed.[106]

1.5 Symbolization, Society and Law

All society is made up from the growing processes of *symbolization*. From archaic societies to modern society, *symbolization* was always present, as something constitutive of social life.[107] *Symbolization* characterises society by its meanings, by its symbols, by its rites, by its shapes, by its ideologies and commonly shared beliefs, and end up being determinants for the life of the individual placed in it.[108] In François Rastier's view, the activity of language, the production of meaning, symbolization and communication fundamentally correspond to *social practices*, given that these contain the possibilities generated and the limits of their own use of language.[109]

Indeed, it is from the *symbolic change*, Umberto Eco states,[110] that the possibility of organised life in society emerges, in a way that all society necessarily implies in

[101] *Cf.* Dewey (2010), p. 100.

[102] *Vide* Boas (2015), pp. 98–99.

[103] *Cf.* Carontini and Peraya (1979), p. 19.

[104] "On entend par icône, à la suite de Ch. S. Peirce, un signe défini par sa relation de ressemblance en l´opposant à la fois à l´indice (caractérisé par une relation de continuité naturelle) et à symbole (fondé sur la simple convention sociale)" ("Icon means, following Ch. S. Peirce, a sign defined by its relation of resemblance by opposing it both to the index (characterized by a relation of natural continuity) and to symbol (based on simple social convention)"—*translation*) (Greimas and Courtés 1993, p. 177, *Iconicité*).

[105] *Cf.* Carontini and Peraya (1979), p. 21.

[106] *Cf.* Plaza (2010), p. 22.

[107] *Vide* Lipovetsky and Serroy (2014), pp. 18–19.

[108] *Cf.* Warat (1995), p. 114.

[109] "L´usage d´une langue est par excellence une activité sociale, si bien que toute situation de communication est déterminée par une pratique sociale qui l´instaure et la contraint" ("The use of a language is par excellence a social activity, so that any communication situation is determined by a social practice which establishes and constrains it" - *translation*) (Rastier 1989, p. 39).

[110] *Cf.* Eco (1990), p. 97.

practices of *languages*. The representation of religious beliefs, the systemisation of a code of communication, the production of levels more refined or less refined of the production of moral, political orders, and the formation of Law[111] are aspects which are intrinsically related to the process of the constitution of a society. Indeed, in respect to language, what linguist Louis Hjelmslev stated can be highlighted:

> Language – speech – is an inexhaustible wealth of multiple value. Language is inseparable from man and follows him in all his actions. Language is the instrument thanks to which man models his thinking, his feelings, his emotions, his efforts, his will and his actions, the instrument thanks to which he influences and is influenced, the ultimate and deepest basis of human society.[112]

A *Socio-semiotics*[113] will recognise the place of the *signs* at the heart of society, and the *processes of significance* as processes implied in *social relations.* It can be noticed, here, closely, how much Law, constructed in society, is entangled in the semantic universe of Culture, and how much the area of Culture encompasses diverse objects to which they are co-extensive.[114] Indeed, this is an interesting point of approximation and of connection between the theoretical perspectives of the *Frankfurter Schule* and the current perspectives of *Semiotics* and the *Semiotics of Law*. It is how interesting connections can be found between the *Critical Theory* and *Semiotics*, in as far as the critical studies are of great interest to the understanding of the *systems of significance*.

Just as Bernard Jackson demonstrates, in the text *Sémiotique et études critiques du droit* (1988), it is clear that the *Frankfurter Schule* encourages important bonds between the universe of the *processes of socialisation* and the universe of the *symbolic exchanges*.[115] If, in the previous study, in the Thesis entitled *Justice and emancipation* (2011), previously published with the title *Democracy, justice and social emancipation* (2013),[116] one can clearly establish the nature of the critical-discursive approach of Law, it is also clear that in order to move forward from these suppositions, it will rediscover the *symbolic* dimension of Law, considering the

---

[111] *Cf.* Araújo (2005), p. 17.

[112] *Cf.* Hjelmslev (1975b), p. 185.

[113] *See Dictionnaire*: "Dans le domaine qui serait éventuellement recouvert par le terme de sociosémiotique, ce n´est que la sociolinguistique qui peut prétendre au statut d´une discipline plus ou moins institutionalisée. (. . .) serait réservé le vaste domaine des connotations sociales, dont on indiquera brièvement certaines dimensions" ("In the field that would eventually be covered by the term sociosemiotics, it is only sociolinguistics that can claim the status of a more or less institutionalized discipline. (. . .) the vast domain of social connotations will be reserved, some dimensions of which will be briefly indicated"—*translation*) (Greimas and Courtés 1993, pp. 355–356, *Sociosémiotique*).

[114] Cf. Greimas and Courtés (1993), p. 77, *Culture*.

[115] "Toujours est-il qu´en raison même de ses sources d´inspiration – ici l´*École de Francfort*, là des travaux de J. Habermas -, la théorie critique engage, par certains côtés, une problématique tout à fait familière aux sémioticiens" ("In any case, because of its very sources of inspiration - here the Frankfurt School, there the work of J. Habermas - critical theory in some respects engages a problematic that is quite familiar to semioticists"—*translation*) (Jackson 1988, p. 66).

[116] *Vide* Bittar (2013a).

nature of the processes of socialisation and the symbolic exchanges as something of great interest in the relation between *Law & language*.

In this line of reasoning, it was without a doubt in the second generation of the *Frankfurter Schule* that it was established, from Jürgen Habermas, a clearer connection between these dimensions.[117] In this regard, it is worth pointing out how the *Critical Theory*, by Jürgen Habermas, reports and relies on *Semiotics*, by Charles Sanders Peirce,[118] as much as the *Semiotics of Law*, by Bernard Jackson,[119] reports and relies on the *Critical Theory*, by Jürgen Habermas. At this theoretical intersection, *languages* are the focus, and the processes of social interaction are observed with all importance and centrality they possess to constitute processes of communicative construction of the coexistence and of the intersemiotic traffic.

1.6 Symbolization, Law and Justice

Law is a highly social phenomenon of *symbolic* implication.[120] To the extent that Law is imposed, it is assumed, that the *symbolic dimension* is not irrelevant, but is indeed *determinant*, for Law;[121] the role of *Semiotics* is relevant, towards taking this dimension as an object of research. In Post-Fácio, entitled *The political semiology*, to the book *The law and its language*, Luiz Alberto Warat noted exactly this.[122] Indeed, it is with the words by Antoine Garapon, that it can be said that:

> Without symbols there is no justice, pure and simple because no justice can do without shapes.[123]

---

[117] *Cf.* Habermas (2004), p. 46.

[118] "The transcendentally oriented pragmatism inaugurated by Ch. S. Peirce attempts to show that there is such a structural connection between experience and instrumental action" (Habermas 1979, p. 22). "The stimulus that encouraged me to bring normative structures into a developmental-logical problematic came from the *genetic structuralism* of Jean Piaget as well, thus from a conception that has overcome the traditional strcuturalist front against evolutionism and that has motifs of the theory of knowledge from Kant to Peirce" (Habermas 1979, p. 125).

[119] "En réalité, la *Sémiotique* tire sa valeur critique de sa généralité même en tant que théorie. Analysant les strategies de signification où qu´elles soient à l´oeuvre, elle est à même d´en faire ressortir la spécificité relative en fonction des univers particuliers - c´est-à-dire des genres des discours ou des domaines de pratiques – où elles s´exercent selon le cas" ("In reality, Semiotics derives its critical value from its very generality as a theory. Analyzing strategies of signification wherever they are at work, it is able to bring out their relative specificity according to the specific universes - that is to say, the genres of discourse or the fields of practice - in which they are exercised as the case may be"—*translation*) (Jackson 1988, p. 68).

[120] *Cf.* Cunha (2010), p. 239.

[121] "La tesi che inizierò a sviluppare, sul punto, è che il diritto ha uno spazio simbolico, e che lo spazio del diritto è simbolico" (The thesis I will begin to develop, on the point, is that the law has a symbolic space, and that the space of the law is symbolic"—*translation*) (Cananzi 2013, p. 81).

[122] *Cf.* Warat (1995), p. 119.

[123] *Cf.* Garapon (1999), p. 311.

Therefore, immediately, one realises that the *Aesthetic Theory*, in the task at hand,[124] has something to say to the *Philosophy and Theory of Law*, just as the *Semiotics of Art* has something to say for the *Semiotics of Law*. It is true that the whole approach about the implications of the *languages* in the field of Law end up being a *reading* of variable *semiotics, symbolics* and *aesthetics* of Law.[125] For this reason it cannot be hidden that the languages partake in the practices of Law, and, in this line of reasoning, everything that pertains to *justice* (defining the 'place' of justice, 'saying' justice, 'representing' justice, 'interpreting' justice, 'consecrating' justice, 'judging' according to justice, 'imposing' justice, 'applying' justice, among others),[126] and despite historical time, it has always somehow been associated to 'symbols', 'representations, 'actions, 'formulas', 'rites', 'ceremonies', 'judgements', mirroring that the *symbolic dimension* accompanies the *history of justice*. For this reason, the *form* has been as relevant as the *content* of the acts of justice to Law, since the Romans up to today. From the point of view of the most ancestral practices of Law in history, the proximity of Law with religion and its sacred rituals is well known.[127]

For the modern world, despite secularism, however, it is interesting to identify how much Law maintains this *symbolic overlap,* and perpetuates its formulating nature. The *symbols of State* substitute the *religious symbols* and mark the shapes for which practices of Law passed on from generation to generation, in a way that the following readings of the *reality* of Law open up:

(i) the medieval torture of a defendant in a public square is a ritual of collective redemption and reaffirmation of the symbolic power of the Church;
(ii) the body of the slave beaten by the 'master' is a map of pain and of suffering in the oppression of freedom;
(iii) the numbers and the statistics of violence are indexes of the lack of justice in society;
(iv) a session of the jury reveals actors, postures, places of speech, rituals, re-enactments, dramatization and the use of persuasive rhetoric that generates discursive effects about the jurors;[128]
(v) a jail is an architecture of control that reveals the logic of the prison;
(vi) the Palace of Justice, where the Tribunals or the Courts of Justice are installed (São Paulo; Paris; Washington; New York), are architectures set with signs of violence, of tradition[129] and of judiciary rituals;[130]

[124]*Cf.* Dewey (2010), p. 73.
[125]*Vide* Bittar (2015a).
[126]*Cf.* Garapon (1999), p. 25.
[127]*Cf.* Dondis (2007), p. 94.
[128]*Cf.* Callejón (2016), p. 336.
[129]*Cf.* Garapon (1999), p. 64.
[130]*Cf.* Garapon (1999), p. 34.

(vii) a forum is a representation of serial sobriety, repetitive, bureaucratic and formulating with which the deeds are judged and the procedural rites executed;
(viii) the lynching in a public square of a criminal is a act of collective revenge that exposes the weaknesses of the institutions of justice and the disbelief in the system of public security;
(ix) the hammer, in the way the North-American judges impose with respect to silence in the sessions of judging, is a symbol of the judicature and the finalisation of the stages of the search for the legal decision;[131]
(x) the ankle-length robes are the garments whose colours and shapes impart a 'solemn' nature to the act of judging and vest people in the position of legal actors in the legal arena;
(xi) the figures, the representations, the crossbows, the swords, the spears, the scales, the busts, the gods and goddesses, the scenes of violence, present in judicial architecture, are manifestations of power and of the violence contained in the universe of justice and of injustice;[132]
(xii) the structural layout of the courtrooms, they reveal the relation between the parts of a legal process and the role of each in a game of representation and in the exercise of ritual roles;[133]
(xiii) the words and the moments of equal opportunities of speech in a collective assembly express the way more or less democratic of promoting justice;
(xiv) the round table of a mediation of conflicts express a circular way of promoting justice and the physical-psychic interaction between those involved in conflict, stimulating cooperative and agreed methods of solutions of conflict;
(xv) the Palaces of Justice are architectonic books, filled with meaning, physical structures spatially open to the eye of its readers, especially considering the relation between violence, justice and injustice, showing the limits of doing justice through the instruments of the State.[134]

In a still preliminary approach, one notices immediately how much the *symbolic* is present and marks the historical definition of *justice*, both by 'way' and by 'content', in the *daily practices* of life in society, affecting the decisive way that is called *Law*. Hence the implication that is noticed, and which is to be explored at further length, it is even possible to *photograph* this reality of symbols, just as Bernard Edelman does, in *Law captured by photography,*[135] in the approach of the lens of analysis about the universe of symbolic practices with surround *Law*.

[131] *Cf.* Garapon (1999), p. 78.
[132] *Cf.* Garapon (1999), p. 200.
[133] *Cf.* Garapon (1999), p. 43.
[134] *Cf.* Garapon (1999), p. 200.
[135] *Cf.* Edelman (1976), p. 41.

References

Agrest D, Gandelsonas M (2013) Semiótica e Arquitetura. In: Nesbitt K (ed) Uma nova agenda para a arquitetura [A new agenda for Architecture]. CosacNaify, São Paulo, pp 129–141

Barthes R (1997) Elementos de semiologia [Elements of semiology] (Izidoro Blikstein Trans), 10th edn. Cultrix, São Paulo

Bittar CA (2015a) Direito de Autor [Copyright law], 6th edn. GEN; Forense, Rio de Janeiro

Bittar ECB (2013a) Diálogo, consciência cosmopolita e direitos humanos. Direitos fundamentais e justiça [Human Rights Justice] 22:98–123

Bittar ECB (2015b) Linguagem jurídica: semiótica, discurso e direito [Legal language: semiotics, discourse and law], 6th edn. Saraiva, São Paulo

Boas F (2015) Arte primitiva [Primitive art] (trans: José C. Pereira). Mauad X, Rio de Janeiro

Buyssens E. (n.d.) Semiologia e comunicação linguística [Semiology and linguistics communication], 3rd edn. (trans: Blikstein I). Cultrix, São Paulo

Calabrese O (2015) Como se lê uma obra de arte [How to read a work of art]. Edições, Lisboa, p 70

Callejón FB (2016) Verdad y certeza en el Derecho y en la Literatura. In: Franca Filho M, Leite GS, Filho RP (eds) Antimanual de Direito & Arte [Anti-manual of Law and Art]. Saraiva, São Paulo, pp 333–351

Cananzi DM (2013) Formatività e norma: elementi di Teoria Estetica dell'interpretazione giuridica. G. Giappichelli Editore, Torino

Carontini E, Peraya D (1979) O projeto semiótico [The semiotics project] (trans: Lima AD). Cultrix, USP, São Paulo

Courtés J (1979) Introdução à semiótica narrativa e discursiva [Introduction to the narrative and discoursive semiotics] (trans: Tasca NB). Almedina, Coimbra

da Cunha PF (2010) Direito, poder e pró-vocação artística [Law, power and artistics provocation]. Boletim da Faculdade de Direito da Universidade de Coimbra 101:209–239

da Cunha PF (2013) Filosofia do Direito [Philosophy of law], 2nd edn. Almedina, Coimbra

Deely J (1990) Semiótica básica [Basic semiotics] (trans: Pinto JCM). Ática, São Paulo

Dewey J (2010) Arte como experiência [Art as experience] (trans: Ribeiro V). Martins Fontes, São Paulo

Didi-Huberman G (1999) The molding image: genealogy and the truth of resemblence in Pliny's natural history. In: Douzinas C, Nead L (eds) Law and the image: the autorithy of art and the aesthetics of Law. Chicago, Chicago Press, pp 36–67

Dondis DA (2007) Sintaxe da linguagem visual [Visual language syntax] (trans: Camargo JL). Martins Fontes, São Paulo

Douzinas C, Nead L (1999) Introduction. In: Douzinas C, Nead L (eds) Law and the image: the authority of art and the aesthetics of law. Chicago Press, Chicago, pp 01–15

Eco U (org) (1990) O signo [The sign] (trans: Fátima Marinho M) 4ª. edn. Presença, Lisboa

Edelman B (1976) O direito captado pela fotografia [The Law captured by photograph]. Trad. Soveral Martins e Pires de Carvalho. Coimbra, Centelha

Filho F, Toscano M (2011) A cegueira da justiça [The blindness of justice]. Sergio Antonio Fabris, Porto Alegre

Filho F, Marcílio T, Leite GS, Filho RP (Coords) (2016) Antimanual de Direito & Arte [Anti-manual of Law & Art]. Saraiva, São Paulo

Fiorin JL (2009) Para uma definição das linguagens sincrética. In: de Oliveira AC, Teixeira L (eds) Linguagens na comunicação [Languages in communication]. Estação das Letras e das Cores, São Paulo, pp 15–40

Fontanille J (2015a) La sémiotique face aux grands défis sociétaux du XXI [e] siècle. Actes Sémiotiques 118. https://www.unilim.fr/actes-semiotiques/5320. Accessed 26 Dec 2019

Fontanille J (2015b) Semiótica do discurso [Semiotics of discourse]. Contexto, São Paulo

Garapon A (1999) Bem julgar [Well judge] (trans: Henriques PF). Instituto Piaget, Lisboa

Geertz C (2014) O saber local [The local knowledge]. 14th edn (trans: Joscelyne V). Vozes, Rio de Janeiro

Gorsdorf LF (2014) Direitos humanos e arte: diálogos possíveis para uma episteme. In: Silva EF, Gediel JAP, Trauczynski SC (eds) Direitos humanos e políticas públicas [Human Rights and Public Policies]. Universidade Positivo, Curitiba, pp 51–66
Greimas AJ, (1987) De l´imperfection. Pierre Fanlac, Périgeux
Greimas AJ, Courtés J (1993) Sémiotique: ditionnarire raisonné de la théorie du langage. Hachette, Paris
Greimas AJ Landowski É (1981) Semiótica e Ciências Sociais [Semiotics and Social Sciences] (trans: àlvaro Lorencini and Sandra Nitrini). São Paulo: Cultrix
Habermas J (1979) Communicaion and the evolution of society. Beacon Press, Transl. Thomas McCarthy. Boston
Habermas J (2004) Verdade e justificação [Truth and justification] (trans: Milton C. Mota). São Paulo, Loyola
Hermann N (2005) Ética e estética [Ethics and aesthetics]. EDIPUCRS, Porto Alegre
Hjelmslev LT (1975a) A estratificação da linguagem [Language stratification]. Os pensadores (trans: Coelho Netto JT). Abril Cultural, São Paulo, pp 157–182
Hjelmslev LT (1975b) Prolegômenos a uma teoria da linguagem [Prolegomena to a theory of language] (trans: Coelho Netto JT). Os pensadores. Abril Cultural, São Paulo, pp 183–219
Honneth A (2015) O direito da liberdade [The right of freedom] (trans: Krieger S). Martins Fontes, São Paulo
Jackson B (1988) Sémiotique et études critiques du droit. Droit et Société 8:61–71
Jacob R (1994) Images de la justice. Éditions Léopard d'Or, Paris
Kristeva J (1981) Semiotica [Semiotics] (trans: Arancibia JM). Fundamentos, Madrid
Landowski E (1993) La sociedade figurada (trans: Hernández Aguilar G et al). Universidad Autónoma de Puebla; Fondo de Cultura Económica, México
Landowski E (2005) Para uma semiótica sensível. Educação & Realidade [Education and reality] 30:93–106
Landowski E (2017) Interactions (socio) sémiotiques. Actes Sémiotiques 120:01-20. epublications.unilim.fr. Accessed 6 June 2017
Leonardi Filho SL (2006) Descrição semiótica do Direito [Semiotics description of law]. Editora Scortecci
Lipovetsky G, Serroy J (2014) O capitalismo estético na era da globalização [The aesthetic capitalism in the age of globalization]. Transl. Edições, Lisboa, p 70
Mathias R (2016) Antropologia visual [Visual anthropology]. Nova Alexandria, São Paulo
Netto JTC (1980) Semiótica, informação e comunicação: diagrama da teoria do signo [Semiotics, information and communication]. Perspectiva, São Paulo
Nöth W (2005) A semiótica no século XX [Semiotics in the XX century] 3rd edn. Annablume, São Paulo
Pietroforte, Antonio Vicente (2016) Análise do texto visual: a construção da imagem [Analysis of the visual text]. 2nd São Paulo: Contexto
Plaza J (2010) Tradução intersemiótica [Intersemiotics translation]. Perspectiva, São Paulo
Radbruch G (1997) Filosofia do Direito [Philosophy of Law] (trans: L. Cabral de Moncada), 6th edn. Arménio Amado, Coimbra
Rancière J (2009a) O inconsciente estético [The aesthetic unconscious] (trans: Netto MC). Editora, São Paulo, p 34
Rancière J (2009b) A partilha do sensível [Sharing the sensitive] (trans: Netto MC). Eixo Experimental; Editora, São Paulo, p 34
Rancière J (2011) El malestar en la estética (trans: Petrecca MÁ, Vogelfandg L, y Burello MG). Capital Intelectual, Buenos Aires
Rapoport NB (2013) Analysis and the arts. In: Bankowski Z, Del Mar M, Maharg P (eds) The arts and the legal academy. Ashgate, England, pp 101–118
Rastier F (1989) Sens et textualité. Hachette, Paris
Rastier F (2017) De la sémantique structurale à la sémiotique des cultures. Actes Sémiotiques 120:01–13. epublications.unilim.fr. Accessed 6 June 2017

Santaella L (1992) A Assinatura das coisas [The signing of things]. Imago, Rio de Janeiro

Santaella L (2007) Linguagens líquidas na era da mobilidade [Liquid languages of the era of mobility]. Paulus, São Paulo

Santaella L (2016a) Memória e perspectivas da semiótica no Brasil [Memory and perspectives of Semiotics in Brazil]. Intexto 37:22–33

Santaella L (2016b) Temas e dilemas do pós-digital [Themes and dilemmas of the post-digital]. Paulus, São Paulo

Santaella L, Nöth W (1998) Imagem [Image]. Iluminuras, São Paulo, p 1998

Terré F (2015) Introduction générale au droit, 10th edn. Dalloz, Paris

Tore GM (2011) L´art comme création, ou la règle de nier la règle. Actes Sémiotiques 114:01–11. epublications.unifilm.fr. Accessed 6 June 2017

von Oertzen de Araújo C (2005) Semiótica do Direito [Semiotics of Law]. Quartier Latin, São Paulo

Warat LA (1995) O direito e sua linguagem [Law and its language], 2nd edn. Sergio Antonio Fabris, Porto Alegre

Chapter 2
Semiotics, Art and Experience

2.1 Semiotics, Art and Artistic Languages

Not even the processes of modernisation have meant a collapse of the *artistic forms*, quite, to the contrary, as Jacques Rancière states, they are multiple contemporary *artistic experiences*.[1] In *L'incoscient esthétique* (2001), Jacques Rancière can confirm that:

> There is no episode, description or sentence that does not carry in itself the potency of the work. Because there is not anything that does not carry in itself the power of language.[2]

Indeed, throughout history, the arts have been expressed via diverse channels and in diverse ways: handicrafts; music; theatre; sculpture; drawing; painting; photography; dance; architecture; literature; cinema; cartoon strips; illustration; calligraphy; visual arts; computer games; graphic art; digital art; *design*; graffiti; *street art*.[3] The arts, currently, have increasingly unlimited and varied boundarics and languages, the example of *body art*. Often, art arises in confined spaces and ways, often in academic strongholds, but, at other times, it is done freely and represents the city—or, the urban space—like the *panneaux* within which *street art* is inscribed, the example of the languages of *graffiti* in urban and suburban spaces in the megalopolis of Brazil.[4]

From the arts closer to *Beaux Arts* to those closer to applied arts, the square of arts is the *pluralism of languages*,[5] and its field of languages is found in a permanent state of development, dependent on the developments of culture, on the boundaries of knowledge, and on technique itself. The languages of the works of art are those that express what cannot be expressed in words:

---

[1] *Cf.* Rancière (2014), p. 24.

[2] *Cf.* Rancière (2009a, b), p. 37.

[3] *Cf.* Dondis (2007), p. 09.

[4] *Vide* Malland (2012).

[5] *Cf.* Dewey (2010), p. 215.

E. C. B. Bittar, *Semiotics, Law & Art*, Law and Visual Jurisprudence 2,
https://doi.org/10.1007/978-3-030-58880-9_2

In fact, each art speaks a language which transmits what cannot be said in any other language, but stays the same.[6]

In contrast to *eclipsing*, the forms of art alternate in predominance in history, not exactly dying out—yet, in fact, are marginalised and falling into temporary oblivion, being redeemed or not in new historical cycles, following the example of handicrafts—,[7] unfolding new perspectives at each step of the opening of the boundaries generated by the *aesthetic experience* itself, merging together intricately, and mutually transforming.[8] For example, this does not mean that the *pluralism of the forms* and contemporary *artistic modalities* involve the abandoning the value of indigenous crafts, or the forgetting the meaning of the tribal religious forms, or the significance of medieval illustration, or even, the burying of classic architecture.

The new boundaries of the arts have been remodelled, in contemporary art, especially, in the light of *digital art*,[9] of *technological art,* of *media-art*,[10] of *industrial design*, of *video art*, and of diverse manifestations of *popular arts*. In this field, it is clear that contemporary technology—which stimulates intertextual, intervisual and intersensory interactions—,[11] like the example of the relation between digital arts and traditional graphic arts, is deeply moved with what has been stabilised since the invention of the mobile types by Gutemberg.[12] And it is in this sense that the understanding of *art*, of the sensitivity, of the aesthetic fields, of the aesthetic meaning and of the visual intelligence should adapt themselves to the new dynamics of the understanding of the artistic universe.[13] What is interesting in the artistic practices is their entangling, in the history of art, as well as the impossibility of speaking about an evolutionary breakthrough. And this is because there is not actually any evolution in the history of art, since the temple of Zeus, in *Paestum* (Italy), continues to suggest—still and unmoved—the pride of ancient classic Greek beauty, without a shadow of a doubt; *Van Gogh* did not 'exceed' *Van Eyck*, since 'they represented' the world with 'different interpretations'.

Consequently, the *plurality of* artistic *languages* opens up a field to inumerous boundaries, application, uses and perspectives of intervention.[14] For no other reason, it has been the focus of attention of *Semiotics*, a science that, in the definition of Umberto Eco, treats the various *languages* as an object of study.[15] Here, therefore, in the *plurality of languages* the *art-sign* appears, in other words, art as what is for

[6]*Cf.* Dewey (2010), p. 215.
[7]*Cf.* Dondis (2007), p. 210.
[8]*Cf.* Rancière (2014), p. 119.
[9]*Cf.* Santaella (2016a, b), p. 235.
[10]*Cf.* Santaella (2016a, b), p. 231.
[11]*Cf.* Plaza (2010), p. 13.
[12]*Cf.* Dondis (2007), p. 205.
[13]*Cf.* Dondis (2007), p. 27.
[14]*Cf.* Rancière (2014), p. 81.
[15]*Cf.* Pignatari (1987), p. 19.

something else (*aliquid stat pro aliquo*).[16] This is how it can be repeated, with Leonardo Da Vinci:

> La pittura è una poesia che si vede e non si sente, e la poesia è una pittura che si sente e non si vede.
>
> The painting is a poem which can be seen and not heard, and the poem is a painting which is heard and not seen.

Besides the *pluralism of the forms of art*, it is important to highlight that, for each modality of art, a *syntax* is developed, the example of visual arts, for which they can speak of a *visual syntax*,[17] according to which inumerous combinations relevant to the process of the constitution of the meanings of the work of art arise. And it is how, following this grammar, one can promote and cause certain stimuli, taking into account the types of elements, and its combinations with each other,[18] it can be highlighted, as Umberto Eco does, how much contemporary art is free and creative,—breaking semiotic barriers—,[19] with regard to other historical models, towards the combination and recombination of *possible languages* that are applied to the work of art.[20]

2.2 Semiotics, Concept of Art and Aesthetic Experience

When one comes up against a debate about the *concept of art*—a central question in this field of definitions—, one stumbles upon a very complex, polemic and open-ended question.[21] For no other reason, Umberto Eco, in *The definition of art,* from the outset, recognises the limits of this exercise.[22] The constant movement of the boundaries of art makes the whole *concept of art* something elusive. For no other reason, all art always refers to the universe of culture, as North-American anthropologist Cliford Geertz confirms,[23] and culture is not something static, but something that is always changing. *Art* is in constant movement of questioning of its own boundaries, playing with the dichotomy between *artistic shape* and *artistic content.* Therefore, the debate about the concept of *art* appears to be the *vexing question* for numerous sciences, from *Aesthetic Philosophy* to the *Semiotics of Art*, as well as

[16] *Cf.* Eco (1991), p. 60.

[17] *Cf.* Dondis (2007), p. 18.

[18] *Cf.* Dondis (2007), p. 58.

[19] "Ed eliminato l'apparente scoglio della pittura astratta, è chiaro che tutte le altre opere d'arte passano agevolmente sotto la categoria del segno" ("And having eliminated the apparent obstacle of abstract painting, it is clear that all the other works of art pass easily under the category of the sign"—*translation*) (Brandi 1986, p. 09).

[20] *Cf.* Eco (2016), p. 226.

[21] *Cf.* da Cunha (2010), p. 229.

[22] *Cf.* Eco (2016), p. 144.

[23] *Cf.* Geertz (2014), p. 113.

from the *Sociology of Art* to the *Anthropology of Art*, as the studies of North-American anthropologist Cliford Geertz report.[24]

This means that one should bear in mind how much the *experience of art* is *rebel* to the *Aesthetic Theory*, in so far as the 'concept' is not always—and with such precision—able to contain the whole potential of aesthetic 'experience',[25] from where the tension permanently runs between *aesthetic experience* and the *concept of art*.[26] This tension can be well expressed in the words of German philosopher G.E. Lessing (*Laocoonte*), who confirms:

> The true objective of science is the truth; in contrast, the true object of art is pleasure.

Or even, it can be felt even more alive in the statement by Spanish painter Pablo Picasso:

> Art is the lie which allows us to know the truth.

In this respect, it is clear that the sole approach of these aesthetics through the 'concept' impoverishes *art*, and this, because *art* manages to say more than its 'concept'. The *arts* allow numerous *aesthetic experiences* that make us to get in touch with our own humanity, and see internal dimensions that are often unknown to us, as Gabriel Perissé reveals,[27] acting in a way of awakening enthusiasm, critical vision, love, wonder, compassion, shock, revolt, emotion, happiness, solidarity, envy, dazzle, offering plenty of 'experimental possibilities' of access to the world, creating internal mutations that touch the dimension of *being*.

Now, to the extent *art* requires *sensitivity*.[28] *Art* requires *sensitivity*, just as it also requires *emotion*.[29] *Art* requires *emotion*, just as it also requires *reason*. *Art* requires *conscious*, just as it also requires *unconscious*. But still, *art* cannot be reduced to the *dimension of the rational concept*, because it also involves the evasion of the *pulse of life*, releasing the *unconscious*,[30] and, in this respect, its reduction to something more fixed and static is far from being capable of *signifying* the completeness of the *human experience*—sublimated in the *work-of-art*—, as a *conscious experience* and *unconscious experience* in the processes of artistic expression.[31] The personal testimony of jazz musician and drummer *Art Blackey*, creator of *Bebop,* is, in this point, of sufficient meaning to express the importance of this *experience of art*:

[24]*Cf.* Geertz (2014), p. 98.

[25]*Cf.* Hermann (2005), p. 31.

[26]*Cf.* Lacoste (1986), p. 108.

[27]*Cf.* Perissé (2004), p. 77.

[28]*Cf.* Geertz (2014), p. 103.

[29]*Cf.* Xerez (2016), pp. 456–457.

[30]*Cf.* Pastore (2009), p. 20.

[31]*Cf.* Pastore (2009), p. 22.

> All kinds of tragedy could have happened to me, but when I am playing, everything passes. When I leave, I will take with me again, but the stage is my sanctuary. I often call it my cocoon.[32]

Indeed, it is proper and unique to the *aesthetic experience* the fact that *art* allows the enhancement of our *experience of the world*,[33] and, for this reason, it helps us to understand it, interact with it, transform it, create the "surrounding" (objective; social; cultural). Another of the singularities of aesthetic experience arises from the fact of all work contains in itself great strength, either for those who make it, or for those who enjoy it. From this it follows that all *works of art* live a duplicity between *material* and *shape*,[34] besides being the record of one or more *human personalities*,[35] containing in itself what can be called the *rhythm of work*,[36] being this unique, original and unrepeatable, highlighting that the *rhythm* of its author, or its authors, can again be felt and experienced, even with new insights, by appreciators.

It should be emphasised that one of the more subtle, sensitive and well mobilised movements by *aesthetic experience* is precisely that of escaping to the domain of the conscious, control, reason and analytic. Contrary to the commitment to truth, reason, certainty, solution, the arts are reluctant to any attempt to being reduced to the realm of the 'concept', being more adequate than being presented as *truths* or *illusions*, as *reasons* or *emotions*, as *vague certainties* or *assumed doubts*, as *solutions* or *questioning*, enabling, with this, the creation of symbolic space for the exercise of other dimensions of our humanity, such as, *perception*, *intuition*, *sensation*, *taste*, *suddenness*, *incalculable*, *unconscious*, *desire*, *criticism*, *error*, *falsity*, *withdrawal*, *fantasy*, *illusion*. Art helps immensely in the transformation of the 'concept' (abstract; rational; general; universal; distant; ethereal) in 'experience' (concrete; sensitive; playful; specific; real; sensorial; material). For this reason, *art* has always meant *local*,[37] despite being a universally recognised practice. For this reason, also, *art* does not only speak to the head, but speaks to the body, tact, eyes, heart, the unconscious.

The poem by Manoel de Barros states this well, as can be read in the poem *Unword (photography sessions)*:

> Today I achieved the kingdom of images, the kingdom of the unword.
>
> (...)
>
> From there comes what the poets should raise the world the word with its metaphors.
>
> What the poets can be pre-things, pre-worms, can be pre-moss.

[32] *Vide* Calado (2007), p. 47.
[33] *Cf.* Hermann (2005), p. 42.
[34] *Cf.* Rendon (2014), p. 135.
[35] *Cf.* Salazar (1961), p. 183.
[36] *Cf.* Salazar (1961), p. 48.
[37] *Cf.* Geertz (2014), pp. 100–101.

From there comes what the poets can understand the world without concepts.

What the poets can remake the world by images, by emanations, by affection.[38]

Everything leads us to believe that it is possible to affirm that the artist does not need '*concept of art*' in order to plunge into the '*experience of art*' and to work with the *symbolic universe*; he does not depend on the *concept of beautiful* to produce a *work of art*. Indeed, some icons of the history of music cultivated their musical art without dominating the '*lettered culture*', or even, the erudite 'concepts' of musical art.

The hoarseness of *Louis Armstrong*.

The melancholy tone of *Billie Holiday*.

The vocal lightness of *Ella Fitzgerald*.

The high level of the art of *Miles Davis*.

The sonorous bliss of the saxophone of *John Coltrane*.

In the area of *jazz*, there are lots of artists, talent and musical virtuosity. The indisputable artistic affinity, in contexts of racism and ethnic antipathy in the United States, in the deep and permanent significance of creativity of Louis Armstrong.[39] The difficult life, but admirable *musical sensitivity*—the musical *feeling*, the vocal timbre, the ability to flutter over the musical lyrics, the melodic sensuality and the dramatization—that makes *Billie Holiday* stand out, among many female voices of *jazz*.[40] And what more can be said, about the musical contribution *Ella Fitzgerald*—from the vocal range and timbre, tuning and perfection of diction—which makes her contribution to the history of contemporary music unique.[41] Furthermore, the sonorous bliss and the spirituality at the head of the saxophone is what makes *John Coltrane* a musician who reached the limits among the expulsion of anger, the expression of pain, the distillation of anguish and the elevation of beauty, just in the gesture of playing the saxophone and making the musical notes turn into a frantic, exhaustive and almost anaesthetic way.[42]

In these examples, of the history of music, it becomes evident how much *art* demands *sensitivity* of the artist, without demanding a commitment for the *truth*. For this reason, *art* disturbs by its lack of commitment to the *truth*, but at the same time means a lot for the preservation of memory. The few remnants of history, which make us access traces of other civilisations, people and cultures, are provided by the arts. *Art* is conservation of the past and announcer of the future, but still, *art* is one of the things that is done with the *body*, that is experienced with the *feelings*, but which

[38] *Cf.* de Barros (2010), p. 383, *translation*.

[39] *Cf.* Calado (2007), pp. 07–09.

[40] *Cf.* Calado (2007), pp. 07–10.

[41] *Cf.* Calado (2007), p. 08.

[42] *Cf.* Calado (2007), p. 07.

sprouts in the *mind* and in *material*,[43] and which works meaning in existence with the world and with the others, which reacts to stimuli and create stimuli. *Post-modern art* itself[44] abuses this perspective, taking art to the furthest limits as *aesthetic*, in other words, as *experience, feeling* and *living* the work of art synthetically through the body.[45]

Art does not 'bend' to 'concepts', but behaves diversely in the manner of a receptacle. For this reason, the whole *philosophical* and *rational attempt* to 'take art in hand', to bottle them up via a "unifying and universal concept", can once again be questioned and put up for discussion, as far as the *infinite* creativity of art gives it the impossibility of being understood and described by the abstract plane of the 'concept', leading to the path of the vanguards and political struggles[46] by the establishment of the disputed *concept of art*.[47] Indeed, what one sees, progressively, throughout the twentieth century, is a disassociation between *art* and *beautiful*—or, an *ideal of beauty*—, in a way which the terms currently walk separately. Even more so, when looking for the *object of art*, supposedly the *beautiful*, the question becomes even more problematic in the area of *contemporary art*, since the *beautiful, abject, critical, ugly, sick,*[48] *misery, humorous, fantastic, dreamy, unfinished, without-meaning* also are objects of art, as the North-American philosopher and art critic Arthur C. Danto points out, in *The abuse of beauty*.[49]

In this collection, the synthesis elaborated by Lucia Santaella is virtuously capable of demonstrating this *cross-border* nature of the arts:

> There is art of artefacts, objects, material, specific sites, earth and dust. There is art of sky and space. There is art of not objects, intangibles, light and breeze. There is art of construction and deconstruction, of representation and anti-representation, of anti-art, of shortfall and outside of art. There is art of spectacular and hidden, of noise and discretion. There is art of the gesture that remains and of the gesture that fades, of action and silence. There is art of the unique object, the distributable, reproducible, transmissible and ubiquity. There is art pre-media, media and post-media. Pre-photographic, photographic and post-photographic. There is art contemplative, responsive, performative, participative, interactive, collaborative. The art today spills over all the limits, of which it passes until even the dissipation of old boundaries manifests but current expressions as post-cinema and post-video.[50]

---

[43] *Cf.* Dewey (2010), p. 431.

[44] *Cf.* Rancière (2009a, b), p. 42.

[45] "L'impiego estetico del linguaggio (il linguaggio poetico) implica dunque un uso emotivo delle referenze ed un uso referenziale delle emozioni, perché la reazione sentimentale si manifesta come realizzazione di un campo di significati connotati" ("The aesthetic use of language (the poetic language) therefore implies an emotional use of references and a referential use of emotions, because the sentimental reaction is manifested as the realization of a field of connotations"—*translation*) (Eco 1993, p. 84).

[46] *Cf.* Pignatari (1995), p. 52.

[47] *Cf.* da Cunha (2010), p. 233.

[48] *Cf.* Eco (2007), p. 302.

[49] *Cf.* Danto (2015), p. 65.

[50] *Cf.* Santaella (2016a, b), pp. 232–233.

The borders of art are so open and instigating, that they turn the *concept of art* into a *filter* (cultural, ethnical, technical, ideological),[51] that it can often signify an *unjust* process of the *exclusion* of the vanguards. For this reason, it is preferable to consider that the boundaries of art are always moving, and that the boundaries of art abuse the possibility of affirmation and solidification of a *concept of art*.[52] This becomes even more notorious, since art can be so extravagant and so disruptive that, the example of the context of *ready made*, the iconoclast work in porcelain signed with the name of the maker (R. Mutt, 1917), entitled *Fountain* (*Fountain,* 1917), by the French artist Marcel Duchamp,[53] and, also, the example of the context of *pop art,* the work in serigraphy entitled *Cans of Campbell's Soup* (*Campbell's Soup Can*, 1962), or even, the work in synthetic polymer entitled *Brillo Box* (*Brillo Box, Soap Pads,* 1964),[54] both of North-American artist Andy Warhol, resonate strongly both in the feeling of acceptance as an act of *genius*,[55] and in the feeling of the rejection of artistic themes and vulgarised concepts,[56] where it is under discussion whether the *serial repetition, industrial objects* and the *publicity* can be seen and accepted as artistic objects. The vanguardism of these artistic attitudes did not only alter the *history of art*, but fertilised a *new philosophy of art*, much more likely to *comprehend art*, than to *define art.*[57]

But, even so, if the concept of art is kept close to the dimension of *aesthetic experience*, the attempt to *trace its* main characteristics, keeping the boundaries open, seem to be the least aggressive way of approaching the complex question that it implies. Therefore what can be said is that *art* corresponds to the re-elaboration of experience to the level of intelligent sensitivity, working at the *symbolic* level and at the *material* level, producing the meeting of *shape* and *material.* It is from this exercise that all art is incorporated. And it is how art has everything to do with the meeting of *shape* and *material*,[58] mediated by human creativity.

---

[51] *Vide* Eco (2007), p. 10.

[52] *Cf.* Nazario (2005), p. 51.

[53] *Vide* Danto (2015), p. 10.

[54] *Cf.* Nazario (2005), p. 24.

[55] *Cf.* Danto (2015), p. 05.

[56] "Nous lisons ainsi chez Warhol : «La toile est un objet absolument quotidien, au même titre que cette chaise ou cette affiche». Applaudissons à cette conception démocratique, mais reconnaissons qu'elle est bien naïve ou de bien mauvaise foi. Si l'art veut signifier le quotidien, il ne l'est pas : c'est confondre la chose et le sens. Or, l'art est contraint de signifier, il ne peut même pas se suicider dans le quotidien" ("We read at Warhol's: 'The canvas is an absolutely everyday object, just like this chair or this poster'. Let us applaud this democratic conception, but let us acknowledge that it is naive or in bad faith. If art wants to signify the everyday, it is not: it is confusing the thing with meaning. But art is forced to signify, it can't even commit suicide in everyday life"—*translation*) (Baudrillard 1972, p. 123).

[57] *Cf.* Danto (2015), p. 17.

[58] *Cf.* Dewey (2010), p. 227.

2.3 Semiotics, Concept of Art and Human Experience

Within the philosophical conception of John Dewey's pragmatism, it becomes evident that the arts were not made to be 'entified'. From art as copy, from art as imitation, from art as representation, from art as contemplation, from art as geniality, here it adopts the idea of John Dewey's pragmatism, that is, from *art as experience*. Art is here inserted in experience as a way of avoiding the split—caused by the modern world—between the useful and the useless, between work and leisure, between beauty and ugliness. After all, only the vulgar materialism of the brutalisation of life in work can create a disassociation between art and life. In this vision, one cannot separate the *artistic objects* from this regular background of *human experience.*[59] Indeed, this is an important finding from the point of view, also from the studies of the *Anthropology of Art.*[60]

The vast majority of *artistic objects* did not appear in the *museums* and *collections of art,*[61] but appeared in social contexts, historical moments, religious practices, regular necessities of life,[62] providing some meaning for a particular social group. To be separated from regular life, and situated in *museums*, they become a target of aesthetic adoration that refutes their original meaning. Hence, the importance of returning them back to experience, to its genesis, there where they represent something entangled in a bigger mesh of meaning.[63] For this reason, the royal shields, Romanesque churches,[64] gothic cathedrals, royal palaces, religious symbols and rituals, religious objects, works of stone of the New Zealanders,[65] and the Christian relics are testimonies of life and death of historical times, where the things have their own *social meaning*, in the wider scope of *common life*.

Therefore, the *museologisation* of works of art, and its removal from ordinary life, is a modern construction that is the result of the segregation of works of art from their origin, or from the definition of works of art as an extraordinary-object formed separately from ordinary life, or as a result of a process of destruction, conquest and war.[66] This is the *vision* of the world built by the capitalist society, in the sense of *enthroning* the works of art separately from *mundane life.*[67] And this due, in the explanation of sociologist Gilles Lipovetsky, precisely because capitalism radically opposes *art* and *common experience.*[68] This not only isolates the *works of art*, in the place of the collection and of the museum, but this also isolates the *artist*, who

[59] *Cf.* Dewey (2010), pp. 59–60.

[60] *Cf.* Boas (2015), p. 15.

[61] *Cf.* Dewey (2010), p. 63.

[62] *Cf.* Dewey (2010), pp. 64–65.

[63] *Cf.* Dewey (2010), p. 61.

[64] *Cf.* Argan (2013), p. 285.

[65] *Cf.* Boas (2015), p. 15.

[66] *Cf.* Dewey (2010), p. 67.

[67] *Cf.* Dewey (2010), p. 67.

[68] *Cf.* Lipovetsky and Serroy (2014), p. 26.

becomes seen as an *isolated creator* of social life, dedicated and committed to his *task of isolated creation.*[69] As they shift from their place of origin, the meaning of *works of art* also changes, hence the difficulty in understanding the works of art, once they are decontextualized from their use, their origin and, thus, their deeper, more complete and genuine meaning.[70] The result of this is no different from:

> Joining the action of all these forces, the conditions which they create the abyss that is used to existing between the producer and the consumer, in modern society, they act towards also creating an abyss between common experience and aesthetic experience.[71]

The *Aesthetic Theory*, regularly, makes the mistake of '*mystifying*' the works of art, and therefore ends up by contributing to constructing a mistaken vision of them. Numerous artificial conceptual divisions are charged by certain philosophical conceptions about the works of art, from which John Dewey wants to distance himself, among them: subject and object; artistic objects and objects of use; artistic authorship and collectivity; nature and culture; work and art.[72] John Dewey's aesthetic pragmatism seeks to avoid this type of attitude, by valuing the origin and the normal process of production of art in its regular sense within the life of organised communities, producers of theatre, music, paintings, architecture.[73] Consequently, the philosophical task of:

> . . .recovering the continuity of aesthetic experience with the normal processes of living.[74]

This task, in the field of Philosophy, makes John Dewey's conception something distant from Immanuel Kant's conception, and from its *rationalism*,[75] or, on the other hand, by Arthur Schopenhauer, the command of the *will* that is found there.[76] Neither *artistic experience* reduces itself to a mere exercise of *reason*, nor does it place itself only in terms of *will. Artistic experience* is something broader, more complex, fuller, and, at the same time, more complete than the segmentation of these parts.[77] Consequently, the important task undertaken by Dewey, with the intention of putting the terms of the approach of art back into a diverse perspective of these conceptions. Last but not least, *art* does not confuse itself with the mere *representation and/or imitation* of the natural world,[78] and here it goes one step further than Dewey's conception imposing the Western philosophical traditions, here

[69] *Cf.* Dewey (2010), p. 69.

[70] *Cf.* Dewey (2010), p. 251.

[71] *Cf.* Dewey (2010), p. 69.

[72] *Cf.* Dewey (2010), p. 452.

[73] *Cf.* Dewey (2010), p. 65.

[74] *Cf.* Dewey (2010), p. 70.

[75] *Cf.* Dewey (2010), p. 441.

[76] *Cf.* Dewey (2010), p. 504.

[77] "L'arte è il frutto dell'ingegno e dello spirito più nobile dell'uomo" ("Art is the fruit of man's noblest genius and spirit.") (Mazzucco 2017, p. 11).

[78] *Cf.* Dewey (2010), p. 492.

appropriately the vision of Plato.[79] With these gaps, the field of definitions is clearer announcing the statement what John Dewey intends, in the field of the *Aesthetic Theory*.

The philosophy is very accustomed to the *concept*, and the artist is very accustomed to *artistic experience*, and these worlds cross paths with difficulty. In order to formulate his philosophical conception, John Dewey has to reject the legacy of René Descartes, from which comes the radical separation between the *I* and the *world*, between *subject* and *object*.[80] But, appropriately, in the Deweyan conception, the *Aesthetic Theory* is only able to comprehend the meaning of works of art when resorting to *artistic-practice*, as this is where the genesis of works of art is found. Hence, the importance of recovering the *originality*, *singularity* and *uniqueness* of aesthetic experience, as a focus of philosophical reflection.[81] In the words of Dewey:

> It is to aesthetic experience, that the philosopher needs to consult in order to comprehend what is experience.[82]

Amongst the various radical and artificial separations produced by modern society, it is the separation between *life* and *art*. Art, in the modern world, is seen as *something fantastic*, as *something magical*, as *something extraordinary*, as something that is far beyond *regular life*. And this, fundamentally, because *art* is separated from *life*, and *life* lost meaning through the modern reduction of *experience*, in its original and fully sensorial meaning. And this because, for John Dewey, *experience* itself has something *artistic*, in a way which *art* is not something *separate*, but the revelation of the very *shape of being* in our humanity. This is the meaning of the statement according to which:

> For being the realisation of an organism in its struggles and conquests in a world of things, experience is art in germinal state.[83]

Here it goes, implicitly, the conception according to which the *modern world* impoverishes the genuine meaning of *experience*, by reducing *experience* to *labour*. Where speed, acceleration, productive rhythm, the logic of quickness dominate all the corners and the spaces of *life*, from it disappears the possibility of *delighting oneself* with *experience*, in a genuine and full sense, original and whole, something that John Dewey's pragmatic philosophy only intends to recover. The dullness of meanings,[84] the supremacy of work, the centralisation of money in the processes of social organisation, the destitution of meaning of experience are some factors that make the arrangement of modern life so densely problematic for the *artificial separation* between *life* and *art*. And this is noted by the very sociological analysis by Hartmut Rosa, for whom *modern experience* is the proper *experience of*

[79] *Cf.* Dewey (2010), p. 497.

[80] *Cf.* Dewey (2010), pp. 434–435.

[81] *Cf.* Dewey (2010), p. 472.

[82] *Cf.* Dewey (2010), p. 472.

[83] *Cf.* Dewey (2010), p. 84.

[84] *Cf.* Dewey (2010), p. 89.

acceleration.[85] The modern society, here understood as the society of acceleration[86] is what produces significant failures on the plane of the *world experience.*

But, for experience to be valid as *whole experience,*[87] in the vision of John Dewey, it should be re-established at its optimal point, and not *divided, segmented, sliced* and *cut up*, as the *experiences* normally produced in the modern world. Therefore, it should be seen with watchful eyes, and, in this respect, *art* is already in *life*, and *life* is already *art*, in a fusion of conceptual horizons that makes it possible to state:

> Art, thus, prefigures us proper processes of living.[88]

Or even, in this even simpler and more straightforward definition:

> Art is a quality of doing and of that that is done.[89]

The processes of living are to do with the configuration of the *shapes of life*, in living conditions, set and contextualised, which, largely, form a plot of insertion in the meaning of work of art. This, indeed, is an important finding, when wanting to be italicised in the area of the *Anthropology of Culture* where *work of art* is a significant part of the life of people[90] or of a civilisation.[91] It is clear, therefore, that *art* is a *way of doing things*, which expresses *life*, *history* and *creation*, in such a way of imprinting itself as a mark over the world, translating itself into shapes of clothing, architecture, paintings, illumination of texts, writing, sculptures, digital art, and so on.

2.4 Semiotics, Art and Permanence

Art reinforces life of spirit, and this because art, like love for life (*amor fati*),[92] is the desire to perpetuate and persist in the destructive *story of disappearance*, which harvests humanity from its cultural blossoming, expressing the human desire for historical transcendence, in other words, revealing human desire for integration

---

[85] "The initial hypothesis of this work runs as follows: *the experience of modernization is an experience of acceleration*" (Rosa 2015, p. 201).

[86] "Thus the guiding hypothesis of this work runs as follows: *modern society can be understood as an "acceleration society" in the sense that it displays a highly conditioned* (voraussetzungsreich) *structural and cultural linkage of both forms of acceleration* - technical acceleration and an increase in the pace of life due to chronic shortage of time resources - and therefore also a strong linkage of acceleration and growth" (Rosa 2015, p. 68).

[87] *Cf.* Dewey (2010), p. 139.

[88] *Cf.* Dewey (2010), p. 92.

[89] *Cf.* Dewey (2010), p. 381.

[90] *Cf.* Franca Filho (2011), p. 25.

[91] *Cf.* Boas (2015), p. 87.

[92] *Cf.* Salazar (1961), p. 09.

between the '*I imagetic*', '*society-culture*' and '*objectuality*' of the objective world. In *Odes* (III, 30, 1–7), the Latin poet Horácio, states something revealing, in this respect:

Exegi monumentum aere perennius
I finished a work more golden than bronze
Regalique situ pyramidum altius,
And higher than the royal pyramids,
Quod non imber edax, non Aquilo impotens
That neither corrosive rain nor impetuous wind
Possit diruere aut innumerabilis
Could destroy, no countless
Annorum series et fuga temporum.
Number of years and the swift passing of time.
Non omnis moriar;multaque pars mei
I will not die completely, and large part of me
Vitabilit Libitinam.
Will escape to the grave.

And this because *art* mobilises material, in order to transform it, in the passage from mortar, marble, wood, scene, image, paint, in works of art. The intangible nature of the symbol and of what it abstractly represents needs to be stabilised into material. *Art* is, indeed, interestingly, *culture* that also incorporates *nature*, and that is not able to rival *nature*;[93] furthermore, it is material (*nature*) that incorporates *culture*, and this because normally the lions, falcons, eagles, lizards, snakes, infernal beasts, flying angels, gargoyles, monsters, hybrid creatures are scarily summoned to participate in the symbol, attracting to its interior the strength of the 'animal kingdom', or 'plant' or 'natural', or even 'imaginary'. Specifically, it is John Dewey who values this perception, when he states:

> Art denotes a process of doing and creating. These both apply as much to beautiful-arts as to technological arts. Art involves moulding clay, carving marble, melting bronze, applying dyes, constructing buildings, singing songs, playing instruments, performing roles on stage, making rhythmic movements in dance. All art makes something with some physical material, the body or something outside of it, with or without the use of intervening instruments, and with views of the production of something visible, audible, or tangible.[94]

Art materialises into a *thing*, an *object-of-the-world*, but it is preserved in its *dimension-of-spirit*, for this reason, it incorporates the material which is not found, bestowing on it new meaning and, now, human, symbolic, semiotic, social, cultural value, and, hence, *aesthetic value*. For this reason, interacting with *art* is interacting with the inaccuracy of the meaning, with the active subconscious, vital energy in original and creative condition,[95] with the obscure trace of real, with human creative strength, with historical memory, with the human heroic search for discovery, with shape, but also with the human capacity to convert *raw material* into a *work of art*.

[93] *Cf.* Dewey (2010), p. 198.
[94] *Cf.* Dewey (2010), p. 126.
[95] *Cf.* Galeffi (1979), p. 27.

For example, a great set of iron metal became the *Eiffel Tower* (1889), this conversion that perpetuates presence in the structures in Paris in the nineteenth century, but also in the twentieth and twenty-first.[96] And this, it does, through the technique, from where among the *Greeks techné* is a term so cited.[97] But, unlike conceiving the *idea of work of art* that only transforms *material*, it should be also be perceived how much material 'make-learning' to the artist, in as far as that:

> The sculptor conceives his statue not only in mental terms, but also in clay, marble or bronze.[98]

The first step in this direction is to recognise that *art* is *work*, something that is recognised in its *making*, chisel, paintbrush, stick, pencil, body, *mouse*, *spray*, lens, camera, photographical technique.[99] It constitutes a form of work that, it even professionalises. In this respect, it recognises as much work as the sickle, hoe, pen, computer, lorry. It is, without a doubt, a form of creative work:

> An incredible dose of observation and the type of intelligence exercised in the perception of qualitative relations characterises the creative work of art.[100]

If it is *creative work*, it has a lot to do with craftwork common to all that is woven, that is, all *text* (*textus,* lat.; *tecere,* lat.). From the semiotic point of view, thus, it can be noticed that *artistic text* is that confirmation that human culture is able to imprint material and objectuality of the things of the world. *Aesthetic text* appears as well as the *locus* of convergences of numerous artistic, cultural, social, political and economic strengths. It is accompanied by the rationality of Walter Benjamin, in *The image of Proust*, which arrives at this conclusion:

> If *text* meant, for the Romans, that which it weaves, no text is more woven than that of Proust, and in a more solid way.[101]

2.5 Semiotics, Art and Power

Art, as any symbolic field, is a place of *social disputes*, especially when bearing in mind its *power-of-significance*. The 'works of art' give material, body, voice, place, evidence, space, a way of self expressing, the questions of the historical moment, and, because of this, they perform a decisive role in the field of disputes, fights and clashes of ideologies, conceptions, projects, identities, cultures, systems, world visions. It is in this regard that Jacques Rancière, in *The emancipated spectator*

---

[96] *Vide* Pignatari (1995), p. 34.
[97] *Cf.* Lacoste (1986), p. 187.
[98] *Cf.* Dewey (2010), p. 169.
[99] *Cf.* Dondis (2007), p. 51.
[100] *Cf.* Dewey (2010), p. 132.
[101] *Cf.* Benjamin (1996a, b, c, d), p. 37.

(2008), talks of an *aesthetic of politics* and, also, of a *politics of aesthetic*.[102] It is in no other way that all 'works of art', especially when of broad visibility and recognition, fame and historical significance, originality and spotlight, brings to itself a field of significance that becomes attractive and wide-reaching. But, art is not political for *politicising themes*, for questioning *aspects of life*, or even, for blasting the *legitimacy of power*, since, considering the vision of Jacques Rancière, in *Unrest in aesthetics* (2004), *art is political* by being constituted in *another reality*, which implies putting in place a proper language, a time and a proper meanings.[103] In this connection, the *sensitive experience* is itself emancipatory,[104] and this in so far as it frees us from the *hetermonies of the real.*

For this reason, *art* reveals *power*, exercises *power*, even if it is bound to the *power-of-attraction* that stems from the *fascination* exercised over people, bearing in mind the *sensitive literacy* that it implies.[105] For no other reason, *art* and *Aesthetic* became object of social dispute. For no other reason, 'beauty' is disputed, as much as the 'concept of beauty' is disputed, in as far as, after all, 'beauty' is valued as 'social wealth'. It is how 'beauty' accumulates factors which instigate *social power* and, for this reason, also starts to be desired by the holders of power, that, in turn, look to surround themselves by it, taking into account that 'beauty' becomes a *symbolic-accessory-of-power*, that is, an 'ornament of power', a 'label of power', in a way which the *fascination created by the work of art* is glued to the service of the *fascination by the holder-of-power*. This is the meaning and weight that the portraits of court possess, especially between the sixteenth and eighteenth centuries.[106]

The *near-transfer* of the 'aura' of the work of art to the *person-of-the-holder-of-power* is a strategy of those who hold the power (economic, political, social, cultural, communicative, bureaucratic).[107] The elite of all the historical periods surrounded themselves by the *works of art*, or, had themselves represented in the *form of art*, and

[102] *Cf.* Rancière (2014), p. 63.

[103] "El arte no es político, tampoco, por la manera en que representa las estructuras de la sociedad, los conflitos o las identidades de los grupos sociales. Es político por la misma distancia quc toma con respecto a sus funciones, por la classe de tempo y de espacio que instituye, por la manera en que recorta este tempo y puebla este espacio" ("Art is not political, either, because of the way it represents the structures of society, conflicts or the identities of social groups. It is political because of the distance it takes from its functions, because of the class of time and space it establishes, because of the way it cuts out this time and populates this space"—*translation*) (Rancière 2011, p. 33).

[104] "Porque la autonomia estética no es la autonomia del 'hacer' artístico que el modernismo há celebrado. Es la autonomia de uma forma de experiência sensible. Y es esta experiencia la que aparece como el germen de una nueva humanidade, de una nueva forma individual y colectiva de vida" ("Because aesthetic autonomy is not the autonomy of artistic 'doing' that modernism has celebrated. It is the autonomy of a form of sensitive experience. And it is this experience that appears as the germ of a new humanity, of a new individual and collective form of life"—*translation*) (Rancière 2011, p. 44).

[105] *Cf.* Dondis (2007), p. 185.

[106] *Cf.* Castelnuovo (2006), p. 17.

[107] *Cf.* Castelnuovo (2006), p. 103.

this is not different in the modern world and under the logic of modern capitalism, as John Dewey states.[108] However, art has an autonomy guaranteed by its own condition of *artistic language*. In spite of the fact that it can desire the *dazzle, magic, aura, intoxicating, futurist, ecstasy, sublime* brought by the work of art, it can only concede to the world of power—and, even, to its contrary, to the world of emancipation—in place of the work of art, and its artistic languages, corporal, verbal and *nonverbal signs*. This is the vision of Jacques Rancière, about the relation between art and power.[109] This means that emancipation is never full, by the work of art, and total control, also, is never full, by the work of art.

Therefore, *art* maintains an ambiguous relation with power, since, in fact, art can appear as an ally of power, contester of power—the example of the evocation of the arts in street protests—,[110] or even a victim of power, every contextual and historical arrangement, of conformity with its tasks, purposes and objectives. In the complex game of social powers, and its contexts,[111] *art* as *exercise of sensitivity*, may even confirm power, or even, ignore power, or more, articulate with power, challenge power, dilute power,[112] and in this is a long history of *meetings* and *misunderstandings*, whether in the *Aesthetic Theory*, or in *aesthetic experience*.

The innocence or the decency of *signs/symbols* seem to be something that directly affects passions, fervours and history, because they were not a few episodes in which a *sign/symbol* was at the centre of *iconoclastic* processes.[113] As John Dewey explains, often, this is due to the fact that:

> The refusal to recognise the boundaries established by convention is the source of frequent accusations of immorality against the objects of art.[114]

Equally, the political caricature has often found the way to consecrate itself, as a method of construction of the *symbol* of the other as the *social enemy, political enemy* or *religious enemy.*[115] Often, it is the power of the *signs/symbols* that starts the process of intolerance, and, sometimes, it is the intolerance that reaches the centrality of the *sign/symbol*. Therefore, with the *Talmud,*[116] with *Buddhism,*[117] with

---

[108] *Cf.* Dewey (2010), p. 67.

[109] *Cf.* Rancière (2009a, b), p. 26.

[110] *Cf.* Bucci (2016), p. 107.

[111] *Cf.* de Campos Barros (2016), p. 209.

[112] *Cf.* Rancière (2014), p. 60.

[113] "Fra il 726 e l'842 d.C. l'Oriente e l'Occidente sono scossi dalla crisi iconoclasta. Cioè dalla grave lotta sulla legitimità del culto delle immagini e sulla legitimità del potere che intende disciplinare tale culto" ("Between 726 and 842 A.D., the East and the West were shaken by the iconoclastic crisis. That is, the serious struggle over the legitimacy of the cult of images and the legitimacy of the power that intends to regulate this cult"—*translation*) (Tuzet 2014, p. 175).

[114] *Cf.* Dewey (2010), p. 343.

[115] *Cf.* Eco (2007), p. 190.

[116] *Vide* Báez (2006), p. 132.

[117] *Cf.* Báez (2006), p. 96.

Lutheranism,[118] in the most varied contexts of history and, at different moments and in different countries, in the West and in the East, the situation of the Biblecaust caused by the Third Reich, in Germany, being of prominence.[119]

On the same topic, the events that took place in Charlottesville, Virginia, in the USA, throughout 2017, when the discussion about the removal of the statues of the Confederates in view of the decision by the City Council, especially of the equestrian statue in bronze of confederate *Robert Edward Lee*, in 1924. The protests around the subject reignited the debate about the racial issue in the USA, as well as causing confrontations between black groups and white supremacist groups. It is indeed worth remembering, in the song *Strange Fruit,* the repulsion of the North-American racism and the lynchings of Afro-Americans at the beginning of the twentieth century, in the USA, in the musical version by *Billie Holiday* of the poem by Abel Meeropol, sung for the first time in 1939, in *Café Society*, in *Greenwich Village*:

Strange Fruit
Southern trees bear strange fruit,
Blood on the leaves and blood at the root,
Black bodies swinging in the southern breeze,
Strange fruit hanging from the poplar trees.

Pastoral scene of the gallant south,
The bulging eyes and the twisted mouth,
Scent of magnolias, sweet and fresh,
Then the sudden smell of burning flesh.

Here is fruit for the crows to pluck,
For the rain to gather, for the wind to suck,
For the sun to rot, for the trees to drop,
Here is a strange and bitter crop.

Art talks of the horrors of history, as well as the inhumanity of human actions. Moreover, art should not be colonised by politics, since its *autonomy* is its survival. For no other reason, there are countless times where *art* shows itself as *aloof* of its possession by politics and therefore makes it possible for the redefinition of aesthetic experience to continue slipping along the edge and transforming the boundaries of the known from *aesthetic rebellion*. In the vision of Herbert Marcuse, against the powers of religion, of morale, of politics, *autonomous art* can be the target of all types of attacks and rejections.[120] In *Minima Moralia*, Theodor Adorno states:

The mission of art is, today, introduce chaos to order.

Artistic productivity is the ability of arbitrary within the unintentional.

Art is magic, free from the lie of being truth.[121]

---

[118] *Cf.* Báez (2006), p. 159.

[119] *Cf.* Báez (2006), p. 241.

[120] *Cf.* Marcuse (2007), p. 62.

[121] *Cf.* Adorno (2001), p. 231. *See* too Hermann (2005), p. 31.

But, this is a more specific way of seeing the role and the mission of the *Aesthetic Theory*, and what it mobilises as instigation in the field of arts, according to socio-economic factors created from injustice and oppression. In turn, the photographer Sebastião Salgado affirms,[122] about his mission in front of the lenses of the camera and the product of his work:

> No photo, alone, can change what it wants in the poverty of the world. However, added to texts, films and the entire acts of humanitarian and environmental organisations, my images form part of a broader movement of the denunciation of violence, of exclusion or ecological issue. This information means contributing to sensitising those which they consider in respect of the capability that we have to change the destiny of humanity.[123]

In fact, the *arts* have diverse postures, in front of various factors that condition life in society. There have already been *official-arts* of political regimes,[124] as there has already been art of the Ideal State, as the Ideal Sate has also already been banished, the example of its expurgation from the *Republic*, of Plato, as Erwin Panofsky notes very precisely.[125] In the plan of architecture, the Mirrored City, filled with sky-scrapers, that is, of modern buildings of high phallic stature (height; slender; fullness; strength; linearity; safety; assurance; importance; imperativity) shape, in the vision of Décio Pignatari, a '*urbograma*' of the power of urban life.[126]

2.6 Semiotics, Art and Symbolic Role

But, it is an undeniable fact that the wealth of the arts that makes them able to carry with great skill plenty of potentials of *production of meaning*, of *representation of things* and *sensitive affectation*, and it is in this that they perform the significant *symbolic role* amongst the circulation of linguistic and non-linguistic *signs*, as can be read in *The sign*, by Umberto Eco.[127] The various possible aesthetics and the pluralist school aesthetics they unload upon society their *arsenal of meanings* through their *aesthetic texts*, stimulating even more multivocity, plurivocity and the emergence of readings and possibilities of meaning.[128] From there, art always

[122] *Cf.* Martins (2017), p. 98.

[123] *Cf.* Salgado (2014), p. 56.

[124] *Cf.* Bucci (2015), p. 27.

[125] *Cf.* Panofsky (2000), p. 08.

[126] *Cf.* Pignatari (1995), p. 133.

[127] *Cf.* Eco (1990), p. 97.

[128] "Le poetiche contemporanee, nel proporre strutture artistiche che richiedono un particolare impegno autonomo del fruitore, spesso una ricostruzione, sempre variabile, del materiale proposto, riflettono una generale tendenza della nostra cultura verso quei processi in cui, invece di una sequenza univoca e necessaria di eventi, si stabilisce come un campo di probabilità, una ambiguità di situazione, tale da stimolare scelte operative o interpretative volta a volta diverse" ("The contemporary poetics, in proposing artistic structures that require a particular autonomous commitment of the user, often a reconstruction, always variable, of the proposed material, reflect a general

being accompanied with the capability of defining the forward and backward march, creating controversy, divergence, ambivalence and vanguard.

There are arts more able of *representing things, producing meanings and creating affectation* than others, depending on the function and on the field in which it is. Each one, evidently, performs one or more functions, but are distinguished by their own channels of which they are valued, to designate and signify. The example of music, in comparison to photography, is that which has poor capacity of reproducing reality,[129] but expresses the states of the soul very well, while this other has the capacity of maintaining the most accurate record possible of the photographed object.

In the field of the *production of meanings*, arts can be seen as *arts-arms*, since they trigger senses, being (or not) capable of creating (more or less) transforming effects (in society, in culture, in the conscience) about the *state-of-things* of society. In the statement of Soviet poet V. Maiakovski this proposal is somewhat contained:

> Art is not a mirror for reflecting the world, but a hammer to forge it.

But, in this field, it is also possible to say nothing already fulfils a function, the poetic function, properly said, which makes each aesthetic exercise a free form of expression of beauty. In *Boy of the Bush* (2nd Part, *Apprentice's Notebook*, 9), the poet Manoel de Barros affirms:

> For my taste the word need not signify– it is only chanting.[130]

In the field of the *representation of things* the capacity that a photograph has of being read, without captions, in every single part, without translation and with little mediation, highlights its capacity of dissemination and its value of the representation of things. It is by Charles Baudelaire (*Music and suggestion*) the following reflection:

> I always heard it said that music cannot boast of translating accurately, like it happens with the word or the painting. This is true up to a certain point, but it is not entirely true. It translates in its own way, and with the means that are its own. In music, as in the painting and even in the written word, that is however the most positive of the arts, there is always a gap to be filled by the imagination of the listener.[131]

In the same way, the references made by the photographer Sebastião Salgado and by the poet Décio Pignatari are tracks of this dimension of the arts:

---

tendency of our culture towards those processes in which, instead of a univocal and necessary sequence of events, is established as a field of probability, an ambiguity of situation, such as to stimulate different operational or interpretative choices from time to time"—*translation*) (Eco 1993, p. 95).

[129] *Cf.* Gomes (1985), p. 19.

[130] *Cf.* de Barros (2010), p. 458.

[131] *Apud* Gomes (1985), p. 43 (translated).

> The photograph is such a powerful writing because it can be read throughout the world without translation.[132]

> Poetry attempts to be or imitate the object to which it refers, by means of analogue forms ('rain rainfall raining), whereas, in prose, we attempt 'to tell' what is happening ('the rain is falling'). It is for this reason that I can 'summarise' a romance or a thesis, but I cannot summarise a poem, a picture or a symphony.[133]

In the field of *sensitive affectation* the elocutive power of each work of art distinguishes itself, according to the writing of Umberto Eco, considering the capacity of coming closer to smell, touch, taste, sight and hearing, reaching the sensorial channels of the human body in a more intense way, or less intense, more whole or less whole, closer or more distant, more plural or more focal.[134] The *arts* are, thus, made of *affectation*, stimulating *perception*, sharpening the *sensations*, attracting by the moving of *sensorial stimuli*, those which *impact* us; work in a way of being mobilisers of *sensations, intelligence, perception, feelings, emotions*, stirring superficial and/or deep layers in these dimensions.

2.7 Semiotics, Art and Creation

The *passion* for art—next to the *transpiration* in the craft of art—moves every true artist, whose creative and genuine movement feeds back to his own passion. The shifts provoked by the passion for creation are forms free from *re-constitution of the world*, now with the aim of freedom conferred by artistic languages.[135] This is why the centre of artistic activity is the *creation*. Indeed, it is what highlights the analysis of the *Semiotics of Art* well.[136] In this respect, the creation is nothing more than what is done in "...field of possibilities open by available means...", in the definition by Gian Maria Tore.[137]

In fact, *creation* is the greatest beauty of the artistic process; it is what uncovers the horizons of difference, making the new possible. For this reason, the horizon of the artist is situated at the threshold of a boundary in the path of the *unknown, unknowable, uncontrollable*. The artist works *at-the-threshold, between-tendencies, at-the-limit,* and, it is in this sense, that the universe of artistic creation, from the semiotic point of view—as Julio Plaza affirms, in *Inter-semiotic Translation*—,

[132] *Cf.* Salgado (2014), p. 58.

[133] *Cf.* Pignatari (1987), p. 21.

[134] *Cf.* Eco (1990), p. 44.

[135] *Cf.* Xerez (2016), p. 468.

[136] "Dès lors, il est indispensable pour une sémiotique de l'art (c'est le corollaire épistémologique) de pouvoir étudier quelque chose en tant que 'création'" ("From then on, it is indispensable for a semiotics of art (this is the epistemological corollary) to be able to study something as a 'creation'"—*translation*) (Tore 2011, p. 01).

[137] *Cf.* Tore (2011), p. 04.

makes an *icon* of the past, of the present an *index* and of the future a *symbol*, in processes of creation and interaction with time that are unique.[138]

It is in this regard that the *new*, the *original*, the *genuine* can come to the light. In this respect, it is worth a tour around *jazz* and the way *jazz* allows the *pulse* of the new, creation and improvisation. *Jazz* is a type of syncopated and improvised music,[139] a result of the crossing of cultural origins and diverse music,[140] of popular origin,[141] arising in the USA, which opens countless rhythmic possibilities, melodies and harmonies.[142] Being the improvisation,[143] in collective movement,[144] one of its main characteristics, despite the lack of uniformity in the self-definition of the term *jazz* and of the boundaries of *jazz*, amongst the other musical modalities, it is clear that the process of creation of *jazz* musicians arises, above all, from the very spontaneous process of musical production—which means a degree of greater *freedom*, if compared to European classical music, with respect to its relation with the *musical norm*—, in the form of a game, normally the result of *jam sessions.* In the good overview by *Herbie Hancock*:

> Jazz is the music that expresses the best of human spirit. It is to do with the idea of sharing, not of competing. Jazz is to do with working in a group.[145]

Within this musical tradition of the twentieth century—structured on the basis of the relation between *theme* x *improvisation*,[146] and which hides within itself the magic of the *blue note*—, flows, trends and lineages were being formed, taking into account common roots (*work songs*; *military music brass band*; *negro spiritual*; *African musical tradition*; *Afro-Cuban rhythmic elements*; *ballads*; *popular music*; *ragtime*; *gospel songs*; *church music*), that opened up into the more varied expressions, from *Swing* to *Bebop,* from *Cool* to *Hard Bop,* from *Fusion* to *Free Jazz*, to the more contemporary trends.[147] Many of these flows, were captained, or assimilated, by five decades of participation on the jazz scene by *Miles Davis*—also nicknamed Chameleon of *Jazz*—which demonstrates the musician's enormous capacity for adaptation, the enormous diversification in musical directions within the music, and the persistence of what was an artist recognised for his leading edge on the front of *Cool Jazz*.[148]

---

[138] *Cf.* Plaza (2010), p. 08.
[139] *Cf.* Junqueira (2014), pp. 39–42.
[140] *Cf.* Hobsbawn (2008), p. 61.
[141] *Cf.* Hobsbawn (2008), p. 61.
[142] *Cf.* Hobsbawn (2008), p. 47.
[143] *Cf.* Calado (2007), p. 10.
[144] *Cf.* Hobsbawn (2008), p. 53.
[145] *Cf.* Calado (2007), p. 41.
[146] *Cf.* Pietroforte (2016), p. 21.
[147] *Cf.* Pietroforte (2016), p. 21.
[148] *Cf.* Calado (2007), p. 07.

In this respect, examples abound in the history of *jazz*, regarding the power of *artistic creation*, among them: the combination between the saxophone of *John Coltrane* and the trumpet of *Miles Davis*, in the performance of *So What* (9:24), song of *modal jazz* composed by *Miles Davis*, in 1959, for the album *King of Blue*,[149] or even, the same duo in the performance of *Some day my prince will come* (9:04), composed by *Frank Churchill* and *Larry Morey*, for the namesake album, launched in 1961;[150] in *Impromptu* (5:22), *Dizzy Gillespie* demonstrates which point *Bebop* reached, through his trumpet, as *virtuosi*, in the song;[151] the *soul* of *Hard Pop* of the song *Jody Grind* (5:47), by *Horace Silver* (*Woody Shaw*, on the trumpet, *Tyone Washington*, on the tenor sax, *Horace Silver*, on the piano, *Larry Ridley*, on the bass, *Roger Humphries*, on the drums), recorded on 02/11/1966, for the album *The Jody Grind*;[152] the sophisticated composition of *Cantaloup Island* (5:29), in 1964, by the pianist Herbie Hancock, with Herbie Hancock on piano, Freddie Hubbard on trumpet, Ron Carter on the bass and Tony Willians on the drums;[153] at the front of the band *Jazz Messengers, Funky jazz,* sub-style of *Hard Bop*, by drummer *Art Blakey*, in *Moanin'* (9:36), the masterpiece of pianist *Bobby Timmons* and of *John Hendricks*, achieves redefining the meaning of *jazz* at its time;[154] the inventive and improvised character of the style of *Bebop* of *Charlie Parker*—something noticeable in the song *Cool Blues*, by *Charlie Parker* himself—[155] who changed the history of *jazz* in the twentieth century.[156]

Umberto Eco draws our attention to the presence of the unconscious and unfathomable trait of the artist, when manifested in the *single, unique* and *improvised* character of the *work of art*, this which appears to be the materialised result of its artistic action.[157] It is in this sense that the *physical object* formed by the *work of art* (picture; wood engraving; enactment; lyrics of song; musical performance) is a *unique* record of the personality (ies) of the artist(s).[158]

It is also in this sense, for example, *creation* can be the result of an intuition, of a furtive creative act, of an *insight,* of a *state-of-soul,* of the *combination* between certain musicians, or, the result of the tuned collective *improvisation* by various musicians, as occurs in the musical improvisation promoted by *jazz*.[159] The improvised and harmonic connection between musical notes and the dialogue between instruments and musical distinctiveness that *creates* and *re-creates* the universe of

---

[149] *Cf.* Calado (2007).
[150] *Cf.* Calado (2007).
[151] *Cf.* Calado (2007).
[152] *Cf.* Calado (2007).
[153] *Cf.* Calado (2007).
[154] *Cf.* Calado (2007).
[155] *Cf.* Calado (2007), p. 8.
[156] *Cf.* Calado (2007), p. 07.
[157] *Cf.* Eco (2016), p. 15.
[158] *Cf.* Eco (2016), p. 29.
[159] *Cf.* Calado (2007), p. 11.

rhythmic, melodic and musical possibilities makes *jazz* what *jazz* is. Here, it is interesting that it is not the execution of *strict rule* that creates *good music*, because as good music, *jazz* also makes the spontaneous connection between united instrumentalists and as creative individuals, in a curious relation between *collective identity* and *subjective distinctiveness*. No other musical style demonstrates with such might and intensity the contribution of the individual in the group or the support of the group for the *solo* of the individual, in addition to a *mix* so virtuous of the *individual* and of the *collaborative*.[160] In this respect, João Francisco Franco Junqueira affirms:

> Improvisation is like a digital impression. Rather more: a defining characteristic of the grandeur of jazz.[161]

Omar Calabrese, in *How a work of art is read,* draws attention to the fact that it is there that the *idioletto* is found, in individual work, and in collective work, the *socioletto* of the work of art.[162] And, for his part, the French philosopher Jean Baudrillard draws attention to the fact that it is there that *material* (screen; paper; wood; marble; paint; body) is converted into a *cultural object*, by stating:

> Thus the painted *work* becomes a *cultural object* by signature: it is not anymore just read, but perceived within its differential value – a single state of 'aesthetic' emotion often confusing critical reading with signage perception.[163]

But, it is important to make clear that creation is not a *pure unilateral stand* of the artist.[164] Not even the *intentio auctoris* will be the only predominant factor in the future and previous acts of intellection and comprehension, fruition and use of the work of art, as the *intention* of the artist does not control the work of art.[165] There is repair and correct, there are errors that become patterns, there are lines that become curves, and there are moulds that are converted into works, in the process of creation. Therefore, the *work determines* the artist, as much as the artist is personified in the work of art. The process is of two paths, in so far as the *form* is not simply *established* in *material*, since *material* is also established in an *artistic form.*

---

[160] *Cf.* Pietroforte (2016), pp. 21–22.

[161] *Cf.* Junqueira (2014), p. 42.

[162] *Cf.* Calabrese (2015), pp. 17–18.

[163] *Cf.* Baudrillard (1972), p. 114.

[164] *Cf.* Nöth (2012), p. 16.

[165] *Cf.* Xerez (2016), p. 462.

2.8 Semiotics, Art and Pluralism of Meanings

No work of art is univocal, being the multiplicity of writings a characteristic of the way of understanding the meaning(s) of which all art is a bearer. The work of art is an open-ended field,[166] or even, in the definition by Umberto Eco, all works of art are an *open-ended opera.*[167] The open-ended work cannot be ended, encapsulated or stopped from being *re-read*, now from another look, even if the author wishes.[168] The look of the artist is completed with the look of the user, and the look of the art is richer in as far as it is fed on *interpretation*, and *re-interpretation*, on *creation* and on *re-creation.*[169] Hence, pluralism, wealth, depth and the infinity of the *artistic look.* In fact, the infinite dimensions of meanings, writings and interpretations conferred to the works of art as *semiotic texts*[170] are an invitation to the relativisation of everything that is said to be absolute, and a unique opportunity to *turn over* in the dimension of the place of the artist-creator.[171] This vision feeds Umberto Eco's understanding of the work of art, both in the field of *theoretical Semiotics*, in the works of *The sign* and *Semiotics and the philosophy of language*, and in the field of the *Theory of Art,* in the work *The definition of art.*[172]

Consequently the magic of the language of arts happens, capable of charming, creating dazzle, and it is from this 'spell' that the *power-seducer* of the works of art moves. In this aspect, the reflection of Walter Benjamin, in *The doctrine of the,* brings this dimension of the work of art to the surface precisely: "This dimension – magic, if one wishes to say– of language and of the writing is not developed separately from the other dimension, semiotics. All the mimetic elements of language constitute a founded intention, that is, they can only come to light on a foundation that is strange to them, and this foundation is not other than the semiotic and communicative dimension of language".[173] Therefore, the work of art does not mean because it represents nature or reality, simply, because the *work of art*, in fact, *creates* a *new reality.*[174]

---

[166] *Cf.* Santaella and Nöth (1998), p. 53.

[167] *See* Eco (1993), p. 34.

[168] "L'apertura quindi è, sotto questo aspetto, la condizone di ogni fruizione estetica e ogni forma fruibile in quanto dotata di valore estetico è aperta. Lo è, como se è visto, anche quando l'artista mira a una comunicazione univoca e non ambigua" ("Openness is therefore, in this respect, the condition of every aesthetic use and every usable form because it has aesthetic value that is open. It is, as if it is seen, even when the artist aims at a univocal and unambiguous communication"—*translation*) (Eco 1993, p. 89).

[169] *Cf.* Franca Filho (2011), p. 83.

[170] *Cf.* Eco (1990), p. 150.

[171] *Cf.* Eco (1991), p. 31.

[172] *Cf.* Eco (2016), p. 30.

[173] *Cf.* Benjamin (1996a, b, c, d), p. 112.

[174] *Cf.* Marcuse (2007), p. 18.

2.9 Semiotics, Art and Memory

Art-memory is a form of access and comprehension of history, appearing as a revealer of history, intentional or not intentionally. The works of art, by their nature of *corpus* material, are records of time, documenting history and freezing circumstantial, exceptional and unrepeatable pictures; for precisely this reason, they make humanity know more about itself. The example of the drawings *Pregnancy of Monsters* and *Brazil 68*, by Antonio Benetazzo, the place of horror, within the work of art, as a portrait of a *political context,* indicates that *artistic text* is a record, and, also, memory,[175] and that suppression of memory is a proper artifice of authoritarianism.[176] For this reason, in this respect, Herbert Marcuse states, in *The aesthetic dimension*, something of relevant interest in this reflection:

> In amidst the sensitivity arises the paradoxical relation of art with time – paradoxical because what is experienced through sensitivity is present, although art is not able to show the present without showing it as the past. What became a form in the work of art already happened: it is recorded, *re-presented*. The mimesis translates reality to memory. In this recollection, art recognised what is and what could be, inside and outside of social conditions. Art derived this understanding from the sphere of the abstract concept and implanted it in the domain of sensuousness.[177]

For this reason, a photographic record is a work of art, uniquely considered, or a mere familiar record, but, it still can be a *document of history*, be it of macro-history of social events, as much as of the micro-history of a given individual. By comparing art of the photographer to the art of the architect, both arts highly documentary and constitutive of memory, Sebastião Salgado states that the images of photography:

> They are fractions of seconds that contain complete stories.[178]

References

Adorno TW (2001) Minima moralia (trans: Morão A). Edições, Lisboa, p 70

Argan GC (2013) História da arte italiana [History of Italian art] (trans: de Katinsky V). Cosac Naif, São Paulo

Báez F (2006) História universal da destruição dos livros [Universal history of book destruction] (trans: Schlafman L). Ediouro, Rio de Janeiro

Baudrillard J (1972) Pour une critique de l'économie politique du signe. Gallimard, Paris

Benjamin W (1996a) A imagem de Proust. In: Magia e técnica, arte e política [Magic and techniques, art and politics] (trans: Rouanet SP), 7th edn. Brasiliense, São Paulo

Benjamin W (1996b) Pequena história da fotografia. In: Magia e técnica, arte e política [Magic and techniques, art and politics]. 7th edn. Brasiliense, São Paulo

[175] *Vide* Seligman-Silva (2012), p. 72.

[176] *Cf.* Cardenuto (2016), p. 21.

[177] *Cf.* Marcuse (2007), p. 63.

[178] *Vide* Salgado (2014), pp. 48–49.

Benjamin W (1996c) A obra de arte na era de sua reprodutibilidade técnica. In: Magia e técnica, arte e política [Magic and techniques, art and politics] (trans: Rouanet SP), 7th edn. Brasiliense, São Paulo
Benjamin W (1996d) Sobre o conceito de história. In: Magia e técnica, arte e política [Magic and techniques, art and politics] (trans: Rouanet SP), 7th edn. Brasiliense, São Paulo
Boas F (2015) Arte primitiva. [Primitive art] (trans: José C. Pereira). Mauad X, Rio de Janeiro
Brandi C (1986) Segno e immagine. Aesthetica, Palermo
Bucci E (2015) O Estado de narciso [Narcissus state]. Companhia das Letras, São Paulo
Bucci E (2016) A forma bruta dos protestos [The crude form of the protests]. Companhia das Letras, São Paulo
Calado C (2007) Coleção Folha de São Paulo (Charlie Parker; Art Blakey; John Coltrane; Dizzy Gillespie; Horace Silver; Miles Davis; Herbie Hancock; Miles Davis). Mediafashion, Rio de Janeiro
Calabrese O (2015) Como se lê uma obra de arte. [How to read a work of art]. Edições, Lisboa, p 70
Cardenuto R (2016) Antonio Benetazzo, permanências do sensível. In: Benetazzo A (ed) Reinaldo Cardenuto. Prefeitura de São Paulo, São Paulo, pp 09–30
Castelnuovo E (2006) Retrato e sociedade na arte italiana [Portrait and society in Italian art] (trans: de Mattos F). Companhia das Letras, São Paulo
da Cunha PF (2010) Direito, poder e pró-vocação artística [Law, power and artistics provocation]. Boletim da Faculdade de Direito da Universidade de Coimbra 101:209–239
Danto AC (2015) O abuso da beleza [Beauty abuse] (trans: Süssekind P). Martins Fontes, São Paulo
de Barros M (2010) Poesia completa [Complete poetry]. Leya, São Paulo
de Campos Barros VS (2016) A civilização chutou as portas do *Saloon*. In: Filho MF, Leite GS, Filho RP (eds) Antimanual de Direito & Arte [Anti-manual of law and art]. Saraiva, São Paulo, pp 200–242
Dewey J (2010) Arte como experiência. [Art as experience] (trans: Vera Ribeiro). Martins Fontes, São Paulo
Dondis DA (2007) Sintaxe da linguagem visual [Visual language syntax] (trans: Camargo JL). Martins Fontes, São Paulo
Eco U (org.) (1990) O signo [The sign] (trans: Marinho MF), 4ª. edn. Presença, Lisboa
Eco U (org.) (1991) Semiótica e filosofia da linguagem [Semiotics and philosophy of language] (trans: Fabris M, Fiorin JL). Ática, São Paulo
Eco U (org.) (1993) Opera aperta. Milano: Bompiani
Eco U (org.) (2007) História da feiúra [History of ugliness] (trans: Aguiar E). Record, Rio de Janeiro
Eco U (org.) (2016) A definição da arte [The definition of art] (trans: Aguiar A). Record, São Paulo
Franca Filho MT (2011) A cegueira da justiça [The blindness of justice]. Sergio Antonio Fabris, Porto Alegre
Galeffi R (1979) Novos ensaios de estética [New essays in aesthetics]. UFBA, Bahia
Gomes ÁC (1985) A estética simbolista [The symbolist aesthetics]. Cultrix, São Paulo
Geertz C (2014) O saber local [The local knowledge] (trans: Vera Joscelyne), 14th edn. Rio de janeiro, Vozes
Hermann N (2005) Ética e estética. EDIPUCRS, Porto Alegre
Hobsbawn EJ (2008) História social do jazz [Social history of jazz] (trans: Noronha A), 6th edn. Paz e Terra, São Paulo
Junqueira JFF (2014) Jazz. Via Impressa, São Paulo
Lacoste J (1986) A filosofia da arte [The philosophy of art] (trans: Cabral Á). Jorge Zahar, Rio de Janeiro
Lipovetsky G, Serroy J (2014) O capitalismo estético na era da globalização [The aesthetic capitalism in the age of globalization]. Edições, Lisboa, p 70
Malland JS (2012) *Tropical spray*: viagem ao coração do grafite brasileiro (trans: Régnier BAL, Noronha JMG). Martins Fontes, São Paulo

Marcuse H (2007) A dimensão estética [The aesthetic dimension] (trans: Costa ME). Edições, Lisboa, p 70

Martins J d S (2017) Sociologia da fotografia e da imagem. [Sociology of the photopgraph and the image], 2nd edn. Contexto, São Paulo

Mazzucco E (2017) Il crimine e l'arte. Tippi, Roma

Nazario L (2005) Quadro histórico do pós-modernismo. In: Guinsburg J, Barbosa AM (eds) O pós-modernismo [Post-modernism]. Perspectiva, São Paulo, pp 23–70

Nöth W (2012) Fundamentos semióticos do estudo das imagens [The semiotic fundamentals of the study of images]. Tabuleiro das Letras 05:01–19

Panofsky E (2000) Idea (trans: Neves P). Martins Fontes, São Paulo

Pastore JAD (2009) A arte do inconsciente. In: Ciência e Cultura [Science and culture]. SBPC/FAPESP, São Paulo, pp 20–24

Perissé G (2004) Filosofia, ética e literatura [Philosophy, ethics and literature]. Manole, São Paulo

Pietroforte AV (2016) Análise do texto visual [Analysis of the visual text], 2nd edn. Contexto, São Paulo

Pignatari D (1987) Semiótica e literatura [Semiotics and literature], 3rd edn. Cultrix, São Paulo

Pignatari D (1995) Semiótica da arte e da arquitetura [Semiotics of art and of the architecture]. Cultrix, São Paulo

Plaza J (2010) Tradução intersemiótica [Intersemiotics translation]. Perspectiva, São Paulo

Rancière J (2009a) O inconsciente estético [The aesthetic unconscious] (trans: Netto MC). Editora, São Paulo, p 34

Rancière J (2009b) A partilha do sensível [Sharing the sensitive] (trans: Netto MC). Eixo Experimental; Editora, São Paulo, p 34

Rancière J (2011) El malestar en la estética (trans: Petrecca MÁ, Vogelfandg L, Burello MG). Capital Intelectual, Buenos Aires

Rancière J (2014) O espectador emancipado [The emancipated viewer] (trans: Benedetti IC). Martins Fontes, São Paulo

Rendon PA (2014) Hacia uma semiótica del arte: implicaciones del pensamento peirceano en el estúdio del arte contemporâneo. Cuadernos de Filosofía Latinoamericana 11:127–145

Rosa H (2015) Social acceleration (trans: Trejo-Mathys J). Columbia, New York

Salazar A (1961) Que é arte? [What is art?] 3rd ed. Arménio Amado, Coimbra

Salgado S (2014) Da minha terra à Terra. [From my land to the Eartth]. Transl. Julia da Rosa Simões. Paralela, São Paulo

Santaella L (2016a) Memória e perspectivas da semiótica no Brasil [Memory and perspectives of semiotics in Brazil]. Intexto 37:22–33

Santaella L (2016b) Temas e dilemas do pós-digital [Themes and dilemmas of the post-digital]. Paulus, São Paulo

Santaella L, Nöth W (1998) Imagem [Image]. Iluminuras, São Paulo

Seligman-Silva M (2012) Imagens do trauma e sobrevivência das imagens: sobre as hiperimagens. In: Cornelsen EL, Vieira EA, Seligman-Silva M (eds) Imagem e memória [Image and memory]. Rona Editora, FALE-Faculdade de Letras da UFMG, Belo Horizonte, pp 63–79

Tore GM (2011) L'art comme création, ou la règle de nier la règle. Actes Sémiotiques, no. 114: 01–11. epublications.unifilm.fr. Accessed 6 June 2017

Tuzet G (2014) Contro le immagini. In: Carla F, Gigliotti V, Heritier P, Mittica MP (eds) Il Diritto tra testo e immagine. Mimesis, Milano, pp 175–188

Xerez RM (2016) A norma jurídica como obra de arte. In: Marcílio FF, Leite GS, Filho RP (eds) *AntiManual de Direito & Arte [Antimanual Law & Art]*, pp 453–476

Chapter 3
Society, Law and Art

3.1 Modern Society, Law and Justice

The gradual *derision of the human*, in modern society, is a great threat that hovers, as a possibility, like the point of approximation to *barbarism*, that is, to *extreme injustice*. The *human* became, paradoxically, *stranger to man*. We were ourselves wild, and diluted ourselves in what 'we are made', by social conditioning, with weak power of autonomous reaction. This type of finding brings with it much dismay, and, for this reason, opens space to philosophical reflection. And the first step is recognising that modern society brought numerous benefits, technological, scientific, economical, cultural, social and political, but it is interesting to notice that it was not without the support of *reason*, as the manifestation of *Instrumental Reason,* that *Auschwitz,* as a modern phenomenon, went from the 'possibility of absolute evil' to the 'effective reality' in civilisation. In *Education after Auschwitz,* Theodor Adorno makes it clear that this *admonition* is constitutive of a conception of education, as emancipated education.[1] For this reason, in the perspective of the *Critical Theory of Society*, the *reading of the rational* was accompanied by the *reading of the irrational*, and the *criticism of barbarism* must keep up with the *analysis* of modern society, and of its classes and institutions, if it wishes to defend modern society from itself, in other words, from its *anthropophagic* nature.

It is also Theodor Adorno, in the fragment *Palace of Hanus*, in *Minimum Morality,*[2] who states that the *universalization* of the merchandise accompanies the *dehumanisation* of human relations. This is largely how, the paradox of modern life becomes apparent, precisely to highlight the necessity to review the '*project of modernity*', especially considering the exhaustion and the deviations from the project of *Enlightenment*. Indeed, it was in the *Dialectic of Enlightenment* (1944)

[1] *Cf.* Adorno (1995), p. 119.

[2] *Cf.* Adorno (2001), pp. 150–151.

E. C. B. Bittar, *Semiotics, Law & Art*, Law and Visual Jurisprudence 2,
https://doi.org/10.1007/978-3-030-58880-9_3

that Max Horkheimer and Theodor Adorno gave the most critical outlines possible to the dawning of modernity, not leaving a shred of doubt that the diagnosis of dialectics between shadows and lights made the apparition of *barbarism* possible in its modern form.[3] Apart from all the promises of the '*project of modernity*', identified with the ideas of *liberty*, *equality* and *fraternity*, the *instrumentalising* deviation in the historical turn, took us to a society whose nature is such that *enlightenment* has been lost as a possibility.

By no other path, can one arrive at the set of the pathologies of contemporary societies, for which the rule that the *appearance* became the *essence*, and the *having* dominates the *being*;[4] under the imperative of *individualism*, the capacity for alteration has faded; the accentuation of *social inequalities* only leads to the subjects of *social justice* and of the *redistribution* being placed aside; under the pressure of many forms of *violence*, *conviviality* and *solidarity* fade away; in the culture of market, the space for the practices that value *humanisation* become less probable; under the insignia from cult to *technification*, the cultivation of *autonomy* is dissolved into the space of *no-place*; under pressure of blind and consumerist *materialism*, the human capacity to pay attention to the *moral development* of personality is unfocused; before the empire of short-sighted and egolatric consumerism,[5] the things are entified, and in place of them serving only as things, the relation between *men* and the use of *assets* is denatured;[6] as a devouring society of natural resources, life becomes paradoxically *devastating*, and, in this sense, less capable of respect for *planetary life*;[7] in the *indifference* of urbanised life, reflected on computers and television, *tablets* and modern technological apparatuses, the *planetary inequality* is only accentuated, and entire populations of the planet find themselves kept from the minimum for *survival*;[8] the technologically advanced society, at the same time pathologically diverted from its self-conscious, produces *pandemic* conditions of reproduction of *individuals-standards,* for whom the reality of disease, and of the exhaustion in the plane of *depression*, *anguish*, *bewilderment* and *lack of direction*, are expected gaps.

From these brief outlines, one clearly notices, how much the *diagnostic of the present* is critical,[9] especially, considering the scenario of a society grief-stricken by the already traced *economic crisis*[10] and *social return,*[11] favourable to the most *repressive* attitudes and to the most *authoritarian* solutions, that are revealed as weakly democratic, to the extent of becoming *frightening* and *alarming*, in the daily

---

[3]*Cf.* Adorno and Horkheimer (1985), p. 20.

[4]*See* Fromm (1987a, b).

[5]*Cf.* Hermann (2005), p. 49.

[6]*See* da Costa (2009).

[7]*Vide* Boff (2012).

[8]*Vide* Davis (2007).

[9]*See* Bittar (2011).

[10]*Cf.* Bittar (2012), pp. 259–294.

[11]*See* Ferry (2010).

way of coping with the collective *despair* and *hopelessness*, to the extent of the *need for utopias* and *alternative ways* of the construction of historical horizons. It is how the culture of the present makes it possible to identify, because of this, a *'dis-orientated' society*, in the inability to think its own paths, becoming, for this reason, inefficient, with the incapability to mobilise new social energies productive and creative for the confrontation of the necessities and urgent challenges, at the same time weakened, before the *anti-democratic scream.*

To the same extent, the '*re-ascending*' from *intolerance* in contemporary society is identified in face of the other and in face of differences, at times of great political, ideological, religious, partisan and intellectual intolerance, hindering the exercise of the forms of being and acting freely, thus becoming a *policing* and *criminalising* society, having in sight the growth of the powers of exception and the distancing from the rules, causing the *logic of persecution* and *institutions-police* to prevail. The pretext of being the society of information, became the *society of vigilance*, and, for this reason, informed in noisy excess of the 'superficial', which ends up meaning 'uninformed' and 'disorientated' by the informational 'bombardment' that leads to the *criticality* and to the *impossibility* of autonomous and critical reading of reality; in the digital and fast communication era, it produces a hectic pace of circulation of data and information, becoming a noisy, tormented and fast society, creating incapability of self-knowledge, promoting *detachment* and *alienation* in the immediacy of the flows of virtual communication.

In these conditions of socialisation, *Law* and *Justice*, are smudged, are liquefied in the face of the politics of occasion, lost in an *entropic chaos* of powerful contextual issues, threatening the very survival of historical conquests on the plane of *human rights*, in addition to many other challenges that have a direct relation to the growth of *intolerance* and *forms of violence*. The whole context of crisis is a context of the apparition of the most ghostly forms of oppression, *symbolic* and *real*, there is nothing more correct than the vigilant attitude of the organised civil society and the political public sphere (*Public*), attentive to the dimension of *citizenship.*[12]

But, the anaesthesia of the *culture of rights*, the *respect of human dignity* and *social vocation* for the search of Justice, can only promote the tendency of *dessocialisation*, of the return to *barbarism*, as well as the possibility of installing itself in the economy of *contention* and *cynicism*, the culture of 'free-for-all', that is so specific to contemporary times. Therefore, the loss of taste of our times for the *culture of integrity*, *respect* and of the definition of the contours of *minimum values* for life in common, when bowing down to the *irrationalities* and *pathologies* of our times, it is possible that the clouding of the spirit offered in the field open to the *banalisation of existence*, with risks of social, political, cultural setbacks can only damage fundamental conquests in the fields of Law and Justice.

For no other reason, *Critical and Social Philosophy of Law* should give the 'alarm signal', bringing to awareness the class of social risks in which we are immersed, to ascertain from this, what affinities and correlations exist, in the exchange between *Philosophy of Law* and *Aesthetic Theory*, for the collaboration towards the

[12] *Vide* Habermas (2003). *See* Bittar (2013).

reaffirmation of social culture of rights, even if this implies the very internal change of culture within the proper Law. The hypothesis of disabling the progress of the social *culture of rights*, in contemporary society, places us in face of the *historical option of no return*, that is, the one that stumbles in the *ravages of the abyss,* of the *ruin of any design* and of the *stumble* in the plane of civilisation.

It is at this point, and in face of this scenario, that *art* can be an alternative of life, in the libidinal gamble for civilisation.[13] And this because, in modern society, *art* represents a dimension of great meaning and importance. In *The aesthetic dimension*, Herbert Marcuse points out the fact that, exactly because it is different from the *principle of reality* that marks the organisation of modern society, with the fortunes and misfortunes that consequently take place, it is possible to set a concrete perspective of action in the field of *art*, on the *front* in favour of *freedom*.[14] After all, the open dimension for *art* is, in this respect—faced with the kingdom of *non-freedom-*, capable of being contrasted with frank clarity, in order to make *artistic freedom* thrive,[15] from where they draw interesting practices and experiences to awaken the *sensitive gaze*, which makes the experience of *art* valuable, especially considering its epochal framework.

3.2 Modern Society, Art and the Reification of the Look

The history of human culture dates back to the wide spectrum of time, where the human *visual experience* holds primitive records that evoke a long process of maturity of the capability of human expression, throughout the centuries.[16] The archway of the history of art indicates fruitful moments crossed by the development of artistic techniques, by the capability of human expression, as well as dialectic transformation of the paradigms of *art*, of both shape, and content. The history of art registers the important spectrum of visions open to the *symbolic universe* as constitutive of our world vision, of our social organisations, of our institutions, of our form of representation of reality. Therefore, there is no doubt that human history is fraught with traces and characteristics in the periodization of the conceptions of art. Even less, one can leave aside the idea that *art*, before unfolding as a theory, faced with the history of art and its periodizations, as Erwin Panofsky points out, arises as *art-imitation*, with the ancient,[17] or as *art-interiorisation*, with the medievals,[18] or as *art-geniality*, with the modern ones.[19]

---

[13] *Vide* Bittar (2011), pp. 125–147.

[14] *Cf.* Marcuse (2007), p. 47.

[15] *Cf.* Marcuse (2007), p. 66.

[16] *Cf.* Dondis (2007), p. 07.

[17] *Cf.* Panofsky (2000), p. 18.

[18] *Cf.* Panofsky (2000), p. 43.

[19] *Cf.* Panofsky (2000), p. 67.

But, it is important to note, in the philosophy of Walter Benjamin, and, especially in the essay of 1934/35, *The work of art at the time of its technical reproducibility*, the process of the reconstitution of the history of art, now considering the possibility of evaluating it from the perspective of two poles, which are, the pole of the *value of worship* of the work of art and the pole of the *value of exhibition*.[20] This theoretical point of view about the unfolding of the history of art is enlightening, in so far as it points out the reversal produced about it, in the context of modernity.[21] And its analysis intends to get across that the character of *text* in a *context* was what marked the work of art, before modernity, and the ritual use had to do—the example of Venus de Milo, for the ancient Greeks, and, also, the example of an image of Crucified Christ for the medieval Fathers–[22] with the *meaning of the work of art* immersed in its architectonic, political, social, cultural relation, in the 'ritual environment' where it served its purpose: the Temple, in the middle of the Greek *agora*, the Gothic Cathedral, in the centre of the medieval city, the Statue, in the middle of the *piazza* of the Italian Burgo.

In modernity, what the processes of *technification, industrialisation, fabrication, repetition* and *economisation* produce—and, together with this, of the *modern museulogicalisation* of work of art[23]—knowing that this 'turn' takes place in the scope of the passage of proper techniques and modern art (were of iron and of glass),[24] at the peak of aesthetic capitalism of publicity,[25] cinema and photography—[26] is a process of *pendular emphasis* in favour of the *value of exhibition* to the detriment of the *cult value* of the work of art, to this is it can add the dimension of the *economic value* in the market of art.[27]

This perception is important, because it situates the *work of art* in history and time. Therefore, it is in the face of the pressure of the market economy, that modernity leads to advances on the plane of technique and the massification of culture, which, at the beginning of the twentieth century, allows the appearance of the phenomenon of the *cultural industry*, which decisively impacted, and in many dimensions, *reality* and the *significance of the works of art*.[28] This perception, arises from various *Frankfurter Schulle* analyses—which represent this theoretical movement of contra-modernity, in the vision of Jacques Rancière—[29] undertaken by Theodor Adorno, Herbert Marcuse, Max Horkheimer and Walter Benjamin, notes

---

[20] *Cf.* Benjamin (1996a, b, c, d), p. 173.

[21] *Cf.* Lipovetsky and Serroy (2014), p. 155.

[22] *Cf.* Benjamin (1996a, b, c, d), p. 171.

[23] *Cf.* Dewey (2010), pp. 66–67.

[24] *Cf.* Lipovetsky and Serroy (2014), pp. 158–159.

[25] *Cf.* Lipovetsky and Serroy (2014), p. 251.

[26] *Cf.* Barros (2016), p. 209.

[27] *Cf.* Benjamin (1996a, b, c, d), p. 173.

[28] *Cf.* Pignatari (1995), p. 08.

[29] *Cf.* Rancière (2009a, b), p. 40.

that the *sphere of cultural objects* were affected by *technification*,[30] by *dessublimation*[31] and by *objectualisation* which consecrate themselves in the world of merchandise, and, that, is now also responsible for converting the *work of art* into *merchandise*, flavoured on the dimension of taste as an exercise of the act of consumption, a consumption that includes being exercised as a form of distinction of classes.[32]

For precisely this reason, the *merchandisation* of culture and art makes it possible for the place to *think* to be abolished, substituted by the *enjoying- oneself*.[33] This is how *sensitive reason* loses its force of *reflection*, diluting itself in the dimension of *leisure* and *distraction*, uncompromising, disconnected and separate. Art, now qualified as a form of *fun, distraction, amusement*, is what makes possible its immense *expansion*, to reach the masses,[34] and, at the same time, its immense *insignificance*.[35] Especially, in *The cultural industry*, Adorno and Horkheimer affirms that fun appears as a form of expression of the very mechanism of alienation at work,[36] to the extent that experience of *without-meaning* of the world of work now reaches the need for constitution in the field of leisure as a place of the obligation of existential enjoyment, that works with the same *logic of excess, disposal, goals of success* and *usefulness*, imperatives that they arise from the world of work.[37]

For this reason, *beauty, aesthetics* and the *arts*—as experiences of freedom—enter into paradox, in so far as the *reification* contradicts and denies them this *emancipatory place*.[38] This is how *beautiful-refied* is *pseudo-art*, since it is revealed as *beautiful-incarcerated* in the *technique of reproduction* more than in *creative vision*,[39] wrapped in the clothes of merchandise and, for this reason, reduced by meaning, since it is now no longer a "single work", "spontaneous creation", creative eruption", beautiful singular and rare", but indeed "repetition", "sameness", "reproduced object", "serial mimesis" with relation to its original. In the essay of 1934/35, *The work of art at the time of its technical reproducibility*, Walter Benjamin identifies this movement of transformation of the work of art, where the *originality* is lost, in favour of *reproducibility*.[40]

Therefore, what there still was in the constitution of the work of art different from the rest that accompanies the process of modernisation, ends up being lost definitely, namely, the '*aura*'. All works of art, as original work, were hidden by an 'aura', a

[30] *Cf.* Benjamin (1996a, b, c, d), p. 173.

[31] *Vide* Lipovetsky and Serroy (2014), pp. 244–245.

[32] *Cf.* Adorno (2001), p. 207.

[33] *Cf.* Adorno and Horkheimer (2006), p. 41.

[34] *Cf.* Hermann (2005), p. 39.

[35] *Cf.* Adorno and Horkheimer (2006), p. 30.

[36] *Cf.* Adorno and Horkheimer (2006), pp. 30–31.

[37] *Cf.* Adorno and Horkheimer (2006), p. 61.

[38] *Cf.* Lipovetsky and Serroy (2014), p. 25.

[39] *Cf.* Adorno and Horkheimer (2006), p. 14.

[40] *Cf.* Benjamin (1996a, b, c, d), p. 180.

result of originality, creativity, personality, historicity, which made its language confused with something from the dimension of incomprehensible, unconscious, dreamlike, magical, mythical, unique. Indeed, for some authors, the proper concept of art implies the concept of *magic*.[41] And this because art flirts with the mysterious, to the extent that it elaborates the *experience*. From the dimension of unique and singular existence, historical and unmistakable, the work when going into circulation in the market of things takes on a new life, that is, its *serial, repeated, copied, fabricated, industrialised, wrapped* existence. This stretch of *The work of art at the time of its technical reproducibility*, by Walter Benjamin, is illustrative of this respect: "The concept of aura allows you to summarise these characteristics: what was atrophied at the time of technical reproducibility of the work of art is its aura. This process is symptomatic, and its significance goes way beyond the sphere of art. Generalising, we can say that the technique of reproduction highlights the domain of tradition the object reproduced. To the extent that it multiplies the reproduction, it replaces the unique existence of the work for a serial existence".[42] However, the warning of Walter Benjamin must be well written, to mean that this not only affects the work of *art*, but the proper form of life, in the modern world, in which everything loses its *perceptive aura* of the *attitude of contemplation* and *respect for things of the world*.[43]

The impoverishment of the meaning of experience,[44] the reduction of all experience to repetitive processes, the weakening of reflection, the discouragement to the sharpness of perception, the stimulus to the possession of the *art-object*, the dissemination of the fetish of things, the decrease of the singularity of things, and the effect of distraction conferred to everything, are characteristic features of the predominant *reified culture*, resulting from the modern extraction of the *aura* from things.[45] From '*beautiful-original*' to '*beautiful-standard*', follows a great distance, and the analysis of the *Franfurter Schulle* takes the matter as the basis for reflection about the form of socialisation in the modern world. In this regard that the field of publicity is full of examples, in so far as the *publicitary image* is responsible for creating the *image-standard*, which generates *illusions* and *exclusions*, to the extent that it creates the *rule-standard* of 'beautiful', 'standardised' and 'imposed by repetition', as 'obliged beautiful', as 'regulated beautiful' by the market, which ends up being converted into 'unjust-beautiful'. Equally, with regard to the power of *televised-image* and its gender stereotypes.[46] Nothing clearer to identify, at the time of individualist hedonism,[47] how the fixation of a '*media-standard-of-beauty*' damages the mobile

---

[41] *Cf.* Salazar (1961), p. 192.

[42] *Cf.* Benjamin (1996a, b, c, d), p. 168.

[43] *Cf.* Benjamin (1996a, b, c, d), p. 101.

[44] *Cf.* Dewey (2010), p. 123.

[45] *Cf.* Benjamin (1996a, b, c, d), p. 170.

[46] *Cf.* Lopes and Marques (2016), p. 250.

[47] *Cf.* Lipovetsky and Serroy (2014), p. 405.

boundaries of aesthetics, in so far as it creates exclusions, and erases diversity;[48] the fixation of a *dictator of beauty*, in the contemporary world, lures masses of individuals to body alteration, and to the appeal of aesthetic surgery, to consented and industrially guided self-injury, as a form of conforming to *shape-of-body* to the standardisation of the *standard-of-beautiful-body* of the *beauty industry*.[49] The consequence is none other than the *reification of the look*. For this reason, North-Korean philosopher Byung-Chul Han, in *The salvation of beautiful,* in this respect affirms:

> The sexualisation of the body does not uniquely follow the logic of emancipation, once it accompanies a commercialisation of the body. The industry of beauty explores the body sexualising it and making it consumable.[50]

Furthermore, in addition to the *loss of aura*, and of the *reification of the look*, it can be seen that modern society has been producing the *saturation of meaning* for toxic waste that affects states of the soul, producing in the hypnotised *frenzy* of new flows of information, also, the *hyper information* which leads to *disinformation*, creating with this the *anaesthesia of sensitivity*, *comprehension* and *reflection*. And this because modern society is a society of noise, pollution, junk and excess. In a society of audible pollution, visual pollution and informational pollution becomes tumultuous to the possibility of audible knowledge, visual knowledge, informative knowledge, since selective and careful purification is necessary. But, as Adorno and Horkheimer state, in *The cultural industry,* contemporary culture, while it remains associated to the excess of visual appeals, audible appeals, sensorial appeals, informative appeals only *mocks* the possibility of the conscience setting anything, because everything becomes indifferent in the face of the homogenised mass of multiple appeals,[51] for which the rule that *quantity* substitutes *quality* is valid.[52] To *reflect* is necessary, in fact, silencing the excess of exterior noise in order to give itself, for example, the experience of 'listening to the music within', namely, the 'symphony' that rules the uniqueness of the personality within each one.

This is how the *loss of aura*, *reification of the look,* and the *saturation of meanings* settle where they find themselves given the empire of *instrumental reason* about *sensitive reason*, and in this the imbalance for the interest in things detrimental to people is converted into pure *existential* and *co-existential emptiness*. The sickness of the modern individual is linked to the pathologies of modern society, diverted from its purposes. When all art was converted into mere *entertainment*,[53] and the cultural consumer was bewildered before the *anaesthesia*, *sedation*, and *paralysis* of

---

[48] *Cf.* Lipovetsky and Serroy (2014), p. 409. *See too* Han (2015), p. 84.

[49] *Cf.* de Sant'Anna (2014), p. 167.

[50] *Cf.* Han (2015), p. 61.

[51] *Cf.* Adorno and Horkheimer (2006), p. 07.

[52] *Cf.* Benjamin (1996a, b, c, d), p. 192.

[53] *Cf.* Bucci (2015), p. 118.

the meanings,[54] besides the exhaustion of *sensitive reason*,[55] it should move towards the shift caused by the aesthetic reflection, since this path is of *self-encounter* and of *encounter-with-the-other*.[56]

Within these limits, modern society is one whose marked trends, especially in the field of *sensitive experience*, leads to three main effects: (a) the *lack of preparation* to digest sensitive experience; (b) the *overload* of sensitive experience, hindering the reflection and/or conscious decodification of messages; (c) frantically taken by a repetitive and anti-libidinal practice, *tormented* and over-excited, it is precisely for this reason incapable of producing significant events for the dimension of the spirit in addition to mere labour.[57] The *reification of the look* is a logical consequence, and almost organic, of this social process.

For this reason, the *pathologies of time* place us before the need to *rethink, resume* and *reconsider* fundamental aspects of modern society and of the 'project of modernity', to bear in mind the importance of some classes and certain aspects of *Enlightenment*. This means, from the political point of view, the depth of republican values, of dialogue, of social participation, of deliberative democracy. This means, on another dimension, and on another scale, the resuming of the historical role that arts, humanities,[58] expressions of investigative knowledge and sciences have for the strengthening of the human spirit in the capacity of self-overcoming of their evils and historical cycles of civilisation decline.

The strategy, therefore, of pinpointing the process of affirmation of the resuming of the spirit of *Enlightenment*, through the field of arts, is now the force of *counter-march* to the process of failure of present times, of its anguishes, torments and unrest. This resumption maintains the same meaning of bringing out what was eclipsed by instrumental reason throughout the history of modernity, and, which, for Jürgen Habermas, meant the resumption of the public sphere (*Öffentlichkeit*),[59] and, here, is proceeded in such a way to unravel the *cultural* and *artistic effervescence* of the dawn of modernity. It is to this extent that the pause for critical and detached reflection, as philosophical exercise, in these conditions of socialisation, should lead us to distancing ourselves from the simple process of '*dullness*' and '*brutalisation*',[60] that is halfway of the use of force and manifestations of the forms of oppression of the other, to bring us closer to the process of the *subtlety of the spirit, intellectual, cultural and moral clarification,* as well as the *refinement of meanings*, as one sees at the door opened by the *work of art* an important place of escape to awareness, *contemplation* and *reflection*.[61]

[54] *Cf.* Adorno and Horkheimer (2006), p. 16.
[55] *Cf.* Marcuse (2007), p. 17.
[56] *Cf.* Perissé (2004), pp. 75–76.
[57] *Cf.* Perissé (2004), p. 82.
[58] *See* Ribeiro (org.) (2001).
[59] *Vide* Habermas (1984).
[60] *Cf.* de Aquino (2014), p. 90.
[61] *Cf.* Benjamin (1996a, b, c, d), p. 192.

And this can be done by the way of arts, to the extent that reality installed by a *work of art* is different and superior to the reality of too many things, and starts a 'new story', *story images* in relation to man with *aesthetic dimension.*[62] This is how the *Aesthetic Theory*, at this moment, opens the field for the development of the capability of reading of the multiple 'layers of reality', found in the various repertoires of the languages of the artistic works 'imaginary fields', 'forms of expression and understanding', 'representations', 'creative horizons', in order to be able to face the *principle of reality*[63]—this one that exhausts utopic energies and spaces of socio-aesthetic creativity—from the freedom of the languages of work of art, capable of performing through its channels the *principle of pleasure*.[64] It is in it that casts one of the flashes of light and *over-life* the whole possibility of *life* that *protests*, before the *lack of life*, *freedom*, *alterity*, *critique*, *autonomy*, *dignity*.

3.3 Modern Society, Aesthetic Capitalism and the Homogenization of Art

Modern society, as a society of merchandise, is the producer of *aesthetic homogenization*. This is even clearer, when art was converted into an important instrument of *qualification* of merchandise at the beginning of the twenty-first century, at the time of aesthetic capitalism. The *universalization of patterns*, the *repetition of the same*, as well as the *projection of local as global* are responsible for a process of the *identification of everything, as the same*. At the beginning of the twentieth century, the *Critical Theory* was capable of describing this process and criticising this capability of capitalism of *reproducing* it. For no other reason, they found themselves on walls (*les murs*) in the city of Paris, during the May of 1968, the messages and the protests of the young. There one could read:

> Culture is the inversion of life.[65]

Today, at the beginning of the twenty-first century, the French sociology of Gilles Lipovestky has had the same important role of analysing the ascension—in the sequence of studies about the *era of emptiness*[66] and about the *hyper-modern*—[67] of *aesthetic capitalism at the times of hyper-consumption*.[68] Hence, the perception that *art* (free, autonomous, significative and plural) disappears in times when,

---

[62] *Cf.* Marcuse (2007), p. 53.

[63] *Cf.* Marcuse (2007), p. 59.

[64] *Cf.* Marcuse (2007), p. 19.

[65] *Cf.* Lauthère-Vigneau (2008), p. 174.

[66] *See* Lipovetsky (2003).

[67] *See* Lipovetsky and Charles (2004).

[68] *Cf.* Lipovetsky and Serroy (2014), p. 14.

paradoxically, art receives a generalised and extensive treatment, in fact, without historical precedents, becoming: *art-for-the-market*. In this point, Gilles Lipovetsky affirms:

> After the art-for-the-Gods, art-for-the-princes, and art-for-art, we are now in art-for-the-market which triumphs.[69]

It is in the 'timelessness' of accelerated experience of everyday life in contemporary life that the genuine experience disappears; as time becomes short-lived, genuine experience and the meaning it bears melt away. Therefore, art is shifted from daily life, and situated 'out of experience'. Its contemporary return, associated to merchandise, only 'dull' the meanings, 'disorientate' the mind, 'exhaust' the experience and 'banalise' the artistic practice, wishing with this to point to the 'return' of art, when 'freedom' continues being something strange to the daily experience, because 'experience' and 'time' are disassociated. Here, the accelerated movement of production of the market is piloted by *design*, *fashion*, *publicity*, *decoration*, the cultural industry of *cinema*, *entertainment* and *music*, in a way that the serial nature of the products invades the life of people continuously, creating an exhaustion in the exploration of its meanings.[70]

The *society of hyper-consumption* seeks to associate the *symbolic force, seduction*, *style*, *standard* to all types of objects, representing them on another level, with relation to industrial capitalism of the nineteenth century, or even, the beginning of the twentieth century; now, it applies the same logic to products according to which, the *way* it is imposed on *content*, as well as *aesthetic value*—by the derived social value of economic wealth, standard of social class, social distinction and/or social identity—[71] it is imposed on the *value of use*, or even the *value of exchange*.[72] It is true that in all historical moments, *art* took part in some way in the *model of society*, but in *aesthetic capitalism in times of hyper-consumption*, the association between merchandise and art is even more explicit, imbricated and deep.[73] It is no wonder that—as Jean Baudrillard points out—the work of art is reduced to its *value of exchange*, in the market of art.[74] Not in other ways, the South-Korean philosopher, settled in Germany, Byung-Chul Han, in *The salvation of the beautiful*, goes on to confirm something very similar, in the sense of treating the theme of art in this day

[69] *Cf.* Lipovetsky and Serroy (2014), p. 32.

[70] *Cf.* Lipovetsky and Serroy (2014), p. 16.

[71] *Cf.* Lipovetsky and Serroy (2014), p. 35.

[72] *Cf.* Lipovetsky and Serroy (2014), p. 16.

[73] *Cf.* Lipovetsky and Serroy (2014), p. 18.

[74] "En ce qui concerne plus précisément le marché de la peinture, on peut dire: c'est l'appropriation des tableaux comme signes qui joue comme facteur de légitimation du pouvoir économique et social" ("As far as the painting market in particular is concerned, we can say: it is the appropriation of paintings as signs that plays a role in legitimizing economic and social power"—*translation*) (Baudrillard 1972, p. 131).

and age.[75] This stage of development of capitalism—a fourth stage—corresponds to extreme *individualism, consumerism, aestheticism* and *hedonism.*[76]

In this phase, *art* is not abandoned, it is not cornered, it is not disregarded, but, to the contrary, it rises to the level of '*hyper-art'*, and is stretched all round, invading all spaces and blending with all objects, no matter the dimension and the nature.[77] The artist, before considered an outcast, an eccentric, a stranger, a *dandy*, a non-integrated, or even, someone shifted from the process of modernisation, is now integrated into the process of the production of merchandise, by his aesthetic-creative meaning.[78] Not only objects are converted by the butcher of *design* and the industry of entertainment, but also entire spaces,[79] cities and urban spaces are being *disneyfied.*[80]

The promises of aesthetic capitalism are many, and the invasion of meanings by the seduction of the market only obscures the possibility of coming closer to the path of *justice*. For this reason, the sociology of Gilles Lipovetsky only analyses and identifies how much *aesthetic capitalism in the times of hyper-consumption* produces '*beauty'*, and simultaneously, with this, produces *standardisation, homogenization, acceleration, competition,*[81] *experiential individualism,*[82] *inequalities, misery,*[83] *degradation of the natural environment,*[84] *mediocrity* and *critical anaesthesia.*[85] For this reason, one can be in the *world of objectualised beauty*, but it is not closer to a world of *virtues*, of *citizenship*, and of *justice*, as Gilles Lipovestky affirms:

> The beauties are many, but we are getting closer, in no way at all, to a world of great virtues, with more justice or even with more happiness.[86]

The order of repeated, reproduced, massive and disposable products creates *fungibility* where before it was exactly its opposite, *originality.*[87] Consequently, Walter Benjamin's analysis that the work of art loses the 'aura' is correct, to desecrating itself like a *pendant* of the *merchandise* itself. Art cannot only be a *passive servant* of pricing, commercial strategy, marketing, brand value,

---

[75] *Cf.* Han (2015), p. 87.

[76] *Cf.* Lipovetsky and Serroy (2014), p. 31.

[77] *Cf.* Lipovetsky and Serroy (2014), p. 32.

[78] *Cf.* Lipovetsky and Serroy (2014), p. 129.

[79] *Cf.* Lipovetsky and Serroy (2014), pp. 368 and 392.

[80] *Cf.* Lipovetsky and Serroy (2014), p. 33.

[81] *Cf.* Lipovetsky and Serroy (2014), p. 37.

[82] *Cf.* Lipovetsky and Serroy (2014), p. 70.

[83] *Cf.* Lipovetsky and Serroy (2014), p. 38.

[84] *Cf.* Lipovetsky and Serroy (2014), p. 40.

[85] *Cf.* Lipovetsky and Serroy (2014), p. 45.

[86] *Cf.* Lipovetsky and Serroy (2014), p. 38.

[87] *Cf.* Lipovetsky and Serroy (2014), p. 36.

productification and reification.[88] Under aesthetic capitalism, something happens to *art* that *is not artistic,* but commercial, and degenerates its function, meaning and uniqueness. The destination of the work of art at the times of aesthetic capitalism is, paradoxically, not the consecration of the work of art, but rather the *reification-of-the-work-of-art.*

In short, the promise of aesthetic capitalism is that of '*beauty*', but, in deep down, what is achieved in the place of *art* is the *reduction* of its meanings, the *loss* of its emancipatory function, as well as the *dis-sublimation* of its symbolic missions,[89] given that generally, what is effectively aimed at, is only an *illusion.*[90] This, evidently, goes in the *opposite direction* of emancipatory meaning that the *work of art* can potentially establish, when thought from the sense attributed to it by French philosopher Jacques Rancière.[91]

3.4 Modern Society, the Legal Look and the Artistic Look

The *artistic look* has a lot to say to the *legal look*. And this because art is a *refinement of experience of the world*, and corresponds with the *active refinement of the perception of the world*, for whom produces it (artist),[92] and with the *passive refinement of the perception of the world*, for whom benefits from it (user).[93] Therefore, it does not matter whether the perspective of whom is placed before art is given by the vision of the artist or by the vision of the user—to the extent these boundaries are undetermined-, especially because both are affected by the *transforming process* that is implied in the universe of arts. Henceforth, one starts to notice the importance of the *look at art*, *look with art*, *look through art*, as a form of *action, creation* and *reaction* sensitive to the real or imagery stimuli instigated by the symbolic.[94] In *The emancipated spectator,* Jacques Rancière sees in the spectator a vision as active as that of the artist, because understanding, knowing, learning are attitudes that are integrated in the continuous process of permanent construction and reconstruction of the *field of the symbolic.*[95]

The activity of *looking* while integrated to the human body by the organ of vision—the eye, this symbol of the soul-, and despite its apparent simplicity and

[88] *Cf.* Lipovetsky and Serroy (2014), p. 41.

[89] *Cf.* Lipovetsky and Serroy (2014), p. 80.

[90] *Cf.* Lipovetsky and Serroy (2014), p. 38.

[91] "Pero el cumplimiento de la promessa implica la supresión del arte como realidad separada, su transformación en una forma de vida" ("But the fulfilment of the promise implies the suppression of art as a separate reality, its transformation into a form of life"—*translation*) (Rancière 2011, p. 49).

[92] *Vide* Lacoste (1986), p. 08.

[93] *Cf.* Galeffi (1979), p. 29.

[94] *Cf.* Rancière (2014), p. 17.

[95] *Cf.* Rancière (2014), p. 21.

innocence, implies numerous other processes, that are worth being registered, when one wants to indicate the *complexity of the operations of the look,* that they can be identified as: perceiving, understanding, contemplating, observing, discovering, recognising, visualising, distinguishing, accompanying, examining, reading, looking.[96] In *One-way street*, it is Walter Benjamin who identifies, in the fragment entitled *Oculist*, that:

> The look is the bottom of the cup of the human being.[97]

If the wealth of the universe of the look is connected to a wide range of activities of the spirit, it should be noticed how much *artistic intelligence* can add to *human intelligence*,[98] and, from here, how much can be applied to the refinement of *intelligence* for the exercise of rights. It is worth reinforcing that the autonomy of artistic language is of fundamental importance for this exercise of qualitative change of the *look* and, in this respect, every human being as a participant of the symbolic universe can be impacted by the *meaning*, or by *without-meaning*, by *concert*, or by *disconcert*, of the works of art. In this is the decisive and sensitively differentiated role, of the work of art, among the more social artefacts.[99] This distant and dislocated place from which it speaks, through artistic language, is already a form of resistance to the current, trend and juncture that reign, annihilating the spirit of what is subtle in the human condition.

The change of the look is, for this reason, a process of transformation, costly to *subjectivity* and *inter-subjectivity.* It gives a mere unidemensional perception of reality, immersed in the stipulations of the world of work and of technical and professional specialisation—generally, rational, instrumental, calculating, technical and unifocal-, to the *multi-faceted* and *subtle* perception of the multiple dimensions of reality and *multiple layers* of our *humanity*,[100] it goes a great distance, which is less accidental and more prompted, there considered the imperatives of modern society.

It is even understood that this is a way of breaking the barriers between the *universe of aesthetics* and the *universe of law*, favouring the dimension of the collaborative understanding of knowledge. Here, the position is defended that the jurists should overcome the limits of *legal positivism.* To make the passage from the *legal look* to the *artistic look* is to exercise a form of *humanism*.[101] *Humanism* is, is in this sense, the appreciation of the dimensions of the human, the sensitive, the creative and, also, the socially responsible.[102] Thus, *humanism* points out the appreciation of sensitive abilities that were obscured by modern society. In order

[96] *Cf.* Dondis (2007), p. 05.

[97] *Cf.* Benjamin (2000a, b), p. 49.

[98] *Cf.* Dondis (2007), p. 231.

[99] *Cf.* Marcuse (2007), p. 29.

[100] *Cf.* Gorsdorf (2014), p. 63.

[101] *Cf.* de Aquino (2014), p. 37.

[102] *See* previous studies on humanism in Bittar (2018), p. 45.

for jurists to abandon the *technical look*, which is the *legal look*, and to cultivate the *sensitive look,* which is the look capable of seeing *the human values* of justice, freedom, equality, solidarity and diversity, are efforts required for a leap in the transformation of technical-legal culture.[103] For this reason, jurists should pay more attention to aesthetic works, because of the *symbolic stock* of significances and the *synesthetic power* they bear. This is a finding that in the area of Law—as a whole—has already had in recent years.[104] And this implies that *sensitivity* is more than one option for the jurist; *sensitivity* is an obligation, since it is through the pain of the Other[105] that I humanises myself and make justice a profession of faith.

Therefore, as read in the area of Law with the suffering, pain, injustice and woes of I and the Other, it does not cease to be an exercise of *sensitivity, solidarity* and *responsibility*, exercised in connection with its finality. And this because *art* is one of the paths to the depths of the soul.[106] Art allows *humanity* to contradict the evils that itself creates. Where hate hides, art penetrates. Where shadow hides, art releases light. Where is prejudice, art shows equality. Art allows me to disintegrate in the otherness of the universe of the Other. For this reason, art can address injustice, violence, intolerance, inequality, loss of rights, grave violations of human rights, hunger, misery, war, oppression, discrimination, social hate, neglect.

In previous studies, it has already become clear the importance of the change that the culture of Law has to undergo, in order to make the passage from the *technical look* to the *sensitive look* work.[107] In practice, all the effort in the teaching of Law has been reduced to the study of technical concepts that develop skills around *abstract concepts* and the *reading of legislation*. Therefore, legal professional see the world through the lens of Law, and not Law through lens of reality and human challenges which are involved in the tasks of Law. Thus, legal professionals find themselves divorced from a more critical view of Law and the *teaching of Law*. A more critical and less functional view of the legal professional, would imply a broader task of cultivating humanist knowledge—which would bring Law closer to the Arts-, precisely because they bring the perspective of the *sensitive look* and *culturally situated*.

For this reason, this book defends the position that the formation that the Faculties of Law offer jurists have been, in recent years, too legal and technical, which alienates the professional from an understanding of culture, society and values that would be central to a humanist view of Law. According to Costas Douzinas who points out, in *Law and the image*,[108] the point of view of the culture of Law, means

[103] *Cf.* Perissé (2004), p. 113.

[104] *Cf.* Ibdfam (2017), p. 7.

[105] *Cf.* Eco (2007), p. 185.

[106] *Cf.* dos Santos Coelho (2012), p. 13.

[107] *See* previous studies on humanism in Bittar (2018), p. 45.

[108] "Lawyers live by the text and love the past, they hate novelty and misunderstand new languages. The law is able to appreciate new art only after it becomes a matter of convention, use, and habit, in other words, when art becomes like law. Great art, on the other hand, precisely because it breaks

overcoming the lack of artistic preparation of the look *that* the professional of Law has for the *reality of the things*, especially given the culture of the *legislative reading* of reality, given by the constraints of the *code*, *valid law*, *planning*, *procedures* and *forms.* It is evident the impoverishment of the *reading of world* caused by this strict approach of *modern Law* by these archetypical, abstract and appellant routes, of modern society.[109]

On the contrary, and, precisely for this reason, challenging, the meticulous, detailed apprehension, subtle from reality is a task of the *artistic look,*[110] since it is capable of promoting, stimulating and provoking, at a sensitive dimension, the perception of things of the world by way of the development of the 'artistic sense'. The 'artistic sense', integrant of *sensitive reason*, corresponds to the development of a human potentiality, and is revealed by the capability of refinement of the *colourful palette* of apprehension of the diverse fields of expression of the '*multi-dimensional realities'* of the real.

The 'artistic sense' involves the ability to ascertain the meanings, to sharpen the perception, to capture the difference, and to come close to what is manifested in each thing, with the qualities (amongst others) of details, horizons, conceptions, shapes, models, visions, concepts, roles, techniques, functions, meanings, interpretations, life forms. The power of the 'artistic sense' is in the creative discoveries which promote, breaking through the known horizons, stimulating the *vision of the world*, thereby providing its bearer the capability of expanding the combinatory repertoire of creative relations. Therefore, what is called 'reality', in its complex empiric and symbolic weft, goes beyond *black and white*, protruding into its *colourful* nature, that only the sensitive look is capable of knowing, detecting, capturing, deciphering, decoding.

In this respect, the importance and the value of the '*artistic sense*' for the '*look at the things of justice'* is derived. *Art*, like justice, is an activity of the spirit, integrated to the social setting, but pertaining to the *symbolic world*. By manifesting a high human capability, *art humanises us*. In the same way, *justice humanises* social treatment, while it establishes criteria and forms of parity, exchange, interchange, prevention and repair. It is exactly in this that the *artist like humanist*[111] provides a *method* for the access to the *symbolic world* which cannot be ignored by the *jurist*, hence the connection between the *artistic look* and the *legal look*, as already known and well elaborated by the studies of Luís Alberto Warat.[112] And this because the experience of justice is something of this type, it is made *work in the sentence,*[113] in *legislation,* in *administrative decision,* and, for this reason, it matters who exercises

away from coventions and rules and expresses creative freedom and imagination, is the antithesis of law. The law of art is the opposite of the rule of law" (Douzinas and Nead 1999, p. 01).

[109]*Cf.* Gorsdorf (2014), p. 60.

[110]*Cf.* Dondis (2007), p. 13.

[111]*Cf.* Perissé (2004), p. 192.

[112]*Cf.* Warat (2004a, b), p. 24.

[113]*Cf.* Carneiro (2002), p. 18.

the activity, since the *interpretation* of each *legal actor* is and always will be *unique* and *singular*, in the creative subjectivity of its formulation, despite the generality of the normative precepts, in the objectivity of the rules established by the legal system.

The artist is moved in the midst of the *forest of signs*,[114] mobilizing *symbolic resources* for the allocation of the meanings of the spectator and, in this respect, it is a skilful instructor in the *symbolic world*. Its way of *seeing the world* from the *other place*, and deconstructs the form in which we are used to *seeing things*, and, to the precise extent, *its place* matters like *another place*. For no other reason, the works of art as expressions of artists create *strangeness* in reality, with the most diverse reactions, as far as, exactly, they *bear* some element that distances them from the 'reality of things', of conventions, and from what is established, either shape, or content.[115]

Therefore it can be said that aesthetics hold their relevance in the construction of *aesthetic perception*, and, for this reason, educate the meanings, and develop abilities that are of fundamental importance for the construction of *aesthetic sense*, from whose balance the *sense of justice* is removed, as *sense of proportion* and *balance*,[116] *measure, righteousness* and *measurement*,[117] often required in *legal judgements.*[118] It is exactly this perception that allows South-Korean philosopher Byung-Chul Han to affirm:

> The symmetry, in which also merges with the idea of justice, is equally beautiful. The fair relation implies a manner necessary to symmetric proportion. A total asymmetry causes a sensation of ugliness. The very injustice expresses itself as an extremely asymmetric proportion.[119]

References

Adorno TW (1995) Educação após Auschwitz. In: Educação e emancipação [Education and emancipation] (trans: Maar WL). Paz e Terra, São Paulo

Adorno TW (2001) Minima moralia (trans: Morão A). Edições, Lisboa, p 70

Adorno TW, Horkheimer M (1985) Dialética do esclarecimento [Dialectics of the Enlightenement] (trans: de Almeida GA) Jorge Zahar, Rio de Janeiro

Adorno TW, Horkheimer M (2006) A indústria cultural: o iluminismo como mistificação das massas. In: de Almeida JMB (ed) Indústria cultural e sociedade [Society and cultural industry] (trans: Levy JE) 3rd edn. Paz e Terra, São Paulo

[114] *Cf.* Plaza (2010), p. 19.

[115] *Cf.* Gorsdorf (2014), p. 56.

[116] "*Cf.* Carneiro (2002), p. 18.

[117] *Cf.* Carneiro (2002), p. 29.

[118] "L'ordinamento è il tentativo di individuare la giusta misura, l'ordine. Questo significa che è interpretazione (di quest'ordine). Questo significa che è formatività (di quest'ordine)" ("Sorting is the attempt to find the right size, the order. This means that it is an interpretation (of this order). This means that it is formative (of this order)"—*translation*) (Cananzi 2013, pp. 50–51).

[119] *Cf.* Han (2015), p. 76.

Barros VS d C (2016) A civilização chutou a porta do saloon. In: Marcílio FF, Leite GS, Rodolfo PF (eds) Antimanual de Direito & Arte [Anti-manual of Law & Art]. Saraiva, São Paulo, pp 200–242
Baudrillard J (1972) Pour une critique de l'économie politique su signe. Gallimard, Paris
Benjamin W (1996a) A imagem de Proust. In: Magia e técnica, arte e política [Magic and techniques, art and politics] (trans: SP Rouanet) 7th edn. Brasiliense, São Paulo
Benjamin W (1996b) Pequena história da fotografia. In: Magia e técnica, arte e política [Magic and techniques, art and politics] 7th edn. Transl. Brasiliense, São Paulo
Benjamin W (1996c) A obra de arte na era de sua reprodutibilidade técnica. In: Magia e técnica, arte e política [Magic and technics, art and politics] (trans: Rouanet SP) 7th edn. Brasiliense, São Paulo
Benjamin W (1996d) Sobre o conceito de história. In: Magia e técnica, arte e política [Magic and techniques, art and politics] (trans: Rouanet SP) 7th edn. Brasiliense, São Paulo
Benjamin W (2000a) Rua de mão única [One way street] (trans: Torres Filho RR, Martins Barbosa JC) 7th edn. Brasiliense, São Paulo
Benjamin W (2000b) Charles Baudelaire: um lírico no auge do capitalismo. In: Obras escolhidas [Selected works] (trans: Martins Barbosa JC, Baptista HA) 3rd edn. Brasiliense, São Paulo
Bittar ECB (2011) Democracia, justiça e direitos humanos: estudos de Teoria Crítica e Filosofia do Direito. [Democracy justice and human rights: studies of Critical Theory and Philosophy of Law]. Saraiva, São Paulo
Bittar ECB (2012) Crise econômica, desglobalização e direitos humanos. Revista Mestrado em Direito [J Master Law] 01:259–294
Bittar ECB (2013) Democracia, justiça e emancipação social: reflexões jusfilosóficas a partir do pensamento de Jürgen Habermas [Democracy, justice and social emancipation: philosophical reflections on Habermas thought]. Quartier Latin, São Paulo
Bittar ECB (2018) Introdução ao estudo do direito: humanismo, democracia e justiça. [Introdcution to Law: humanism, democracy and justice]. Saraiva, São Paulo
Boff L (2012) Sustentabilidade [Sustainability]. Vozes, Rio de Janeiro
Bucci E (2015) O Estado de narciso [Narcissus state]. Companhia das Letras, São Paulo
Carneiro MF (2002) Estética do direito e do conhecimento [Aesthetics of law and the knowledge]. Rio Grande do Sul, Porto Alegre
Cananzi DM (2013) Formatività e norma: elementi di Teoria Estetica dell'interpretazione giuridica. G. Giappichelli Editore, Torino
da Costa DB (2009) A crise do supereu [The crisis of the superego]. Juruá, Curitiba
Davis M (2007) Cidades mortas [Dead cities] (trans: Calado A) Record, Rio de Janeiro
de Aquino SRF (2014) O direito em busca de sua humanidade [Law in search for its humanity]. CRV, Curitiba
de Sant'Anna DB (2014) História da beleza no Brasil [History of beauty in Brazil]. Contexto, São Paulo
Dewey, John. (2010) Arte como experiência. [Art as experience] (trans: Vera Ribeiro). São Paulo: Martins Fontes
Dondis DA (2007) Sintaxe da linguagem visual [Visual language syntax] (trans: Camargo JL). Martins Fontes, São Paulo
dos Santos Coelho NMM (2012) Direito, arte e formação do jurista. In: Trogo S, dos Santos Coelho NMM (eds) Direito, Filosofia e Arte [Law, philosophy and art]. RIDEEL, São Paulo
Douzinas C, Nead L (1999) Introduction. In: Douzinas C, Nead L (eds) Law and the image. The Universtiy of Chicago Press, Chicago
Eco U (org) (2007) História da feiúra [History of ugliness] (trans: Aguiar E). Record, Rio de Janeiro
Ferry L (2010) Diante da crise [In the face of the crisis] (trans: Jannini K). Difel, Rio de Janeiro
Fromm E (1987a) Ter ou ser? [To have or to be?] 4th edn. (trans: Nathanael C). LTC, Caixeiro, Rio de Janeiro
Fromm E (1987b) Anatomia da destrutividade humana [The anatomy of the human destructiveness] (trans: de Moura Matos MA) 2nd edn. Guanabara, Rio de Janeiro

Galeffi R (1979) Novos ensaios de estética [New essays in Aesthetics]. UFBA, Bahia
Gorsdorf LF (2014) Direitos humanos e arte: diálogos possíveis para uma episteme. In: Silva EF, Gediel JAP, Trauczynski SC (eds) Direitos humanos e políticas públicas [Human rights and public policies]. Universidade Positivo, Curitiba, pp 51–66
Habermas J (1984) Mudança estrutural da esfera pública [Structural change in the public sphere] (trans: Flávio R. Kothe). Rio de Janeiro, Tempo Brasileiro
Habermas J (2003) Direito e democracia [Between facts and norms]. vs. I. e II. 2nd edn (trans: Siebeneichler FB). Tempo Brasileiro, Rio de Janeiro
Han B-C (2015) A salvação do belo [The salvation of the beauty] (trans: Pereira MS). Relógio d'Agua, Lisboa
Hermann N (2005) Ética e estética [Ethics and aesthetics]. EDIPUCRS, Porto Alegre
Ibdfam (2017) Direito e arte [Law and art]. Revista do IBDFAM, 34
Lacoste J (1986) A filosofia da arte [The philosophy of art] (trans: Cabral Á). Jorge Zahar, Rio de Janeiro
Lauthère-Vigneau, Cathérine (direc.) (2008) Préface de Daniel Cohn-Dendit. In: Mai 68. Denoël, Pearis
Lipovetsky G (2003) L'ère du vide. Gallimard, Paris
Lipovetsky G, Charles S (2004) Os tempos hipermodernos [The hypermodern times] (trans: Vilela M) Barcarolla, São Paulo
Lipovetsky G, Serroy J (2014) O capitalismo estético na era da globalização [The aesthetic capitalism in the age of globalization] Transl. Edições, Lisboa, p 70
Lopes MS, Alves AM (2016) O Direito na Televisão: Construção e Perpetuação de Estereótipos Femininos no Programa "Casos de Família". In: Franca Filho M, Leite GS, Filho RP (eds) Anti Manual de Direito & Arte [Anti-manual of Law and Art], pp 243–280
Marcuse H (2007) A dimensão estética [The aesthetic dimension] (trans: Costa ME). Edições, Lisboa, p 70
Panofsky E (2000) Idea (trans: Neves P). Martins Fontes, São Paulo
Perissé G (2004) Filosofia, ética e literatura [Philosophy, ethics and literature]. Manole, São Paulo
Pignatari D (1995) Semiótica da arte e da arquitetura [Semiotics of art and of the architecture]. Cultrix, São Paulo
Plaza J (2010) Tradução intersemiótica [Intersemiotics translation]. Perspectiva, São Paulo
Rancière J (2009a) O inconsciente estético [The aesthetic unconscious] (trans: Netto MC). Editora, São Paulo, p 34
Rancière J (2009b) A partilha do sensível [Sharing the sensitive] (trans: Netto MC). Eixo Experimental; Editora, São Paulo, p 34
Rancière J (2011) El malestar en la estética (trans: Petrecca MÁ, Vogelfandg L, y Burello MG). Capital Intelectual, Buenos Aires
Rancière J (2014) O espectador emancipado [The emancipated viewer] (trans: Benedetti IC). Martins Fontes, São Paulo
Ribeiro RJ (org) (2001) Humanidades [Humanities]. EDUSP, São Paulo
Salazar A (1961) Que é arte? [What is art?] 3rd edn. Arménio Amado, Coimbra
Santaella L (2016b) Temas e dilemas do pós-digital [Themes and dilemmas of the post-digital]. Paulus, São Paulo
Warat LA (2004a) Literasofia. In: Mezzaroba O, Rover AJ, Junior ADR, Monteiro CS (eds) Territórios desconhecidos [Unknown territories]. Fundação Boiteux, Florianópolis, pp 19–26
Warat LA (2004b) La cinesofia y su lado oscuro. In: Mezzaroba O, Rover AJ, Junior ADR, Monteiro CS (eds) Territórios desconhecidos. Fundação Boiteux, Florianópolis, pp 549–562

Part II
Special Part

Chapter 4
Applied Semiotics, Law and Art

4.1 Semiotics, Law and Painting: The Iconology of Justice

Justice is a value of high significance as a *social regulator*. For this reason, *justice* receives high symbolic treatment. This is how the *symbol of justice* appears as being the archetype,[1] or even, the *semiotic synthesis*, that moves to the understanding of just and unjust, in the way we read the question, at least from the point of view of Western tradition. The *symbolic representation*[2] is an 'aesthetic synthesis' to be translated, by way of symbols, socially relevant values, as Daniele M. Conanzi, points out in his study *Estetica del Diritto* (2016).[3] Here, it is clear the importance of the study of the *symbol* will fall under the analysis of the *Semiotics of Image*, in a way which *Iconology* is to it the specific part of a *Semiotics* applied and specialised in the studies of the *discourses of images*.[4]

As mentioned before (Sect. 1.4), a *symbol* is a modality of sign that represents the object by a relation of *conventional use*, by an arbitrary construction, a socially established comprehension or association,[5] and has *aesthetic appeal*. The *Dictionary*

[1] *Vide* http://www.stf.jus.br. Accessed 11.05.2020.

[2] *Cf.* Garapon (1999), p. 42.

[3] "Il simbolo è quello che manifesta la verità, l'originario, ed è anche quello attorno al quale si ritrova e costruisce la società. Questa infatti non è un semplice insieme di individui casualmente avvicinati, né occasionalmente riuniti. La società è un gruppo che si riconosce in quanto tale; un gruppo che negli emblemi, nella musica, nei simboli, nei dispositivi cerimoniali (per dirla con Legendre), riconosce la sua identità e dunque se stessa" ("The symbol is the one that manifests the truth, the original, and it is also the one around which society is found and built. This in fact is not a simple set of individuals randomly approached, nor occasionally reunited. Society is a group that recognizes itself as such; a group that in its emblems, in its music, in its symbols, in its ceremonial devices (to put it in Legendre), recognizes its identity and therefore itself"—*translation*) (Cananzi 2013, p. 84).

[4] *See* Nöth (2012), p. 02.

[5] *Cf.* Santaella and Nöth (1998), p. 63.

E. C. B. Bittar, *Semiotics, Law & Art*, Law and Visual Jurisprudence 2,
https://doi.org/10.1007/978-3-030-58880-9_4

of symbols points out that the *symbol of justice*, just as we take it in modernity, is used to having the following characteristics: justice is blindfolded, it has a sword in the hand and carries scales.[6] In the thorough and detailed study of the *symbol of justice*, the partial aspects can be highlighted for analysis, extracting that: (a) the scales indicate: equality; equilibrium; weighing; measure; balancing; (b) the sword indicates: force; order; impositivity; coercion; (c) the blindfold over the eyes indicates: decision; impartiality; neutrality, equidistance; (d) more rarely, the hammer indicates: order; respect; obedience. But, in all cases, when the 'notion of justice' is invoked, it appears that, currently one wishes to invoke a set of verbs, such as to ponder, consider, balance, distribute, correct, assign, penalise, observe, equilibrate, which within the *symbol* would be entirely encrypted.

Therefore, in the Western cultural tradition, the presence of the *symbol of justice* is very clear, representing numerous shapes, either by sculpture, or by painting, or by illuminated manuscript, or by architecture.[7] It is in this regard that the *strength* of these symbols in the Palaces of Justice, in Assemblies and parliamentary rooms, Royal Palaces, is amazing, as Antoine Garapon states and analyses.[8] The *strength* of the *symbol* is associated to the meticulous nature of how it is imagined, drawn and thought out, every generation, besides being transmitted and copied, from time to time, in the symbolic universe in which nothing is free.[9] It is interesting that the traditional representation of justice, in Western culture, is of *mythical origin*. Here, art and architecture, religion and wisdom of the Egyptians, decidedly influenced Western civilisation.[10] Whether for the Egyptians, for the Romans, or for the Greeks, the representation of justice is incarnated in the figure of a Goddess, and, ancestrally, the archetype of a female indicates the path of justice.[11] The representation of *Justitia* (Roman representation) and of *Thémis* (Greek representation) are classic, and is multiplied in the most different forms, in a continuity of long centuries of Western tradition. This traditional representation of the idea of justice evokes the *origins*, the *foundations*, the *original paradigm* for Western culture.[12]

The most interesting thing is that the traditional representation of justice has remained classic, even with all the technical, aesthetic and social changes introduced by the process of modernisation.[13] Despite modern society having become technical, secular, rational, the representation of justice continues to maintain the constant traits identified above, given that the mythical representation continues to confer

[6] *See* Chevalier and Gheerbrant (2005), p. 527.

[7] *Cf.* Franca Filho (2011), p. 18.

[8] *Cf.* Garapon (1998), p. 203.

[9] "Elle se donne à voir à travers des forêts de symboles savamment agencés, où rien, ni le geste ni l'ornement, ne fut jamais gratuit" ("It can be seen through forests of skillfully arranged symbols, where nothing, neither gesture nor ornament, was ever free"—*translation*) (Jacob 1994, p. 10).

[10] *Cf.* Argan (2013), p. 26.

[11] *Vide* Garapon (1999), p. 31.

[12] *Cf.* Garapon (1998), p. 205.

[13] *Cf.* Garapon (1998), p. 205.

fundamental traits of what is sought to symbolise righteousness. The stability and survival of the *symbol of justice* indicates the high symbolic value that it accumulates in our culture.

From the historical point of view, this whole *symbolic burden* can be, gradually unveiled, by accompanying the existing studies about the subject, so that it can be noticed, for example, that the *blindfold over the eyes* is a recent element, from the historical point of view, in the visual identification of justice. From this type of note, there has been necessary controversy for a better understanding of the subject, since the representation of justice involved, for the ancient and for the medieval, and, even at the beginning of modernity, the *clear and sharp vision*.[14] It is only in the sixteenth century, the first appearance of blindfolded justice, a record of the importance for the identification that the predominant conception that justice should be *impartial* is modern.[15] By spreading this representation throughout Europe, it is now the symbol of the bourgeois era, Western civilisation and the break from the medieval past, being exhibited, generally, in the middle of public squares, for all to see, as a *civilisation icon*.[16] Therefore, it is in modernity that the characteristics of *equidistance* and *secularism* are fixed to the figure of justice.[17]

Therefore, the artistic evocation of the symbol of justice, whether by painting, or by sculpture, or by illuminated manuscript, or by architecture only reinforces the set of values that should impregnate the practices of a given institution, hence its recurring presence in the rooms of justice and public deliberation, reinforcing the importance of rituals, the role of the judge/legislator, the authority of the decisions made.[18]

The function of the *symbol of justice* is multiple and, in this respect, fulfils various roles: representation of the meaning; beauty and decoration; memory and recollection; values and authority; aesthetic awareness; ritual; symbolic investiture; education; evocation.[19] And evocation of the *symbol of justice* is almost never disassociated from the evocation of images of *injustice, wars, oppression* and *violence*, hence its compensatory nature, on the symbolic level, of human, historical, political, religious, economic, cultural and social irrationalities.[20]

---

[14] *Cf.* Franca Filho (2011), p. 36.
[15] *See* Franca Filho (2011), p. 40.
[16] *Cf.* Franca Filho (2011), p. 42.
[17] *Cf.* Franca Filho (2011), p. 42.
[18] *Cf.* Garapon (1998), p. 205.
[19] *Cf.* Garapon (1998), p. 205.
[20] *Vide* Garapon (1998), p. 206.

4.1.1 The Symbol of Justice: Historic Mirror and Public-Sign

The *symbol of justice* is, normally, considered a *stable*, *constant*, *common* and *universal symbol.*[21] Despite the enormous historical changes, it means a symbol that persists and that resists, even though the wear of time represents the strength that normally buries the most beautiful and deepest human constructions, in so far as the importance and ritual character of the symbol of justice: the repetition is an affirmation of it.[22] From the historical point of view, perhaps the constancy and the survival of its evocation are associated to the need for legitimacy of powers, every new historical cycle, which even the relative variation of its uses and attributes explains.[23]

In this line of reasoning this is what Judith Resnik and Dennis Curtis make very clear, in their great iconographic study, contained in the work entitled *Representing Justice,* that the persistence of the symbol of justice owes its function, to legitimizing the violence of the State.[24] Besides this important point, it must be said that in this history there are variations, and these variations denote the very difficulty of *affirming* an *unambiguous and constant concept* of *justice*, which requires that the *symbol of justice* ends up expressing the *tensions* and *variations* that arise from the *contextual, historical, complex* and *unstable* nature of the *concept of justice*, and the variation in the *use of power.*[25]

On the whole, it can be said that *aesthetic text* is a *public-sign*, for various reasons. Firstly, because it takes place in *public space.*[26] Secondly, because it is made to be seen, observed, imitated, admired, criticised, discussed. And thirdly,

[21] "Moving west across the Pacific Ocean, one can see the entrance to the 1974 building for the Supreme Court of Japan" (Resnik and Curtris 2011, p. 01).

[22] "Le même geste peut être accompli pendant des siècles, se voir attribuer successivement plusieurs significations différentes, il n'en poursuit pas moins de génération en génération le cycle inlassable de ses répétitions. Il n'en va pas autrement des rites et des symboles de la justice" ("The same gesture can be accomplished for centuries, being successively attributed several different meanings, it nevertheless continues from generation to generation the untiring cycle of its repetitions. The same is true of the rites and symbols of justice"—*translation*) (Jacob 1994, p. 10).

[23] "We assume that the survival of her image is related, at least in part, to the conscious use of justice imagery by governments seeking to legitimate their exercices of power by associating themselves with the concept of justice implicit in the imagery" (Resnik and Curtis 1987, p. 1743).

[24] "Instead we argue that Justice's remarkable longevity stems from her political utility, deployed because of a never-ending need to legitimate state violence" (Resnik and Curtris 2011, p. 12).

[25] "The imagery of justice reflects the tensions inherent in defining what is just and what stance judges should take a vis-à-vis their sovereigns" (Resnik and Curtis 1987, p. 1764).

[26] "L'allégorie de Justice doit unir ses spectateurs sur la place publique: parce qu'elle se trouve sur l'agora, l'incarnation de la Vertu du bien juger a une autre fin que strictement artistique; elle est volontariste. L'allégorie nous parle par l'art: c'est une image agissante et fédératrice" ("The allegory of Justice must unite its spectators in the public square: because it is on the agora, the embodiment of the Virtue of good judgment has a purpose other than strictly artistic; it is voluntaristic. Allegory speaks to us through art: it is an active and unifying image"—*translation*) (Hayaert and Garapon 2014, p. 10).

Fig. 4.1 Justice, Front view of the City Hall Building Burg Square, Bruges, Belgium Personal Archive: Photography: © pyo

because its field of work is the production of significances and interpretations. Now, as far as the *symbol of justice* is registered in the world by means of *aesthetic languages*, it acquires this vocation of *public-sign*. In the illustration below (see Fig. 4.1), the *public nature of the symbol of justice* can be seen very clearly, for in *Burg Square* (Bruges, Belgium), it is possible to identify how ostentatious the demand and the presence of a statue of justice is, topping the front face of a public building. The symbol of justice is placed in view of the whole city, and there it sends permanent messages to the citizens, placing itself at the centre of social life.

Indeed, the whole history of the *symbology of justice* is a history of justice as *public-sign*.[27] A *public-sign* designates the bonds between the *individuals* and the

[27] *See* Warat (1995), pp. 28–29.

community.[28] An image of justice condenses, as *symbolic image*, the aspirations, searches, fights, beliefs, projections and representations of the *common desire* for coordination of the *public sphere*. It, also, serves as warning and admonition to the practical exercise of justice, impregnating the legitamatory force the exercise of power.[29] For this reason, the history of the symbol of justice speaks with a history of public sphere, in a way it is *trans-figured* and *re-figured* numerous time, throughout Western history.

It is in the *public sphere* that it makes sense, whether in the Egyptian *temple*, (*Mâat*), or in the Greek *Agora* (*Thémis; Diké*),[30] or in the Roman *Urbis* (*Justitia*), or inside the Gothic medieval cathedral (*Christus*), or on the modern *città*, in the bourgeois *piazza*. In the ancient world, *diké,* as the pagan Goddess of Greek mythology; in the medieval world, justice is divine, and is part of a greater ordernation of life, acting as cardinal virtue, director of good-deed and good governing; at the beginning of modernity, justice is featured as an appendix of the supreme; in the modern world, justice is part of urban, city space, full of fairs and bystanders, where the new culture of coins circulates with freedom, and the art of statuary predominates in its rise as a secular persona of bourgeois life, but now blind.[31] It will exceed itself, even further, from the modern Revolutions, whether in the modern *Declaration*, or in the rational and objective Code, or in the *monumentality* of the Palaces of Justice, in the eighteenth and nineteenth centuries, or in the *abstract modernity* of the functional buildings of justice of the twentieth century, or in the *transparency* and *computer digitality* of the architecture of justice of the twenty-first century, in the large urban contemporary centres, or in the *street art* on the outskirts of the cosmopolitan cities. Of these, the image of justice in virtual environments, in the new settings of public space as *digital space*, at the time of *hyper-information*, the image of justice lends itself to many uses, meanings and

[28]*Cf.* Plaza (2010), p. 19.

[29]*Cf.* Lacerda (2012), p. 43.

[30]"La Grèce avait pu donner à Thémis ou à Dikè des silhouettes féminines. Elle avait aussi connu l'emploi de la balance dans certains rituels judiciaires. Mais jamais la balance à deux plateaux n'y était devenue l'attribut emblématique d'une représentation stéréotypée de la justice" ("Greece could have given Themis or Dikè female figures. It had also known the use of the scales in certain judicial rituals. But never had the double-platter scale become an emblematic attribute of a stereotypical representation of justice"—*translation*) (Jacob 1994, pp. 220–221).

[31]"Of course, Justice is not a solitary icon in the Western tradition. Rather, she is one of a series of images, most in the female form, associated with powerful concepts of virtues and vices. Justice, like many of these images, traces her ancestry to goddesses. Her forerunners seem to have been Maát in Egyptian culture, Themis and Dike in ancient Greece, and then Justitia under Roman rule. When goddesses lost currency as the Church grew in power, Justice appeared in Christian imagery—used not as goddess but as a personification of the ancient virtue. In medieval traditions, Justice achieves a place as one of the four cardinal virtues; the others are Prudence, Temperance, and Fortitude" (Resnik and Curtis 1987, pp. 1729–1730).

perspectives. This is how it becomes capable of being read and understood globally today.[32]

For this reason, a careful approach to the *history of the symbol of justice* allows us to understand that this passes through time, but not in an unchanged way. The whole symbol is composed of certain *figurative attributes*, to the extent that the *symbol* is an encryption, a semiotic *reduction*, a convention, and maintains a strong appeal to a community of meaning. As a *symbol*, it incorporates the whole set of public and collective expectations around what is *common*; consequently, at times, its solemn, divine, serious, enthusiastic, dramatic, ritual, celebrative, admonishing, guttural, equidistant character depending on the adopted *languages* in the 'representation' of justice, from the historic moment and from meanings of Law and of Justice in that context. Furthermore, it is important to affirm, often the representations of the *symbol of justice* are given through artistic techniques, of strategies contained in the *idioletto* of an author, of symbologies and encrypted languages, in a way to hinder the access—without distortions—to the meaning of the *work-of-art*, be it a manuscript, engraving, painting, sculpture, graphics.

But, the *semiotic relation* produced by the *symbol of justice*, is not one of mere *representation* (symbolic/reality), but of degrees of *symbolisation* and *iconisation*, within a broader procedure of *veridictorian persuasion* that appeals to *human meanings*. The symbol of justice is a *place-of-the-common*, a *significant* as *being able-doing-knowing* (*pouvoir-faire-savoir*) placed in *public space*, as a stimulus of a conception of justice that is open to the public and diverse interpretation of its readers. For this reason, it is the *historical* and *inter-textual set* of the symbolic representations of justice that give us a broader *message*, and not the analysis of an *isolated figuration*. Furthermore, its maintenance, its constant invocation in the modern palaces of justice, its constant representation in the paintings of great artists, or even, in the frescos in cathedrals and churches, points to the *symbolic weight* exercised by *visual tradition* of representation of the *symbol of justice*.

Yet, it is fact that the *symbol of justice* is used to being paired with other *virtues* and *vices*, or even, used to being represented in a shielded form by the best forces of nature (or of the human soul), in a way that the *symbol of justice* is *public-sign* (1), of constant presence in history (2), and, also, of enormous symbolic strength (3). As a *public-sign*, made up in the *historical form* of possible representations, contrary to what it is used to affirming, it is *not* stable in history, and only serves a *catalyst* of *semiotically instituted* and *conventionally determined* meanings within the arrangement of *relations of power* and *historical forms of justice*, from a socio-historical-cultural context. This demonstrates that, even if there is a certain stability of elements and there is a universal transmission of the *symbol of justice*, the *symbol of justice* is *relative* in its representations in time and space, and plays very clearly with the circumstantial elements.

[32] "These various deployments all rely on the fact that we (people living in Europe, North and South America, Africa, Australia, and Asia) can "read" them" (Resnik and Curtris 2011, p. 08).

This is how some attributes that form it can be located, can be subdivided in two classes, namely: (1) constant attributes; (2) circumstantial attributes. All things considered of historical representations, the symbol of justice, appears in the form of a feminine figure,[33] in every context, or even, in each narrative and figurative investment, the *symbol of justice* is clothed in specific elements that are variable and circumstantial. Thus, the *attributes of the symbol of justice*, normally, are the sword, vision (or, blindfold), scales, throne, crown, sceptre, code, hammer, with detectable variations in each historical context, being certain that determined elements have remained unchanged in *Western representations*, such as the sword and the scales, with higher prevalence. Nowadays, often, only the scales, that it is a *sub-symbol*, is evoked within the *complete symbol*, which represents justice, as the analysis of Portuguese jurist Paulo Ferreira da Cunha points out.[34]

The great consecration and dissemination of the *symbol of justice* brings some creativity to Western art, especially from the end of the Middle Ages, when you see this *symbol* associated to so many other *symbols*.[35] Hence, the figure of a *Goddess* with *traditional-symbols* attached to her (sword, scales), can also be surrounded by *attributes* (constant; circumstantial),[36] *objects* and/or *associated* to other innovative and contextually significant *symbols-strength* (to the building, to the historical moment, to the commissioner of the work, to the author of the work of art), such as: (1) crown (queen, attribute of royal power); (2) throne (place of decision); (3) dove (symbol of peace); (4) snake (pointing to vices, poison, astuteness or prudence); (5) people (popular sovereignty); (6) penalty (power of the written); (7) scrolls of laws (Roman *codex*; divine laws); (8) angels (celestial, purity, naivety); (9) sayings, such as, *Lex Duodecim Tabularum* (tradition of Roman Law); (10) sayings, such as *Lex* (legislative body of Positive Law); (11) horses and lions (strength of nature); (12) book (wisdom; erudite culture; study); (13) virtues (Truth, Prudence, Courage, Study, Strength, Temperance); (14) skull (mortality; finiteness of human things); (15) the eye of the law (all-seeing; all-controlling). This is why, given this enormous variety of *attributes* (constant; circumstantial), one tries here to stop the analysis to dedicate oneself to the understanding of something more stable, such as the blindfold, scales and sword.

[33]"And yet it must be acknowledged that blindfolded Justitia, with all of her warlike attributes, was primarily a female figure, as had been the Egyptian Maat (goddess not only of justice but of truth and order) and the Greek Dike, a daughter of Zeus. Male images of divine justice, such as that of God at the Last Judgment or that of Saint Michel, had not been prevented from exercising the power of vision" (Jay 1999, p. 27).

[34]*Cf.* da Cunha (2013), p. 210.

[35]"Elle garde comme attributs dominants la balance, le glaive et le bandeau" ("She keeps as her dominant attributes the scales, the sword and the blindfold"—*translation*) (Jacob 1994, p. 238).

[36]*Cf.* da Cunha (2013), p. 210.

4.1.1.1 The Symbol of Justice: The Blindfold

Justice with the blindfold is not a constant representation in the history of the *symbology of justice*. Its emergence is late, in the tradition of the *symbology of justice,* and dated to the sixteenth century.[37] And this because the *blindness* did not always accompany the *representation* of justice in the traditional and ancestral representations of Western culture (sculpture; painting; manuscript; numismatics). On the contrary, the vision is a more explicit attribute of the Goddess *Diké.* And, with great consistency, among the Greek, Roman and Medieval worlds, the *symbol of justice* is always combined with the attribute of *super-vision*, in other words, the *eye of justice.*[38] It is a good example of importance of the vision for justice, the representation by Albrecht Dürer, entitled *Sol Justititae*, in 1498. This allows us to affirm that the *vision* was always a strong attribute to qualify the capacity of analysis, action, observation and actuation of justice, from the old world to the modern world.[39]

In Medieval and Renaissance imagery, *iconography* that possesses blindness as a characteristic is linked to bad aspects, which are, Death, Greed, Ignorance, Error, Wrath, as Robert Jacob indicates.[40] And, in fact, the studies undertaken by Judith Resnik and Dennis Curtis arrived to the same conclusion, evaluating that *blindness* hitherto is a negative attribute, in a broad sense.[41] The *blindness* of the Goddess of justice, as a bad attribute, that is, linked to a deficiency and to the madness, in the representation contained in the engraving by Albrecht Dürer in the poem by Sebastian Brant (1494),[42] in the *Ship of Fools* (*Das Narrenschiff*),[43] is rapidly transformed in the *paradigm* of modern justice,[44] in other words, converted from

[37]"Consider also the many meanings possible for blindfold. The blindfold is a relatively late addition to the imagery of Justice" (Jacob 1994, p. 233).

[38]*Cf.* Franca Filho (2011), p. 33.

[39]*Cf.* Franca Filho (2011), p. 36.

[40]"D'ailleurs, avant le XVIe siècle, personne ne s'était avisé qu'il fallait être aveugle pour être impartial. Au contraire, le discernement et la vision aiguë passent pour les qualités nécessaires d'une bonne justice" ("Besides, before the XVI century, no one knew that one had to be blind to be impartial. On the contrary, discernment and sharp vision are considered necessary qualities of good justice"—*translation*) (Jacob 1994, p. 233).

[41]"Rather, for Medieval and Renaissance audiences, the blindfold was laden with negative connotations" (Resnik and Curtris 2011, p. 62).

[42]"The first appears in a late fifteenth century woodcut by Dürer to illustrate a book by Sebatian Brant. Justice is shown being blindfolded by a fool…" (Resnik and Curtris, http://digitalcommons.law.yale.edu/fss_papers/917, Acesso em 07/04/2017, 1987, pp. 1756–1757). Em outra parte: "Brant, who was a noted lawyer and law professor, trained (as he said at the front of the book) in both civil and canon law, saw blindness as a fault" (Resnik and Curtris 2011, p. 67).

[43]*Vide* da Cunha (2013), p. 211. *See too* Franca Filho (2011), p. 36.

[44]"But suddenly at the end of the fifteenth century, a blindfold began to be placed over the goddess's eyes, producing what has rightly been called the most enigmatic of the attributes of Justice". Perhaps the earliest image showing the change is a 1494 wood engraving of a Fool covering the

something negative into something positive in the configuration of justice,[45] namely, blindness as a quality of impartiality and non-sense of people who engage in the attitude of those who judge, starting to become predominant as *figurativisation* from 1530.[46] From there on, the first appearance of justice blindfolded, in a positive sense, as a sign of impartiality, came in 1531, in the Wormser Reformation, Worms. According some analyses, perhaps the image of Sebastian Brant was imposed in such a way, and was scattered in the general mindset, that jurists had to render themselves to its *figurativity*, in a way of converting its meaning into something positive, in the process of judgement.[47] Consequently, there was already a concern to denounce, in an aberrant way, the problem of *judicial error* as something dangerous, and that aroused the attention of scholars, lawyers and jurists.[48]

The *symbol of justice*, which needed new characteristics for new times, would burst, in the middle of the Medieval city, in the transition to the modern world, thirsty for representing the strength and power of the bourgeois, and, for this reason, as a *symbol,* the synthesis of a *new time*, disruptive in relation to the times of the representations and power of the Catholic Church.[49] And this occurs mainly from Northern Europe, in a way that a historical process connected to the *laicisation* and to the ascension of the Protestant Reform is revealed there.[50] In addition, it means a demand for resource no longer in the same forms of justice subject to judicial error, but, by the force of the demands of the legal community, the resource increasingly less than *judicial discretion* and increasingly more than *legislation* and *Roman codification*.[51]

It spreads as an *image-of-the-city*—and is found, generally, in the middle of the public square—,[52] equally distanced from the power of the Church and the power of

eyes of Justice, illustrating Sebastian Brant's *Narrenschiff* ('Ship of Fools') wich was rapidly reproduced in translations throughout Europe" (Jay 1999, pp. 19–20).

[45] *Cf.* da Cunha (2004), p. 87.

[46] "By 1530, however, this image seems to have lost its satirical implication and the blindfold was transformed into a positive emblem of impartiality and equality before the law" (Jay 1999, p. 20).

[47] *Vide* Lacerda (2012), p. 48.

[48] "The artist who created *The Fool Blindfolding Justice* was Constitutio not the only one of his era to deploy a blindfold as a warning against judicial error" (Resnik and Curtris 2011, p. 67).

[49] *Cf.* Franca Filho (2011), p. 82.

[50] "Harbison suggests that in Northern Europe, the Reformation and secularization gave impetus to a need for propaganda to reassure members of society that early decisions paralleled heavenly ones" (Resnik and Curtis 2011, p. 1746).

[51] "These materials were part of a larger effort to professionalize law, to dispossess lay jurists of their authority, and to promote law's codification. The negativity of the blindfold was part of a message about the superiority of Roman statutory law over the customary law used by German lay judges" (Resnik and Curtris 2011, p. 69).

[52] "Le trait est particulièrement apparent dans la statuaire qui s'est développée à partir du XVIe siècle dans les villes du sud de l'Allemagne et en Suisse. La Justice est en général installée sur une colonne qui domine la place publique la plus importante de la ville" ("The line is particularly apparent in the statuary that developed from XVI century in the cities of southern Germany and

the sovereign, and, in this sense, starts to affirm the *publicity* of justice.[53] If this image is spread, affirmed and consolidated between the sixteenth and seventeenth centuries,[54] this coincides with the professionalization of independent magistrates, who were impartial, and not bound to royal power, granting greater autonomy and impartiality, equidistance and seriousness to the act of judging.[55] Furthermore, *blindness* appears to mark a clear break from the Medieval world and its imagery, of a *justice* that was *represented* as superior to men, and, therefore *divine,* towards to a *secular justice*, that no longer needs theological routes to be accessed, since the *laws* now indicate everything that needs to be *interpreted, meditated, interiorised,* pointing to a period in which the *empire of written law* is above the theological discourses about *divine justice.*[56]

Blindness, therefore, goes on to signify: (1) interiority and intimacy with the truth;[57] (2) impartiality[58] in view of arguments and the compromise of the parties involved;[59] (3) equidistance of the parties;[60] (4) caution in walking, not crashing into

---

Switzerland. Justice is usually installed on a column overlooking the city's most important public square"—*translation*) (Jacob 1994, p. 240).

[53]"Robert has argued that it was relatively secular, democratic forms of government (the city-states of central Europe) that typically propagated visual allegories of justice, while the absolutist monarchy continued to rely mainly on the effigy of the king. He relates the allegory of Justice to the city-state's need for an emblem that abstracted power and dissociated it from the individual men at his helm of government. The emblem of Justice not only represented justice but allegorized and legitimated the state and its executive power" (Taylor 1999, p. 169).

[54]*Vide* Jacob (1994), p. 13.

[55]"A political explanation is offered by Judge Otto Kissel, who notes that the blindfold became a popular attribute of Justice during the sixteenth and seventeenth centuries. Kissel argues that inclusion of the blindfold in Justice imagery coincided with the establishing of professional, independent judges, who stood apart from the sovereign and were not simply acting at its behest" (Resnik and Curtis 1987, p. 1757).

[56]*Vide* Jacob (1994), p. 237.

[57]"A blind-folded justice could thus avoid the seductions of images and achieve the dispassionate distance necessary to render verdicts impartially, an argument advanced as early as the jurist Andre Alciati's influential compendium of emblems, the *Emblemata* of 1531" (Jay 1999, pp. 21–24).

[58]"La benda fa segno dell'imparzialità di un giudice deputato a bocca della legge, a mero dichiaratore di una norma generale e astratta. La bilancia esprime la ricerca del punto in cui le forze si annullano, nell'assunto che in giudizio si esprimano pretese più o meno impari; infine, la spada allude al fondamento coercitivo del giudizio, coerzione che (al fine di legittimarsi) risiede nel monopolio dell Stato" ("The blindfold is a sign of the impartiality of a judge deputed by the mouth of the law, a mere declarer of a general and abstract rule. The balance expresses the search for the point at which forces are annulled, in the assumption that more or less unequal claims are made in court; finally, the sword alludes to the coercive foundation of judgment, a coercion that (in order to legitimize itself) resides in the monopoly of the State"—*translation*) (Ziccardi 2014, p. 168).

[59]*Cf.* Lacerda (2012), p. 38.

[60]*Cf.* Lacerda (2012), p. 45.

Fig. 4.2 Symbols of Justice Museum of the Supreme Court of Justice Washington D. C. United States of America Personal Archive: Photography © pyo

taking steps, knowing that the terrain of the future is unknown;[61] (5) disengagement with royal power, and, therefore, judicial autonomy.

Since then, blind justice has spread as a *model* of the idea of justice. The title of the example, in the illustration below (see Fig. 4.2), from the *Museum of the Supreme Court of Justice* (Washington D.C., USA), There is this invocation of blind justice, which accurately records this more widespread conception, that justice is blind.

There are many contemporary criticisms in respect of the role of the *blindfold* in the symbol of justice, in addition to the meanings it bears. For this reason, currently, in the wake of Martin Jay,[62] it is perhaps preferable to notice in the *symbol of justice* neither a justice with open eyes nor a blind justice, but prefer that symbol in which is appears as a bifacial form—the example of the figure entitled *Mundanae iustitiae effigies,* which appears on the title page of the book in the sixteenth century entitled

[61]"There is another powerful justification for the allegorical image of the blindfold. Because her eyes are covered, Justitia must walk cautiously into the future, not rushing headlong to judgment" (Jay 1999, p. 32).

[62]*See* Jay (1999), p. 35.

Praxis rerum civilium—,[63] either with eyes open, or eyes closed, saying that both qualities are indispensable for good judgement, namely, both the impartiality of the blindfolded face (that looks at the scales), and the vision of the face with eyes open (which looks at the sword), in order to not to be deceived by what it sees.[64] Or even, in the wake of Martha Nussbaum and Simone Weil,[65] it is possible to represent justice, taking the blindfold away from it,[66] so that the cognitive range gives it even better conditions of exercise of its socially relevant task.

4.1.1.2 The Symbol of Justice: The Scales

The *sub-symbol of the scales*, internalized as part of the *symbol of justice,* an obviously central part—and that, historically, is increasingly consolidated as a *synthesis of the idea of justice*—, has an Egyptian origin,[67] and not Greek or Roman. The Greek and Roman uses are already much more contemporary, since the use of the *scales*, among the Egyptians, pointed to the activity of the *weighing of human actions*, and, thus, as part of the divine activity of judgement in the passage to the kingdom of the dead.[68] The Egyptians would take advantage of this symbology, through religious rite and religious beliefs, and, perhaps, from there, this had influenced other people, cultures and old traditions. It is fact that not only the Egyptian religion took advantage of this symbol, but also Judaism and Islam.[69] The Romans would use, in principle, *coins* as the symbol of justice, and, in her first appearances, already as a woman with the writing *Iustitia* (coins of Emperor Tiberius), but in her more consolidated and constant appearances, she was a

[63]"*Mundanae iustitiae effigies* (A *Portrait of Worldy Justice*) is the title placed above an intriguing Janus-faced Justice from a sixteenth-century book, *Praxis rerum civilium (Legal Practice in Civil Matters*)" (Resnik and Curtris 2011, p. 72).

[64]"The face of the sighted Justice looks toward her large sword, held upright in her right hand, while the face of the blindfolded Justice turns toward her left side, where her left hand holds tipped scales" (Resnik and Curtris 2011, p. 72).

[65]*Vide* Ziccardi (2014).

[66]*Cf.* Ziccardi (2014), p. 173.

[67]"C'est pourquoi les historiens privilégient d'ordinaire la piste égyptienne. On sait qu'en Égypte, la pesée de l'âme du défunt lors du jugement des morts a donné matière à de très nombreuses représentations. La balance y est l'instrument du jugement. La déesse de la Justice, Maât, ne préside pas à la cérémonie, mais elle y participe de manière décisive en posant sur des plateaux la plume d'autruche qui est son attribut principal. La plume de Maât constitue à la fois l'accusation et la mesure exacte de la justice" ("That's why historians usually favor the Egyptian trail. It is known that in Egypt, the weighing of the soul of the deceased at the judgment of the dead has given rise to many representations. The scale is the instrument of judgment. The Goddess of Justice, Maat, does not preside over the ceremony, but she participates decisively by placing the ostrich feather, which is her main attribute, on trays. Maat's feather is both the accusation and the exact measure of justice"—*translation*) (Jacob 1994, p. 221).

[68]*Cf.* Lacerda (2012), p. 35.

[69]*Cf.* Lacerda (2012), p. 36.

Fig. 4.3 Jurisprudence Vatican Museum The Vatican Rome, Italy Personal Archive: Photography: © pyo

woman with scales, affirming herself since the end of the first century A.D. (coins of the Emperors Vespasiano and Titus).[70]

It is, however, from the Middle Ages that the *symbol of the scales* is stereotyped as a more constant, normal *standard*, invoked in various allegories, paintings, sculptures and illuminated manuscripts of the period, demarcating once and for all, in Western imagery, its presence as the characteriser of the idea of justice.[71] In the illustration below (see Fig. 4.3), it is possible to verify, in a painting from the *Vatican Museum* (Rome, Italy), the presence of the scales as a decisive element for the configuration of the idea of justice. The *scales* are not only present, but they *confer geometrical balance* to the artistic composition itself of this painting. Here, the *Goddess of justice* has a writing in verbal signs (*Jurisprudentia*) at her feet, she is surrounded by books and scrolls, and the sword rests, for it is a necessary element, but not so important, for not maintaining a physical connection with the *Goddess of justice*. Here, she prefers the contact of her hands on the task of *balancing* and *handling books*.

This is what the scales point to: (1) balanced decision between two plates, implying judgement; (2) the indication that all arguments have two sides, and it is necessary to listen and give the opportunity to tell both versions; (3) the balance and the harmony of the plates of the scales;[72] (4) the capability to dose, weigh, ponder, consider, in a way to reach the verdict not by a solitary and unilateral process, but from the parts of the argument presented to the plates of the scales; (5) subtlety and

---

[70] *Vide* Jacob (1994), pp. 219–220.

[71] *See* Jacob (1994), p. 224.

[72] *Cf.* Lacerda (2012), p. 37.

Fig. 4.4 Justice front view of public building Burg Square Bruges, Belgium Personal Archive: Photography: © pyo

sensitive dexterity, in the dynamic and sensitive balance of the scales, which is capable of capturing the slightest variation of measure, in the identification of the small differences between the facts and phenomena, indicating that the activity of justice implies the capability of perceiving that the common eye does not differentiate.

4.1.1.3 The Symbol of Justice: The Sword

The *sub-symbol of the sword*, within the *symbol of justice*, points to the dimension of strength, of the coercivity of the decisions of justice.[73] The symbol of justice depends the scales and the sword, which appear to be *sub-symbols* of the most constant in the evocation of the *notion of justice*. The title of the example, as can be seen in the illustration below (see Fig. 4.4), in *Burg Square* (Bruges, Belgium), the

[73]*Cf.* Lacerda (2012), p. 42.

statue of justice is not only a *public-sign* that appears in the main square at the top, but is positioned in the highest part of the public building. There, in the eyes of all, she holds scales with her left hand, and a sword with her right hand. This, the sword, is found right in front of her body, and maintains an active position, communicating to the city that the use of its *force* is at the disposal of public authorities, for the fulfilment of the proclaims of justice.

The *sub-symbol* of the sword, associated to the *symbol of justice*, appears to have been vulgarised from a representation in the fourteenth century, by Andre Pisano, in the *Baptistery of San Giovanni,* in Florence, Italy (1334–1336).[74]

And this because the sword appears to evoke the idea that: (1) justice would be dismantled from the conditions of its application, if it could not impose the decisions of justice; (2) the force, in turn, is a substitute for the force of individuals; (3) the strength indicates that *power* favours the application of justice, and confers to it the conditions of executivity; (4) a form of threat and prevention, as a sword held and directed to all those who intend to commit unjust acts;[75] (5) the balance of the scales without the force of the sword would be destined to denial by those affected by the decisions of justice; (6) its vertical position or at rest, indicates the degree of resource to force and the activity required, more passive or more active; (7) the power of division and partition, to the extent that *attributing to each one* a task of justice.[76]

4.1.2 *Between* Iconology *and* Semiotics of Painting*: The Symbol of Justice in Western Painting*

The *Semiotics of Art* encompasses a *Semiotics of Painting*,[77] given that the *Semiotics of Painting* is only a part of the *Semiotics of Image.* The *Semiotics of Painting* is a segment in the field of studies applied in *General Semiotics*, even in the recent state of development,[78] given that, here, in fact, it is the *sign-icon*[79] that is highlighted in importance and centrality.

In this point, it is worth emphasising, initially, that *Semiotics, Image* and *Painting* are studied by the *Semiotics of Image*, in a way that *Iconology* is the specific part of a *Semiotics* applied and specialised in the studies of the *discourses of images*,[80] in other words, of *imagery texts*,[81] and, to a *Semiotics of Painting*, of *pictorial texts.*[82]

---

[74] *Cf.* Lacerda (2012), p. 43.

[75] *Cf.* Lacerda (2012), p. 43.

[76] *Cf.* Lacerda (2012), p. 45.

[77] *Cf.* da Cunha (2004), p. 23.

[78] *Cf.* Santaella and Nöth (1998), p. 97.

[79] *Cf.* Plaza (2010), p. 24.

[80] *See* Nöth (2012), p. 02.

[81] *Cf.* Santaella and Nöth (1998), p. 33.

[82] *Cf.* Volli (2015), p. 277.

For the analysis of *Visual Semiotics*, or *Semiotics of Image*, more specifically, it is worth the affirmation by Algirdas Julien Greimas and Joseph Courtés of which the *image* is considered the *unit of manifestation*,[83] capable of being submitted to semiotic analysis. Furthermore, the whole debate about *visuality* crosses to the discussion about the *iconicity* of the image.[84]

But, it is important to affirm that *Iconology* was always a part of the *history of art* concerned with the interpretation of the meaning of the works of art, enabling the analysis of the works of art.[85] In this point, the German historian and art critic Erwin Panofsky was, without a doubt, the main reference in this domain.[86] It was only more recently, with the development of the semiotic studies of the image, *Iconology*—for some also called *Iconomy*—that it became possible—simultaneously—a part of the *Semiotics of Image*, as the studies of semioticist Lucia Santaella point out, alongside Winfried Nöth.[87]

The undertaking of *Semiotics* is here, as in other parts, the understanding and the unravelling of the meaning(s), considering wealth and diversity, the dynamics and the plurality of the images in the large field for the decoding of enigmas of social life, symbology and human culture,[88] bearing in mind the symbolic patrimony of humanity.[89] It is certain that this field of *Semiotics* imposes very specific difficulties on the work of readings and decoding of meaning, given that the classes are not symmetrical to the same dimensions of semiotics which tackle linguistic questions.[90]

---

[83]"En sémiotique visuelle, l'image est considérée comme une unité de manifestation autosuffisante, comme un tout de signification, susceptible d'être soumis à l'analyse" (Greimas and Courtés 1993, p. 181, *Analogie*).

[84]"Il est ainsi de l'icône, signe 'naturellement motivé' représentant le 'réferent', et de l'iconicité, concept situé au coeur des débats de la sémiologie de l'image, et qui renvoient tout aussi naturellement à l'ancienne 'imitation de la nature'" ("Il est ainsi de l'icône, signe 'naturellement motivé' représentant le 'réferent', et de l'iconicité, concept situé au coeur des débats de la sémiologie de l'image, et qui renvoient tout aussi naturellement à l'ancienne 'imitation de la nature'"—*translation*) (Greimas 1984, p. 07).

[85]*See* Panofsky (2009), p. 13.

[86]"L'iconografia è quel ramo della storia dell'arte che si occupa del soggetto o significato delle opere d'arte, in quanto contrapposto alla forma di esse" (Panofsky 2009, p. 03).

[87]*See* Santaella and Nöth (1998), p. 98.

[88]*Cf.* Volli (2015), p. 275.

[89]*Cf.* Santaella and Nöth (1998), p. 141.

[90]"La sémiotique générale met à la disposition du sémioticien préoccupé des problèmes de la visualité un outillage conceptuel et procédurier nombreux et diversifié, sans pour autant lui fournir des recettes toutes faites, sans le forcer, surtout, à transposer des procédures linguistiques reconnues, mais probablement mal adaptées à des domaines dont les articulations significantes apparaissent intuitivement fort diferentes de celles des langues naturelles" ("General semiotics provides the semioticist concerned with the problems of visuality with numerous and diversified conceptual and procedural tools, without providing him with ready-made recipes, without forcing him, above all, to transpose recognized linguistic procedures, which are probably poorly adapted to domains whose significant articulations appear intuitively very different from those of natural languages"—*translation*) (Greimas 1984, p. 14).

In any case, Algirdas Julien Greimas, in his text entitled *Sémiotique figurative et sémiotique plastique* (1984), already recognised that *Visual Semiotics* as an innovative and building part of the semiotic studies, whose effort consists of making what is tridemensional captured and juxtaposed to what is flat (painting; photography; graphic arts).[91] According to Ugo Volli, this text in 1984 by Algirdas Julien Greimas was decisive for the constitution of the field of studies of the *Semiotics of Painting.*[92]

4.1.2.1 Semiotics, Image and Justice

The idea of *image* is complexly worked by *Semiotics*, considering the artificial character with which the *aesthetic visual sign* is installed in our imagination,[93] forming the *reality of images* that dwell in our *symbolic universe*. And this because the image has a double dimension, since it is the *image-thing* and *image-imagination*, as Lucia Santaella and Winfried Nöth point out well.[94] In addition to this, as Italian semioticist Omar Calabrese draws to our attention, the *image* has something to do with what the *sign-verbal* does not have, since it is able to function in a syncretic way, besides being able to put on the same plane—without waiting for the succession of signs—, broadening the complex and open perception of *aesthetic text.*[95]

And, even if the research about the image is complex, substantial and extensive,[96] in the area of the *Semiotics of Painting,* it is certain that the *image* appears as something that creates strangeness to the culture of Law. Hence, the reciprocal importance between the studies of the *Semiotics of Painting* and the *Semiotics of Law*, but, above all, the importance of the *Semiotics of Painting* for the *Semiotics of Law*, to the extent of the very deficits found in the area of Law when dealing with the *image*. This has evident historical reasons, and they date back to the nineteenth

[91]"On pense pouvoir en restreindre l'objet d'investigation en définissant la *Sémiotique visuelle* par son *support planaire,* en chargeant ainsi la surfasse de parler de l'espace tri-dimensionnel: les manifestations picturale, graphique, photographique se trouvent alors réunies au nom d'un mode de 'présence au monde' commun" ("'We think that we can restrict the object of investigation by defining Visual Semiotics by its planar support, by charging the surface to speak of three-dimensional space: the pictorial, graphic and photographic manifestations are then brought together in the name of a common mode of' presence in the world"—*translation*) (Greimas 1984, p. 01).

[92]*Vide* Volli (2015), p. 278.

[93]"Il est communément admis de definir d'abord la sémiotique visuelle par son caractere *construit,* artificiel, en l'opposant ainsi aux langues 'naturelles' e aux mondes 'naturels', ces deux macro-sémiotiques à l'intérieur desquelles nous insère, bien malgré nous, notre codition d'hommes" ("It is commonly accepted that visual semiotics should first be defined by its constructed, artificial character, thus opposing it to 'natural' languages and 'natural' worlds, these two macro-semiotics within which we insert, in spite of ourselves, our condition of men"—*translation*) (Greimas 1984, p. 01).

[94]*Cf.* Santaella and Nöth (1998), p. 36.

[95]*Cf.* Calabrese (2015), p. 120.

[96]*Cf.* Nöth (2012), p. 07.

century,[97] when visual culture ceased to be stimulated, prioritizing a literate legal formation and founded in writing, something that prevails in Western culture to this day, when the expression of Law is confused with the expression of *verbal texts*.[98] It is interesting to note that, to the contrary, the predominance until the nineteenth century, and, thus, before the ascension of *juridical positivism*—where the predominance of *linguistic signs* is highlighted, in a way of predominance of the Code, Regulation, Law, Evidence, Judicial Dogmatics, Written Document, Process—,[99] given by the evocation of the image of justice, of the symbol of justice, of the allegory of justice, in various spaces of justice, as, indeed, can be seen in the solid analysis of the works of art that are *read* and *interpreted* in the aftermath. *Juridical positivism* builds the prestige of the *image* in the culture of Law, from the nineteenth century.[100] The search for a *legal iconology,* or, for a *legal iconography*, is not, therefore, of today.[101] Here, therefore, the *legal image*, or even, the *aesthetic text with meaning for Law*, is what one seeks to treat and develop as an object of study, as French historians of Law Nathalie Goedert and Ninon Maillard highlight.[102]

For no other reason, this path of the *Semiotics of Painting* is supportive of the studies of the *History of art* and of the *History of culture.*[103] It is the complexity of the image that attracts the need for which its study to be necessarily interdisciplinary, as Lucia Santaella points out,[104] and, precisely for this reason, circumscribed and revealed, at the same time. It is impossible to cover a complete route of the history of Western painting,[105] here one works with only a brief historical clipping. The history of the *image* has a fascinating route in world history, the example of the *sign of the*

[97] *See* Goedert and Maillard (2015), p. 168.

[98] "L'évolution de la production normative en Occident, marquée par la prédominance de l'écrit, comme source, comme preuve, comme expression du droit, semble en avoir fait un objet textuel. L'énoncé du droit ne saurait pourtant se circonscrire à sa lettre. Car le texte juridique s'inscrit dans un univers normatif plus vaste constitué de référents symboliques et de rituels. Le droit se montre, s'exprime, s'élabore sous des formes diverses dont le juriste peut aussi se saisir pour appréhender sa discipline dans toute sa complexité" ("The evolution of normative production in the West, marked by the predominance of the written word, as a source, as evidence, as an expression of law, seems to have made it a textual object. The statement of the law cannot, however, be confined to its letter. For the legal text is part of a larger normative universe made up of symbolic referents and rituals. The law is shown, expressed and developed in various forms, which the jurist can also use to grasp its discipline in all its complexity"—*translation*) (Goedert and Maillard 2015, p. 18).

[99] See Tuzet (2014), p. 176.

[100] *Vide* Franca Filho (2011), p. 82.

[101] "Dès 1923, Hans Fehr définit l'iconographie juridique comme la "reconnaissance des formes ayant une signification juridique" et invite le juriste à s'intéresser aux figures du droit et à en interpréter les motifs" ("As early as 1923, Hans Fehr defined legal iconography as "the recognition of forms with legal significance" and invited the jurist to take an interest in the figures of law and to interpret their motives"—*translation*) (Goedert and Maillard 2015, p. 19).

[102] *Cf.* Goedert and Maillard (2015), p. 22.

[103] *See* da Cunha (2004), p. 22. *Vide* Jacob (1994).

[104] *Cf.* Santaella and Nöth (1998), p. 13.

[105] *Vide* Argan (2013), p. 22.

bison in a cave,[106] and one could focus on the error of seeking to cover long historical periods that would divert us from the task of interpreting the studied works in a *localised way*. For this reason, given the vastness of the business of covering the *pictorial works* from the Palaeolithic period[107] to the contemporary period—as, indeed, they point out the studies of *Visual Anthropology*—[108] the task of clipping is decidedly relevant.

But, in any case, as it is also highlighted from *Visual Anthropology*, a *clipping of image* is already a substantial portion of the traditions, beliefs, culture, practices and ideologies that govern a whole system of culture.[109] In this sense, art can capture, represent, seize, figure, sensitise, translate, mould, reflect an entire era and all its beliefs. Therefore, it is intended to cover a *short iconological route*, exactly where historian Robert Jacob pinpoints the emergence of a more systematic and coherent artistic and architectonic production, in the medieval period,[110] regarding justice, thus analysing a clipping of *selected images*.

The pictorial image of justice is visited without the pretence of exhibiting is enigmatic character,[111] and without the pretence of covering anything other than the period between the thirteenth century and the sixteenth century, of European art—considering the iconographical mass bequeathed to us—, following a sequential chronological order (1218; 1297; 1303; 1508; 1768-9; 1857; 1937), with only a few representative and strongly symbolic works, in good state of conservation, and which are invaluable cultural heritage of humanity. In this case, the choice implied a route within *Italian art*,[112] given the importance and significance of this, local and universally, including from the point of view of the *history of art*, without disregarding the *Belgian, Spanish, French, English, Brazilian arts*, amongst others.

---

[106] *Cf.* Argan (2013), p. 25.

[107] *Cf.* Argan (2013), pp. 21–24.

[108] *Cf.* Mathias (2016), p. 15.

[109] *See* Mathias (2016), p. 27.

[110] "Les miniatures médiévales les plus anciennes, en effet, comme les premiers tableaux de justice, révèlent déjà un monde ordonné, la justice est forte, mais elle a soif d'exposer aux yeux de tous ses racines et ses fondements. Elle les trouve dans une forme idéale de justice, celle de Dieu, qu'elle s'efforce d'imiter, avec laquelle elle aspire même à se confondre. La délégation de Dieu aux hommes du pouvoir de juger est alors la clef du système iconographique. Elle manifeste tout à la fois la légitimité de la fonction judiciaire et la responsabilité du juge, deux thèmes systématiquement associés, comme en un jeu de miroir, et simultanément présent dans l'image comme ils l'étaient dans la pensée des hommes" ("The oldest medieval miniatures, in fact, like the first paintings of justice, already reveal an ordered world, justice is strong, but it is thirsty to expose to the eyes of all its roots and foundations. It finds them in an ideal form of justice, that of God, which it strives to imitate, with which it even aspires to merge. The delegation of God's power of judgment to men is then the key to the iconographic system. It manifests both the legitimacy of the judicial function and the responsibility of the judge, two themes systematically associated, as if in a game of mirrors, and simultaneously present in the image as they were in the minds of men"—*translation*) (Jacob 1994, p. 12).

[111] *Cf.* Jacob (1994), p. 219.

[112] *Vide* Argan (2013).

This brief historical-pictorial route—where architecture and painting are correlated to each other—[113] draws some meanings of the works analysed, without the pretence of defusing the open character of the *meaning of images*,[114] in its consideration for the *iconology of justice*.[115]

4.1.2.2 The Semiotic Square and Pictorial Text

Before entering into the analysis of each of the works, specifically, it is important to affirm that *Semiotics* allows for an in-depth reading of *pictorial texts*. Therefore, a *pictorial text* can be broken down, considering three levels, the *fundamental*, where the main opposition is stated, the *narrative*, where the investment of subjects around the objects in the scene is stated, and the *discursive*, forming a more superficial layer.[116] If the *meaning* can be constructed in this way, it can, similarly, be br*oken down* in the same ways. To the *enunciation* (E) of *aesthetic text*, it follows the *decodification* (D) of *aesthetic text*. The *semiotic operation* of dismantling of *pictorial text* is a central task of the analytics. The whole narrative structure of the level of expression can be reduced, through the methodology of *Semiotics*, the logical-grammatical structures, providing important *keys-of-reading* for the interpretation of the texts.

And this is because all *text* is elaborated in the form of a mesh. It would be no exception that pictorial text if it was elaborated in a way to form a *mesh*, very difficult to be *disassociated* into parts, or into partial elements, in so far as its appearance at the *discursive level* is always that of a *totality of meaning*.[117] Either for *pictorial texts*, or more complex *syncretic texts*, a formation of the totality of meaning is not by hybridisation, but by a *complex articulated totality*.[118]

Furthermore, a *pictorial text* casts light on a planar support, it is structured on the basis, on the part of the artist, of numerous classes, that complexly cross each other in the determination of the work of art. In *Sémiotique figurative et Sémiotique plastique* (1984), it is Algirdas Julien Greimas who affirms and differentiates the classes of analysis of the *image* into chromatic classes, eidetic classes,[119] and, even, topological classes.[120] This is how these classes can be identified as *chromatic*

[113] *Cf.* Jacob (1994), p. 103.

[114] *Cf.* Santaella and Nöth (1998), p. 53.

[115] *Cf.* Santaella and Nöth (1998), p. 98.

[116] *Cf.* de Oliveira and Teixeira (2009), p. 43.

[117] *Cf.* Calabrese (2015), p. 31.

[118] *Cf.* de Oliveira (2009), p. 84.

[119] "En partant de la constation conventionelle que, sur une surfasse peinte, on peut trouver des couleurs et des formes, la distinction des catégories chromatiques et des catégories éidétiques" ("Starting from the conventional observation that on a painted surface one can find colors and shapes, the distinction between chromatic and eidetic categories.") (Greimas 1984, p. 16).

[120] "Le cadre apparaît comme le seul point de départ sûr, permettant de concevoir une grille topologique virtuellement sous-tendues à la surfasse oferte à la lecture: les catégories topologiques,

classes (black v white; blue v yellow)*, eidetic classes* (hero v bandit; just v unjust), *topological classes* (high v low; left v right), *material classes* (hard v soft; grand v simple), that allow the semioticist to elaborate the *reading of pictorial text.*[121] From a *figurative Semiotics*, it is possible to affirm that a work of art is a *text* which forms a *semiotic system.*[122] It is evident that—as Omar Calabrese analyses—*pictorial text* may contain certain encrypted *caches* objects, which place in the dimension of the secret[123] that which can only be disposed of by the closer look of the *reader* of the work, either within *iconographic tradition*, or within the *copyright tradition* of the artist himself.

Therefore, it is from a *fundamental opposition*—extracted from the text and identified by the semioticist—that it is able to arrive at forming a fundamental opposition of the *semantic axis*. From this, towards the deeper logical structures (disruption; inconsistency; complementarity), it goes on forming the *semiotic square*, to the extent that for Algirdas Julien Greimas, the world is formed by elementary structures of differentiation and of opposition (hot v cold; beautiful v ugly; just v unjust; light v dark).[124]

This is how one arrives at the *semiotic square*, considered, in the reading of Joseph Courtés, as the organisation of the *basic structure of significance.*[125] The *semiotic square* reports a set of *traces of significance* at a deeper level of *structures of significance,* making it possible to see the *pictorial text* only as a superficial tip of an *iceberg*. The *semiotic square* is a figure that represents the articulation of any *semantic class,*[126] implied in a text (white v black; light v dark; divine v demonic; just v unjust; life v death; high v low; being v seeming),[127] and that allows us to access the fundamental structures of *narration* and *discourse*, dissecting the logical structures[128] that permeate what is presented in the *plane of expression*. It can be

les unes rectilignes—telles que haut/bas ou droite/gauche—les autres curvilignes—périphérique/central ou cernant/cerné—(...)" ("The frame appears to be the only sure starting point, allowing the design of a topological grid virtually underlain by the surface offered to the reading: the topological categories, some straight—such as up/down or right/left—the other curvilinear—peripheral/central or surrounding/circumscribed—(...)"—*translation*) (Greimas 1984, p. 15).

[121] *Cf.* Pietroforte (2016), p. 39.

[122] "Dire qu'un objet planaire construir produit des 'effects de sens', c'est déjà postuler qu'il est lui-même un objet significant et qu'il releve, comme tel, d'um *système sémiotique* dont il est une des manifestations possibles" ("To say that a planar constructed object produces 'effects of meaning' is already postulating that it is itself a significant object and as such is part of a semiotic system of which it is one of the possible manifestations"—*translation*) (Greimas 1984, p. 13).

[123] *Vide* Calabrese (2015), p. 55.

[124] *Cf.* Nöth (2005), p. 151.

[125] *Cf.* Courtés (1979), p. 71.

[126] "On entend par carré sémiotique la représentation visuelle de l'articulation logique d'une catégorie sémantique quelconque" ("A semiotic square is the visual representation of the logical articulation of any semantic category"—*translation*) (Greimas and Courtés 1993, p. 29, *Carré Sémiotique*).

[127] *Cf.* Volli (2015), p. 73.

[128] *Vide* Volli (2015), p. 72.

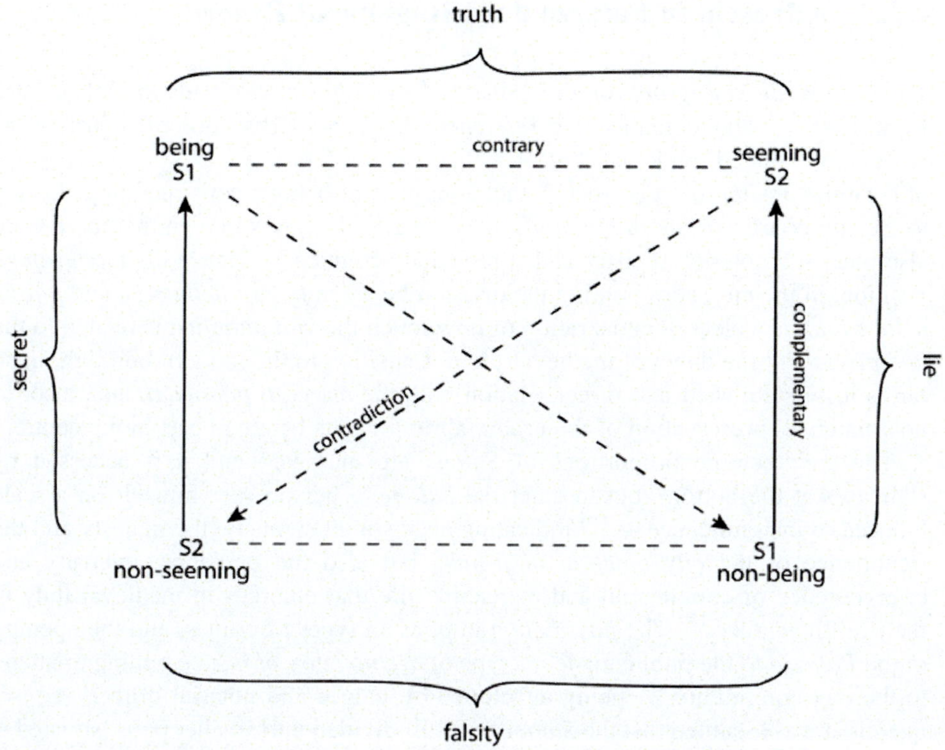

Fig. 4.5 Carré Sémiotique

applied to analyse a *literary text*, a *photographic text*, a *cinematographic text*, an *advertising text*, in the same way as it can be applied to analyse a *pictorial text*. A general example of construction of the *semiotic square*—offered in the *Dictionnaire* by A.J. Greimas and J. Courtés—[129] considers the relation between *being* and *seeming*—which discusses the plane of *truth* and of *lie*—[130] resulting in the following structural configuration of meaning as Fig. 4.5 (*Carré Sémiotique*) shows:

Therefore, it is when exploring a semiotic square that one notices what is contained at the superficial level, of aesthetic and formal appearance of the work of art, at the structural and logical level. To offer us a *minimum narrative* of a text,[131] it becomes a powerful instrument of *narrative* and *discursive analysis*, to be worked and developed by the semioticist.[132]

---

[129] *Cf.* Greimas and Courtés (1993), p. 32 (*carré sémiotique*).

[130] *Cf.* Volli (2015), p. 76.

[131] *Vide* Fontanille (2015a, b), p. 66.

[132] *Cf.* Calabrese (2015), pp. 109–110.

4.1.3 Affreschi *in* Palazzo della Ragione *of Padova*

The *Palazzo della Ragione*, or also called *Salone,* in the city of Padova (Italy), dates from 1218,[133] and contains live references to *justice*. But, not of a justice, as something isolated, punctual, but of justice involved in a *grand symbolic cosmos* of meanings. After all, it is erected with a purpose of being a construction dedicated to the city courts (*tribunali cittadini*) of Padova.[134] But, it is known that there were also practised notarial, registry and contractual activities.[135] Hence, its *topographic* position, in the city, surmounting the division between *piazza delle erbe* and *piazza della frutta,* is a clear demonstration of how much the *vita pubblica* is related to the *vita privata,* at the dawn of medieval life in transition to the modern borough, in so far as it is established in a direct relation with the *mercatti padovani,* and, also, of how much all preservation of the urban fabric finds its beating heart in the centre.

The architectonic proportions of *Salone* are massive—and it is accessed by staircases at the bottom, but to enter the *Salone,* a person sees himself on a scale reduced to insignificance—,[136] indicating also, simultaneously, the majesty and the importance of the *city function of justice*, but also the opulence, intensity and effervescence of commercial and mercantile life that emerges in medieval Italy in the twelfth century.[137] The *jurisdiction* implies all types of crimes, and the opening of the *Palazzo* to the public made it a type of *architecture of justice* willing to attend to the city community,[138] being developed by judges and notarial officers, consequently it was assumed that the *Salone* was sub-divided into smaller parts, situated at

---

[133]"Nel 1218, sotto il podestà Giovanni Rusconi, si eresse il grande Palazzo del Comune, terminato nel 1219, mentre era podestà Malpilio da San Miniato" ("In 1218, under the podestà Giovanni Rusconi, the great Palazzo del Comune was built, completed in 1219, while Malpilio da San Miniato was podestà"—*translation*) (Rossi 2007, p. 23).

[134]"Il Palazzo della Ragione, simbolo del potere comunale e al centro della vivace area dei mercati, dal 1100 non più soggetti alla giurisdizione vescovile, prende il nome dal latino *reddere rationem* e allude alla sua funzione principale, l'amministrazione della giustizia" ("The Palazzo della Ragione, symbol of municipal power and at the centre of the lively market area, no longer subject to bishop's jurisdiction since 1100, takes its name from the Latin reddere rationem and alludes to its main function, the administration of justice"—*translation*) (Rossi 2007, p. 23).

[135]*Cf.* Rossi (2007), p. 66.

[136]*Cf.* Rossi (2007), p. 32.

[137]"Dall XII secolo la crescita urbana ed economica spinse mercati e mercanti a porsi como interlocutori obbligati dei poteri politici e a rivendicari non solo l'autonomia ma anche gli spazi necessari. Il Pallazzo della Ragione si trovava al centro della grande *platea Communis,* con le fronti principali aperte e porticare per consentire il passaggio di uomini e merci" ("Since the 12th century, urban and economic growth has pushed markets and merchants to act as obligatory interlocutors of the political powers and to claim not only autonomy but also the necessary spaces. The Pallazzo della Ragione was at the centre of the large Communis stalls, with the main fronts open and porticoed to allow the passage of men and goods") (Rossi 2007, p. 13).

[138]*Cf.* Rossi (2007), p. 62.

points where the respective *symbolic* functions of the decoration also evoked inspirations for the modality of *justice* for which it was meant.[139]

The *Palazzo* has an interior of wood and is well adorned, but displayed, on the outside, *signs of justice* that appealed less to reason and sensitivity, and more to fear and humiliating public flogging. There, five ropes remained exposed to the view of the city, with a view of serving as public admonition, but also for the enforcement of sentences that were carried out in the form of *public flogging*.[140] Indeed, in addition to pecuniary penalties, the exposure to the crowd, the pronunciation of the sentence out loud to the knowledge of all, the torments, the execution of Reus in the square, despite the sentences that removed part of the ear, tongue or nose, demonstrated the exemplary and symbolic character of the penalties applied under the public scrutiny of *città*.[141] The public exhibition, moral infamy and spectacular character of the sentences were part of the practices of the period, and served as a form of instilling *fear* and *dread* in the population.[142] Now, there would be nothing that increased the interest of the population more than the intensity of *cruelty* applied to offenders, debtors and criminals, and from this arises an even greater interest in the powers of the city, and an even greater veneration of authority, as Umberto Eco points out.[143]

4.1.3.1 Justice in the Centre of the City and Communal Life

The full view of *Salone* gives an impression of being in front of the *kósmos* as a whole, that is, of a *global vision* of life and the worldly and supra-terrain chores, in an immense *coordination* that makes everything function in the way of a *cosmic order,* where the astrological cycles function as if they provide the tonic of the universe. To put together all the *décor* of *Salone* there was the theoretical-philosophical inspiration of thc Aristotclian conccptions of Pictro d'Abano, portraying a clear medieval overlap between theology, philosophy and the zodiacal visions of the universe, in a systemic understanding of things.

Furthermore, in a *Palazzo* of this proportion, the *symbolic burden* is huge, and so that the decorative figures can take on a human feature, the figures are framed in the niches that compensate for the colossal proportion of the ambiance, and the technique used to make up the panels is that of *affresco.* Including, the original frescos are of authorship of Giotto, but they were lost in the fire of 1420.

---

[139] *See* Rossi (2007), p. 62.

[140] *Cf.* Rossi (2007), p. 21.

[141] *Cf.* Rossi (2007), pp. 64–65.

[142] "Sottoporre alla pubblica vergogna era uno dei caratteri fondanti della punizione, così come la spettacolarità: per questo i cadaveri dei condannati a morte erano esposti sulle mura della città" ("Submitting to public shame was one of the founding features of the punishment, as well as spectacularity: for this reason the corpses of those condemned to death were displayed on the city walls"—*translation*) (Rossi 2007, p. 66).

[143] *Vide* Eco (2007), p. 224.

Despite the enormity and diversity of the figures constantly there, there is *thematic unity* in the whole circle of the room, that runs a dynamic turn on the south, north, east and west walls, filling the whole lateral space of the empty dimension of the room. The reasons are *astrological-philosophical*, and there all the *zodiacal signs* are found represented (Aries; Taurus; Gemini; Cancer; Leo; Virgo; Libra; Scorpio; Sagittarius; Capricorn; Aquarius; Pisces), providing a complete loop in the room. Moreover, just as the medieval world will know, since the second to third century, a growing movement of the assimilation of the *animal figures* in the illustrations and the construction of medieval bestiaries, the theme of *real and fictitious animal figures* appear here constantly, something which is not in any way strange in the pictorial decoration of the *Palazzo*.[144] Therefore, the constant evocation in the covering of *Salone* of *animal figures* (real or fictitious), many of which inspired by medieval bestiaries, and which cover all the seasons of the year, closing along the 360° view of the room, a complete cycle of observation of the sky and of daily life.

The big cycle (macro-cosmos) of the zodiac functions dynamically in rotation, while the small cycle (micro-cosmos) of human life is manifested by everyday activities and medieval crafts. These dimensions are related to each other, and are evoked all the time. In this complete rotation, at the bottom, is the human character that is there the whole time represented—and displayed—, by various figures, a form of warning directed at the judges that their office involves the understanding of human attitudes and the ways in which they act in society.[145] There is an emphasis on the significance of the use of *real animals* and of *imaginary animals*, since, in the vision of didactic-moral medieval bestiaries, the human *vices* and *virtues* are related to various *animals*, and its *pictorial function* is of *reminding* the judges of the *vices* and *virtues* that bring the defendants to trial, and the conflicting situations are under the public scrutiny in the *Palazzo*.[146] There is another emphasis on the *Judgement of Solomon*, in the *Salone,* evoking it in a clearly pedagogical way to the circumstances, a clear inspiration of the biblical tradition.[147] In other words, in the complete conception of the *affreschi,* there remains the clear vision that both Divine Providence, and the human effort, both contribute so that human purposes and freedom can be present in common life.[148]

The frescos painted on the lower strip of the walls, on all the sides, correspond to the *strip of the tribunals*. At this level, you can see one of the medieval frescos that reports a scene of a trial taking place, how it was executed, and who its characters were.[149] At this level of frescos, *justice* appears represented with eyes open, carrying a sword and scales, but it is in fact carried out and practised by qualified and learned

---

[144] *Vide* Eco (2007), p. 116.

[145] *Cf.* Rossi (2007), p. 46.

[146] *See* Rossi (2007), pp. 37–40.

[147] *See* Rossi (2007), pp. 40–42.

[148] *Cf.* Rossi (2007), p. 40.

[149] *Vide* Rossi (2007), p. 63.

Fig. 4.6 Palazzo della Ragione Interior view Padova, Italy Personal Archive: Photography: © ecbittar

judges—already in this period—considering the books of laws used at the time, in other words, the *Codice,* the *Digesto,* the *Institutes.*[150] The illustration below allows us to identify the *representation of justice,* in the way it is employed in the *frescos* of *Salone* (see Fig. 4.6)

4.1.3.2 Justice, the System of Laws and the City of *Affreschi*

Its *historical significance* here is precisely that related to the need to overcome *justice of the Barbarian people*, articulating an inspired conception of the Classical Antiquity, and that it was capable of structuring itself as a *zodiacal system* in the organisation of life of the community, in all its tasks and mysteries, regular trades and activities, connected to a *system of laws*, which provokes a symbolic and practical disruption in the order of things then in force of barbaric individual and family punishments, forcing a city resumption of *Roman Law*, as a form of overcoming ordeals and other punishments of Germanic people.[151] This point of mutation is given, exactly, by the *symbolic* and *majestic*, representative and central form in which the *Palazzo* is built and decorated.

If the *Palazzo* is at the centre of communal life, this grants an authority also *central to justice*, in its capacity of intervention in common life. In fact, the *topographical place* of justice is a strong indicator of its *vital function in the* medieval *commune*. This is clear. But, it is still more interesting to observe that the *Palazzo* is at the centre of the *città,* but that at the centre of the *Salone* is the stone of vituperation (*Pietra del Vituperio*), a black stone, the whole astrological cycle

[150] *Cf.* Rossi (2007), p. 62.

[151] *Cf.* Rossi (2007), pp. 61–62.

being fulfilled around the stone and in its atoning function of the evils of the city, to where the insolvent debtors were dragged,[152] made to pronounce three times the ritual words (*cedo bonis;* relinquish my assets), sitting and standing up three times. They could avoid being imprisoned, the first time, with this procedure, but the second time, they were reappointed to a new ritual, being expelled from the city only being able to return only after settling their debts.[153] In other words, the *punishment* is the centre and the end of the *system of justice*.

4.1.3.3 The Semiotic Square and Pictorial Text

In the case of *Afreschi* of the Palazzo della Ragione of Padova, considering the intrinsic relation between *architectonic monumentality* and *artistic frescos,* between the astrological-metaphysical cycle and the four walls of the building, the height of the ceiling of the roof and the amplitude of the physical space required for the distribution of the whole circle of interconnected works, in any case, the presence of the relationship that can be analysed is clear, through the *semiotic square,* which is outlined from the semantic axes of the *philosophical-cosmological narrative*, which are: centre v edge; big v small; macro-cosmos v micro-cosmos; divine v human; general v specific; spiritual v material; order v disorder; common v individual; all v part. As it is not relevant, for the purposes of analysis of the *Palazzo* the observation of a separate painting, but the observation of the *whole aesthetic* formed by the sum of *architectonic force* and *pictorial force*, the result of the analysis of the above mentioned work points, fundamentally, to the relation between the *body of the convicted*, in the *stone of vituperation*, and the *cosmos* that surrounds it, justifying the need for the application of *justice*, to which *injustice* does not imply in *disorder* and *chaos*, in *disorganisation* and *corruption* of which it is common. Consequently, the semiotic square better refers to the tension contained in the opposition between *all* and *part*, to appoint the set of works of the *Palazzo*, according the following diagram in Fig. 4.7 (*carré sémiotique*):

---

[152] "Al centro della sala si trovava la "pietra del vituperio", un sedile in pietra nera dove venivano messi alla berlina i debitori insolventi" ("In the middle of the room was the "stone of the victim", a black stone seat where insolvent debtors were saluted"—*translation*) (Rossi 2007, p. 25).

[153] *Vide* Rossi (2007), p. 67.

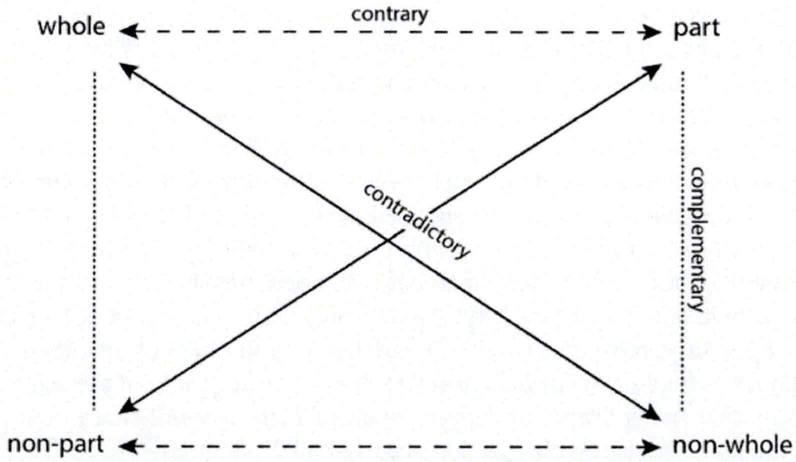

Fig. 4.7 Carré Sémiotique

4.1.4 *Allegoria ed Efetti del Buono e del Cattivo Governo, Palazzo Pubblico di Siena*

In the *Palazzo Pubblico di Siena* (*Palazzo Comunale,* Sienna, Tuscany, Italy, 1297–1310),[154] one finds a very curious model of medieval allegory, fertile for the understanding of the history of the iconology of justice,[155] as well as the relations between law, politics and justice, in as far as the *Sala dei Nove* (*Sala della Pace*), in the recently entitled *Allegoria ed Efetti del Buono e del Cattivo Governo* (1338–1339), whose original name was *La Pace e la Guerra*,[156] whose technique of fresco (*affreschi*) is by artist-philosopher Ambrogio Lorenzetti. The *Palazzo Pubblico* is the headquarters of the government,[157] where the acts of coordination of life in the city and in the field are exercised, spreading justice in the commune.[158]

[154]"Achiudere la piazza, come una preziosa quinta, il Palazzo Pubblico, iniziato nel 1297 e già in uso nel 1310. Alla decorazione del Palazzo furono chiamati i grandi artisti senesi: c'è un'urgenza di bellezza nella Siena del Trecento che invade tutto, dalle sale del potere alle copertine dei libri contabili" ("Close the square, like a precious backdrop, the Palazzo Pubblico, begun in 1297 and already in use in 1310. The great Sienese artists were called to decorate the Palazzo: there is an urgency of beauty in fourteenth-century Siena that invades everything from the halls of power to the covers of account books"—*translation*) (Carlotti 2010, p. 31).

[155]"A particularly good example is in Ambrogio Lorenzetti's well-known fresco, *Allegory of Good Government, in Sienas's* Palazzo Pubblico" (Resnik and Curtis 2011, p. 1744).

[156]"La denominazione di Buono e Cattivo Governo è relativamente recente: infatti fino al 1700, l'argomento degli affreschi è identificato con *La pace e la guerra*" ("The name Good and Bad Government is relatively recent: in fact, until 1700, the subject of the frescoes was identified with Peace and War"—*translation*) (Carlotti 2010, p. 47).

[157]*Vide* Argan (2013), p. 350.

[158]*Cf.* Carlotti (2010), p. 58.

Here, *justice* is an attribute of the *governing,*[159] and not of the *judging*, and it has to do with the general balance of *common life*, of *public things.*[160] This gives rise to a very specific outline to the medieval representation of the *symbol of justice*, since it is associated to the exercise of *royal power* and *political power.*[161]

In order to start the analysis, it is important to verify that the *locus* of the *Palazzo* is the centre of the *piazza del Campo*, where the *centre of the government* is also found, and the centre of communal and medieval civic life. A long linear tower of the *Torre del Mangia,* 88 m high (the fourth highest in Italy), a symbol of power of the autonomous commune, of the emergence of bourgeois power and the political-administrative authority of the city. Around Sienna, in this period, it had served as an emerging city, prosperous and with emphasis on the field of arts, there forming the famous *School of Art of Sienna* (*arte senese*), in full cycle of the Italian do *del Trecento*, that rivals the art of *Florence* and of *Pisa* in significance, and that is a neuralgic point in the big change that occurred in Western art.[162]

The work is of clear Aristotelian-Thomistic influence, resulting from the theological influence of Ambrogio Lorenzetti,[163] there were misgivings about its huge proximity to the *Divina Commedia,* of Dante Aleghieri,[164] with a huge set of *affreschi* that occupies the entire room, the *Sala dei Nove,* from where the city was governed, where *Justice*, and the *Good Government*, *Tyranny* and the *Bad Government* were discussed, placing at the centre of the medieval imagery, the notion of the *Common Good*, and of the necessary virtues to support it. It is a huge *work*, but more important for the fact that it is civil, governmental work containing philosophical-theological conceptions of the world.[165] The allegory is the most complete and multi-dimensional holistic interpretation of communal life, including urban life and peasant life, clearly divided in two parts, namely, that which represents the *Buon Governo* and its effects, and the other which represents the *Cattivo Governo* and its effects. The representation of everyday, urban and peasant life, is not only a mere *representation* of the reality, it is, also, an ethical-political forecast of the *real way of governing*, in a *figurative utopia,*[166] using the artist appropriately as a dichotomy between the *Good* (*Peace; Public Interest; Concord; Spring; Justice*) and the *Bad* (*War; Self Interest; Division; Winter; Injustice*), repeatedly showcased

---

[159] *See* Jacob (1994), p. 228.

[160] "Come suggeriscono, in maniera molto esplicita, le opere veneziane che abbiamo preso in considerazione, il tema della Giustizia si lega strettamente a quello del governo della cosa pubblica" ("As the Venetian works we have taken into consideration suggest, in a very explicit way, the theme of Justice is closely linked to that of the government of public affairs"—*translation*) (Gandolfo 2012, p. 288).

[161] *Cf.* Gandolfo (2012), p. 288.

[162] *Vide* Carlotti (2010), p. 22.

[163] *See* Meoni (2001), p. 16.

[164] *See* Carlotti (2010), p. 63.

[165] *Cf.* Argan (2013), p. 35.

[166] *Vide* Meoni (2001), p. 13.

in medieval eschatology.[167] For this reason, the *concepts of justice* and *common good* are much better depicted, properly than the attempt of representation of reality.[168]

4.1.4.1 The Three States of Justice in *Allegoria*

The *Allegoria* should be read, interpreted and perceived, considering the three levels (divine; institutions; human) at which they are registered—pictorial, symbolic and philosophically—the signs of which Ambrogio Lorenzetti uses to give colour and life to the re-enactment in which it acts out the *Buon Governo.*[169] The *Allegoria*, seen as a whole, contains the *figure of justice*, at three different moments, where it shows *Divine Justice* (on a bigger scale and central symbolic level) as enthroned, there next to the *Buon Governo*, *human justice* as *cardinal virtue* (on a smaller scale and lesser symbolic level), it is in a third form, namely, *justice*, subordinated and tied, stripped of power, at the feet of tyrannical-diabolic figure, disallowed in the *Bad Government.* The observation of the photograph below allows us to identify the three dimensions and the representation of *justice,* on the wall that describes the *Buon Governo* (see Fig. 4.8):

On the wall to the right (it appears north), one finds the *Buon Governo*,[170] where the cycle of life is centralised by the notions of order, harmony, work and production, where the commercial exchanges are equal,[171] looking at the gates of the city topped by the signs written around a feminine figure represented in the form of a winged *Victory*, called *Securitas,*[172] which offers security to all who enter and leave,

---

[167] *Cf.* Meoni (2001), p. 15.

[168] *See* Castelnuovo and Peraya (1979), p. 109.

[169] "L'allegoria del buon governo nella sua composizione è articolata su tre livelli: nella fascia centrale le virtù e le istituzione che devono presidere la vita politica (da sinistra la Giustizia, il Comune e le Virtù), ispirate e rese possibili – in alto – dal dono della Sapienza di Dio e dalla conoscenza dell'essere rivelata da Cristo (Fede, Carità, Speranza), e attuate nella vita della città, dal protagonismo degli uomini, legai liberamente dalla Concordia, l'unica allegoria presente in questa fascia inferiore di figure reali. A completare l'affresco, nella cornice superiore, trovava posto la già ricordata allegoria del Sole, in quella inferiore abbiamo ancora la rappresentazione delle arti del Trivio, Grammatica, Retorica e Logica" ("The allegory of good governance in its composition is articulated on three levels: in the central band the virtues and institutions that must preside over political life (from the left, Justice, the Commune and the Virtues), inspired and made possible - at the top - by the gift of the Wisdom of God and the knowledge of being revealed by Christ (Faith, Charity, Hope), and implemented in the life of the city, by the protagonism of men, I freely bound from Concordia, the only allegory present in this lower band of real figures. To complete the fresco, in the upper frame, was placed the already mentioned allegory of the Sun, in the lower one we still have the representation of the arts of Trivio, Grammar, Rhetoric and Logic"—*translation*) (Carlotti 2010, p. 61).

[170] *Cf.* Carlotti (2010), p. 53.

[171] *Cf.* Meoni (2001), p. 28.

[172] *Cf.* Meoni (2001), p. 23.

Fig. 4.8 Ambrogio Lorenzetti *Il Buongoverno* Palazzo Pubblico Sienna, Italy

allowing the opening of the city (to the outside and to the inside) to provide *external relations* in harmony with other *città*. In the *Buon Governo,* there are two representations of Justice, one of *Divine Justice* (on a bigger scale) and one of justice as *cardinal virtue* (on a smaller scale).

The *divine Wisdom* (*Sapientia*),[173] which inspires *Divine Justice*, and, just below her, *Concord* (the level of the people) which derives from her, are feminine figures that are aligned in such a way, in the left corner of the *Buon Governo,* that they occupy three visual planes, which lead us to understand that *justice* is the fruit of *divine wisdom*, and that *concord in the city* is an effect of the *good administration of justice* in ordinary life. This figure of *Divine Justice* is surrounded by written labels, which derive from the *Sacred Scriptures*: *Diligite Iustitiam qui Iudicatis Terram* (*Amatela la giustizia, voi che governate la terra*).[174]

Divine Justice (woman dressed in red), which accompanies the royal figure of the *Bene Comune,* on the same linear plane of the work, has its arms extended in two different directions, pointing to the left hand, where it is inscribed *commutative justice* (it acts in balance and honesty of commerce),[175] and, pointing to the right side, where it is inscribed *distributive justice* (it acts towards cutting of the head of a murderer).[176] From the plates of the *Scales of Justice* two ropes part, which are united in the hands of *Concord* (consequently, the false origin *cum—cordia*),[177] and,

[173]*See* Carlotti (2010), p. 56.

[174]*Vide* Carlotti (2010), p. 53.

[175]*Cf.* Gandolfo (2012), p. 304.

[176]*See* Carlotti (2010), pp. 56–57.

[177]"La corda lega liberamente i cittadini – alludendo a una falsa etimologia di concordia *(cum chorda*, invece che l'unità dei cuori) - per finire in mano alla figura di vecchio che domina la zona destra: il Comune di Siena" ("The rope freely binds the citizens - alluding to a false etymology of concord (cum chorda, instead of the unity of hearts) - to end up in the hands of the figure of the old man who dominates the right area: the Commune of Siena"—*translation*) (Carlotti 2010, p. 57).

from then on, they are transmitted to the 24 citizens, who hold it, taking it to the hands of the *Buon Governo*. The rope is the symbol of the *fino liame* that unites citizens and government, around justice and common purposes of the city. In contrast, there is the idea that if this concatenated chain arising from this *fino liame* is untied, or even, if this *liame* is broken, there is wretchedness, either from communal life, or from the government.

Above the governor (*Bene Comune*), the three *theological virtues* (*Faith, Hope, Charity*) are found flanking Christ, messenger of the divine universe.[178] In turn, the *cardinal virtues* (*Iustitia*; *Temperantia*; *Prudentia*; *Fortitudo*; *Pax*)[179] they accompany the royal figure of the governor, who acts under the divine protection, under which is inscribed *Commune Senarum Civitas Virgini*, coming back to the achievement of the *Common Good*.

4.1.4.2 The Effects of *Justice in the City* in *Allegoria*

Continuing *Buon Governo*, the ensuing wall is entirely dedicated to the effects of the Good Government (in the city and in the countryside). The effects of justice are those that arise directly from the relation between *wisdom, balance, justice, concord, peace* and *prudence*.[180] The *Allegoria* points to the idea that the Common Good is the centre of communal life, and, of the administration of the government centred in this vision, there are effects felt in the daily routine of life of the citizens. Therefore, the figurative relation of intimacy between *Justice* and *Government*, to the extent that *commutative* and *distributive* justice are made by the hands of the government, where even the organised force of the army is found in a servile and controlled position, also serving as shield and support to the government, just below the figure of the *Buon Governo*.[181] Communal life follows a *slow* rhythm, *daily routine*, where each thing occupies its place, realising that security[182] provides conditions for a prosperous and organised social life.

4.1.4.3 The Effects of *Injustice in the City* in *Allegoria*

On the left hand wall (west wall), one finds the *Cattivo Governo*, and on the same wall where it is inscribed, the effects of the Bad Government are also found.[183] The

[178] *Cf.* Meoni (2001), p. 18.

[179] *Cf.* Ost (2001), p. 428.

[180] *Cf.* Carlotti (2010), p. 67.

[181] *Cf.* Carlotti (2010), p. 67.

[182] *Cf.* Carlotti (2010), p. 75.

[183] "Sulla parete ovest della Sala, c'è un vasto affresco, gravemente danneggiato e lacunoso, diviso in tre zone: l'Allegoria del malgoverno, gli Effetti del malgoverno in città e gli Effetti del malgoverno in campagna" ("On the west wall of the Hall, there is a vast fresco, badly damaged

Fig. 4.9 Ambrogio Lorenzetti *Il malgoverno* Palazzo Pubblico Sienna, Italy Personal Archive: Photography: © ecbittar

Cattivo Governo is a *diabolic figure*,[184] surrounded by the labels of the verbal signs: *Tyranny*. The bad government—whose diabolic enthroned figure is surrounded by beastly figures, carries a dagger and a chalice of gold dirty with blood—has by methods tyranny, vengeance and violence, and governs to obtain personal wealth.[185] Disorder, sterility and devastation dominate the whole configuration of this view, painted with dark and grey colours. On the wall of *Bad Government*, what can be seen in Fig. 4.9, is the diabolical figure of *Cattivo Governo*, and the way of tyrannical administration of the city, with its respective effects:

The same structure of the *Allegoria* here is found present on three planes, *justice* is found on the lowest plane of the work, surrounded by plates of *shattered scales*. On the higher plane, the diabolic figure is surrounded by *Pride* (*Superbia*), *Greed* (*Avarizia*) and *Conceit* (*Vanagloria*); on the plane of the institutions, the figure of the *Bad Government* is enthroned, surrounded by beastly figures and few advisors; on the plane of men, in turn, one feels the absence of the closeness of organised people, that is, of citizens who court the government.[186] With the badly damaged frescos—which makes it difficult to understand and interpret the work—the long wall where

---

and incomplete, divided into three zones: the Allegory of Bad Governance, the Effects of Bad Governance in the City and the Effects of Bad Governance in the Country"—*translation*) (Carlotti 2010, p. 87).

[184] *Vide* Eco (2007), p. 92.

[185] "Nell'affresco vediano infatti una figura diabolica - la Tirannide - ai piedi della quale sta legata la Giustizia, senza corona, tra i piatti di una bilancia spezzata" ("In the fresco they see a diabolical figure - the Tyranny - at the foot of which Justice is tied, without crown, between the plates of a broken scale"—*translation*) (Carlotti 2010, p. 91).

[186] *Cf.* Carlotti (2010), p. 91.

there are the effects of the *Cattivo Governo* are, the cycle of Lorezentti points to the daily routine of a disturbed, disorganised life, surrounded by destruction, governed by fear, violence, abandonment, murders, intrigues and disputes, and the field is unfertile and unproductive.[187] The set of *affreschi* points to a generalised square of *political disorder, imbalance, immorality* and *injustice*.

4.1.4.4 The Semiotic Square and Pictorial Text

In the case of the *Allegoria ed Efetti del Buono e del Cattivo Governo,* in the *Palazzo Pubblico* di Siena, the relation between the two painted panels, considering what the *Buon Governo* is, and considering what the *Cattivo Governo* is, leads to a fundamental opposition which structures the semantic axis in the form of *Good* v *Bad*, in a way that the *Good Government* (inspired by divine forces; just; capable of producing good effects) is opposed to the *Bad Government* (inspired by demonic forces; unjust; capable of producing bad effects), given that the *chromatic classes* (blue v black), *eidetic classes* (king v demon; justice v injustice), *topological classes* (high v low), help to reinforce these charateristics. The *narrative-pictorial programme*, as a whole, is capable of symbolising the effects of good and the effects of bad, and, thus, imprinting the medieval vision of which the *virtue of justice* is something that accompanies the *Good Government* and characterises the Good Governor in the use of legitimate power. The structure as a whole of *iconography* points, in a narrative version, to a story (the example of narrative literary), which can be structured as such in the figurative form (Fig. 4.10).

But, if the attention is given not to the totality of the work, but given in a focused way to the relative *narrative* to justice, and in its studies, it is evident in the *pictorial text* its situation accordingly to which, on a wall, justice operates as a *support and active inspiration of the government*, in the *Good Government*, and, on the other wall, justice is found inactive and inoperative, being stopped in its symbolic-active function, being *inactive, gagged, tied up, overcome* and *defeated,* in the *Bad Government*, where it could be used in the logical relation between *active* (chained to public life; influencing the good government with sword and scales; acting as cardinal virtue) and *non-active* (tied up; subordinated to the bad government; disconnected from communal life; inactive). This implies, also, other internal relations such good v bad, just v unjust, good government v bad government common good v self interest, divine v human.[188] Despite this *iconography* evoking this immensity of other classes, in its wider configuration, when specific attention to the situation of justice is given, one notices the predominance of tension between activity and inactivity, in a way that its figurativisation in the *semiotic square* allows us to see Fig. 4.11.

[187] *Cf.* Carlotti (2010), p. 93.

[188] *Cf.* Calabrese (2015), pp. 104–105.

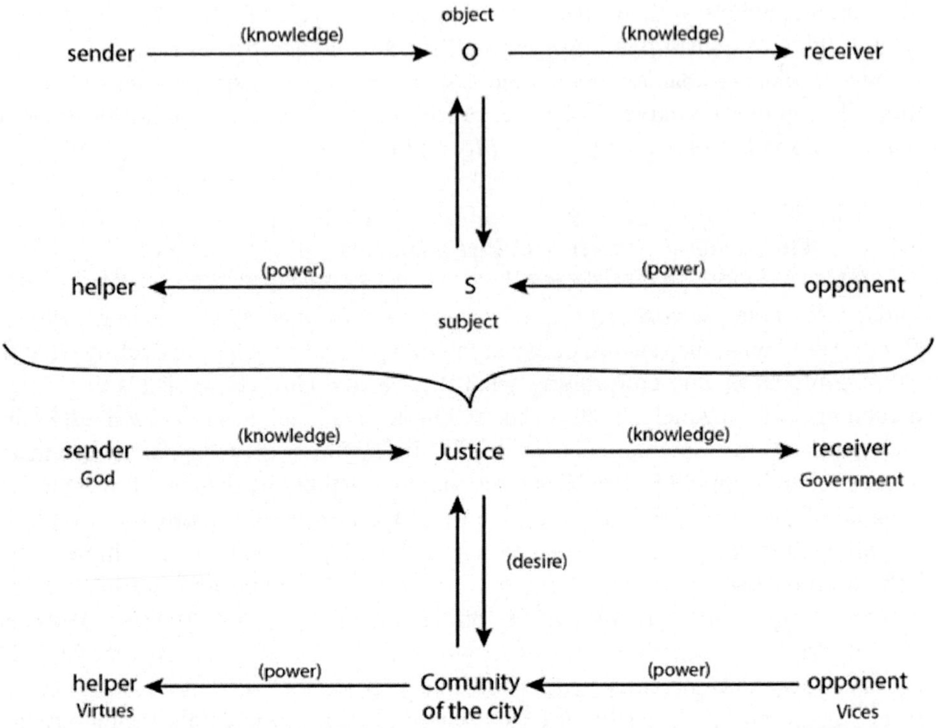

Fig. 4.10 Actants sémiotiques

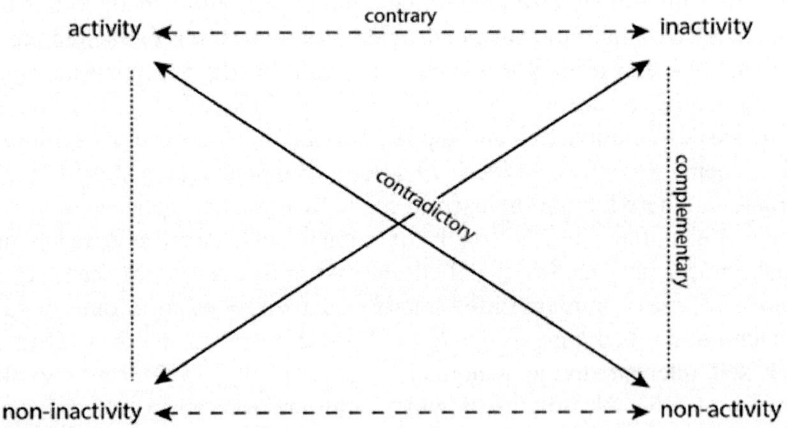

Fig. 4.11 Carré Sémiotique

4.1.5 Affreschi *in the* Cappella degli Scrovegni *of Padova*

The *Cappella degli Scrovegni* (Padova, Italy),[189] holds a work of *affreschi* of Giotto, carried out between 1303 and 1305, under the private order of Enrico Scrovegni, from a rich and usurious Padovian family, which possesses a revolutionary character in the history of art. In this work, Giotto innovates the techniques, and foresees the history of art, through the live spectacle of colours—the example of blue of the starry sky of the *Cappella*—, of realistic figures, of autonomous shapes, and by the depth, unprecedented technical innovations,[190] on the Middle Age plane, pointing out through this work the first indications of the Renaissance.[191]

The *Cappella* as a whole narrates the story of the salvation of the soul, and contains biblical scenes. Treated as a huge *pictorial text* that expresses a true *ethical-devotional pathway*, of a highly pedagogical nature, founded in the vision of the theological-Christian world. It conforms to the task of *communicating* the knowledge about divine things, directing it to converting and teaching Christian devotees. The denseness of the figures, the symmetrical distribution in the *Cappella,* and the vision of the world that guide the construction of the whole global image of the work form, without a doubt, an enormous *philosophical-theological* undertaking, elaborated by means of the *pictorial figuration*.[192] It goes as far as stating, as specialist Giuliano Pisano does so, that this is a *Divina Commedia* of the painting, considering the pictorial legacy it creates.[193] The work holds a cycle of frescos with biblical stories, topped by the spectacular representation of the *Final Judgement*, a recurring theme in the medieval painting, as Umberto Eco[194] points out—which is found on the big wall of the opposite-façade—, between two big walls where *virtues* and *vices* parade.

4.1.5.1 Justice and Injustice at the Centre of the Cycle of Virtues

Human choice is something that is exercised on the basis of *liberum arbitrium*,[195] in the face of two possible routes, namely, that of the *vices* and that of the *virtues*. The cycle *giottesco* of the vices (north wall) and of the virtues (south wall) hedge the whole pathway of the *Cappella*—this pictorial construction is symmetrically divided

---

[189] http://www.cappelladegliscrovegni.it/index.php/en/the-scrovegni-s-chapel/history-of-scrovegni-s-chapel. Accessed 14.01.2020.

[190] *Vide* Argan (2013), p. 25.

[191] "Un'autentica rivoluzione" (Pisani 2015, p. 09).

[192] "Lo schema si rivelò ben presto un sofisticato disegno filosofico-teologico" ("The scheme soon turned out to be a sophisticated philosophical-theological design"—*translation*) (Pisani 2015, p. 12).

[193] *Cf.* Pisani (2015), p. 30.

[194] *Vide* Eco (2007), p. 78.

[195] *Cf.* Pisani (2015), pp. 150–151.

into three virtues and three vices—, having in the *middle the figures* of *Justice* and of *Injustice centralised*, as a pair of opposites, in a total of seven vices and seven virtues.[196]

This effort of placing Justice in the *centre* is so great,[197] in the work of Giotto, that for this to happen, it needs to *invert* the order of distribution of the cardinal virtues, which are distributed as such: *Prudentia; Fortitudo; Temperantia; Iustitia* (four cardinal virtues); *Fides; Karitas; Spes* (three theological virtues). The *virtues* are represented totalling a number of seven. These are opposite to the vices, which are found on the opposite wall: *Stultitia; Inconstantia; Ira; Iniusticia* (cardinal vices); *Infidelitas; Invidia; Desperatio* (theological vices). This is shows the importance and, also, the sanctity, centrality and significance which is found in the pair *Justice/ Injustice*,[198] in the general vision that Giotto imprints to the representation of the *virtues.*[199] They do not only create a division between *theological virtues* (*theological vices*) and *cardinal virtues* (*cardinal vices*), as they are also the centre of all the *virtues* and all the *vices*.

But, the representation by Giotto in the *Cappella degli Scrovegni* is different from the tradition that has been in place, since Dante Aleghieri and São Tomás de Aquino,[200] in this respect. In this tradition, the seven *theological virtues*, oppose the seven *main vices* (pride; envy; sloth; wrath; greed; gluttony; lust), and, in place of these, Giotto represents the *seven cardinal* and *theological vices* (*Stultitia; Inconstantia; Ira; Iniusticia*—cardinal vices; *Infidelitas; Invidia; Desperatio*—theological vices). For this reason, Giotto does not simply follow the most popular *theological tradition*, but represents the virtues and the vices in a very specific way, although with the same salvation finality.[201] This allows us to understand that the vision that pervades the *Cappella* is not simply a *reproduction of the* prevailing *theological vision*, but, in fact, an *innovative creation,* that adds something in particular in the sense of the relation between vices and virtues.

[196]*Vide* Frugoni (2005), p. 91.

[197]"Di qui derivano i concetti etici di giustizia e ingiustizia, la coppia centrale dell'intero ciclo giottesco: *Iniusticia - Iusticia*" ("Hence the ethical concepts of justice and injustice, the central couple of the entire Giottesque cycle: Iniusticia – Iusticia"—*translation*) (Pisani 2015, p. 161).

[198]*Cf.* Gandolfo (2012), p. 303.

[199]"La *Iusticia* è collocata al centro delle sette virtù, in posizione di assoluto rilievo. Un particolare significativo rivela come la *Iusticia* (e specularmente, sulla parete opposta, l'*Iniusticia*) rappresenti il fulcro dell'intero ciclo affrescato..." ("Lusticia is placed at the center of the seven virtues, in a position of absolute prominence. A significant detail reveals how the Iusticia (and specularly, on the opposite wall, the Iniusticia) represents the fulcrum of the entire frescoed cycle..."—*translation*) (Pisani 2015, p. 165).

[200]"Di contro alle sete virtù Dante pone, sempre seguendo san Tommaso, i sete vizi capitali: 1. Superbia; 2. Invidia; 3. Ira; 4, accidia; 5. Avarizia; 6. Gola; 7. lussuria" ("Against thirst for virtue Dante, always following St. Thomas, places the thirst for deadly vices: 1. Pride; 2. Envy; 3. Wrath; 4. Sloth; 5. Greed; 6. Gluttony; 7. Lust"—*translation*) (Pisani 2015, p. 152).

[201]*Cf.* Pisani (2015), p. 153.

Fig. 4.12 Justice cycles of virtues and vices (1304–1306) Giotto di Bondone (1267–1337) *Cappella degli Scrovegni* Padova, Italy Personal Archive: Photography: © echittar

The representation of *Justice* here is of a secular nature,[202] and not divine, in that it appears as one of the various *virtues.*[203] This means that it is within the reach of all human beings to be exercised. However, it is serenely placed in the position of crowned, centralised and enthroned woman.[204] As Fig. 4.12 shows, it is right in the middle of the *Cycle of Virtues* where the Goddess of justice is found, seen as a central virtue:

She is depicted as a woman, with a blue background, seated on a throne, with scales, where on the right-hand, the condemnation of a criminal by a lord is staged, and on the left-hand plate, the coronation of a person, by a winged youngster is staged.[205] It must be accentuated with strong paint the fact that this representation of *justice* does not grant it a sword—the sword is found in the hands of *injustice*, on the

[202] *Cf.* Frugoni (2005), p. 92.
[203] *See* Cananzi (2013), p. 47.
[204] *Cf.* Frugoni (2005), p. 91.
[205] *Vide* Pisani (2015), pp. 163–164.

counter wall—and this because, as historian Robert Jacob states, the medieval resist in granting justice the element of *strength*, understanding it preferably as *balance*, something that is only modified in the modern age.[206]

Fairness and *common good* are the fruits of the diligent attitude of *distribution of the just*.[207] *Justice* has eyes its open serenely, with its look aimed at Heaven from the wall of the *Final Judgement*, and below it, there is the *kingdom of justice*, where there is *order, trade, peace* and *dance*. Justice here is clearly laid out as the condition of the *peace, order* and *harmony* of life in common in the city, invoking a notion broadly worked out by old and classic philosophical thinking.[208] The scenes presented at the feet of the enthroned justice show the *kingdom of justice*, where a man and his wife—who surrender to the war—go out to hunt, and where villagers of a village dance, in addition to two merchants who ride and trade between cities in safety.[209] In other words, while perfect justice is executed, human life is able to develop in a harmonious form.[210] Here is divine therapy, clearly indicated, as a path of effort to acquire cardinal virtues.[211] The complete cycle of the band of virtues of this wall leads, in the *Final Judgement*, to Heaven,[212] to a vision that reveals the clear divine concession for which justice to be done among men, something inscribed very clearly in medieval-Christian tradition, also considering the tradition of the *illumination of justice*.[213]

4.1.5.2 The Masculine Figure of *Injustice*

In contradiction with this feminine figure of *justice*, on the opposite wall, and face to face with *justice*, one finds the masculine figure of *injustice*. The figure is seated and wears grand clothes, he has long white hair, harsh features, holds a sword in his left hand, and in the right hand he holds a harpoon, noting how his nails invoke claws or bestial figures. His air is of contempt, and the environment that surrounds him is not life in the city, urban life, but there is something of woods, an obscure place, where assault and crime can happen in an uncontrolled way, evoking the idea of the dark, fear, and, also, of the obscure fury of lack of control and insecurity, disorder and violence.[214]

---

[206] *See* Jacob (1994), p. 225.
[207] *Cf.* Pisani (2015), p. 164.
[208] *Cf.* Pisani (2015), p. 166.
[209] *Cf.* Pisani (2015), p. 165.
[210] *Cf.* Frugoni (2005), p. 92.
[211] *Cf.* Pisani (2015), p. 166.
[212] *Cf.* Pisani (2015), p. 148.
[213] *Vide* Jacob (1994), p. 28.
[214] *Cf.* Frugoni (2005), p. 93.

Note that, in the whole of the *Cappella,* all the virtues are feminine, and, including, the vices, with the exception of two: *injustice and infidelity.*[215] This uncommon representation of a masculine figure, in order the designate the opposite of the feminine figure, perhaps is the invocation of a tyrant, echoing a tendency that only is accentuated from the end of the Middle Ages.[216]

In this representation, the chromatic background used by the artist is red. The look of the masculine figure of *injustice* is aimed at Hell, and just below the figuration of *injustice*, there is the *kingdom of injustice*, where *violence*, *crime*, *war*, and, hence, *conflict* and *unhappiness* prevail.[217] As Fig. 4.13 shows, it is right in the middle of the *Cycle of Vices* that the masculine figure of injustice is found:

Continuing, when looking at Fig. 4.13, one can also notice that there are scenes of events that take place in everyday life. In this strip, the scenes are of a woman being stripped and wounded, of a man dead and fallen on the ground, and two armed soldiers proceeding towards other wars.[218] The masculine figure of injustice looks directly at Hell, represented on the wall of the *Final Judgement,*[219] given that the complete cycle of the strip of vices of this wall leads the soul to Hell.[220] At the end of the whole cycle, on the big wall at the bottom of the *Cappella,* there is the *Final Judgement.* In the centre of it, the figure of Christ judging shines above everything,[221] opening up the separation between the weeds and the wheat, and exerting his role in the *Final Judgement.*

4.1.5.3 The Semiotic Square and Pictorial Text

In the case of *Affreschi* in the *Cappella degli Scrovegni* of Padova, the masterpiece by Giotto leads to a complete and broader figuration that is to do with a philosophical-theological theme, which opposes the semantic structure in a way of

[215]"Nella cappella tutte le Virtù sono femminili, cosí come i Vizi, ad eccezioni di *Iniustitia* ed *Infidelitas*" ("In the chapel all the Virtues are feminine, as are the Vices, with the exception of Iniustitia and Infidelitas"—*translation*) (Frugoni 2005, p. 90).

[216]"By the late Middle Ages, artists had come to use the male form for certain Vices. How and why words, activities, or abstractions come to be gendered is a topic of feminist theory, for the iconography reflected, produced, and codified sex-role distinctions" (Resnik and Curtris 2011, p. 09).

[217]"Il regno dell'ingiustizia è disordine, violenza, delitto, guerra, somma infelicità" ("The kingdom of injustice is disorder, violence, crime, war, total unhappiness"—*translation*) (Pisani 2015, p. 163).

[218]*Cf.* Pisani (2015), p. 63.

[219]"La *Iusticia* guarda alla sua destra, verso l'uomo che avanza: l'inclinazione del capo ricorda quella del Cristo giudicante. Anche l'*Iniusticia* guarda alla sua destra, ma la testa è di profilo e gli occhi puntano diritti sull'Inferno della controfaciata" ("Iusticia looks to her right, towards the advancing man: the inclination of the head recalls that of the judging Christ. The Iniusticia also looks to her right, but the head is in profile and the eyes point straight to the Inferno of the counterfacade"—*translation*) (Pisani 2015, p. 165).

[220]*Cf.* Pisani (2015), p. 148.

[221]*See* Pisani (2015), p. 236.

Fig. 4.13 Injustice cycles of virtues and vices (1304–1306) Giotto di Bondone (1267–1337) *Cappella degli Scrovegni* Padova, Italy Personal Archive: Photography: © ecbittar

creating the tension between *salvation v damnation* of the soul. The *Final Judgement* consumes the whole scene of the cycle of virtues and vices, in a way that the *philosophical-theological narrative* points to Heaven or Hell, from the path of the individual soul, in its life on Earth. Given the *Final Judgement,* Christ appears in a *central* form, as the *divine Judge*, in opposition to everything else, which is found on the side of the two walls that hold the cycle of virtues and vices. The choice is the fundamental activity of the soul, between one and other perspectives. This is how the virtues lead to salvation and the vices lead to damnation.

But, if focus is given to the *figure of justice*, in the cycle of virtues and vices, it is clear that the opposition takes place using *chromatic classes* (blue v black), *eidetic classes* (justice v injustice; woman v man; order v disorder; harmony v disharmony; peace v war; life v death), *topological classes* (right v left; heaven v hell), which

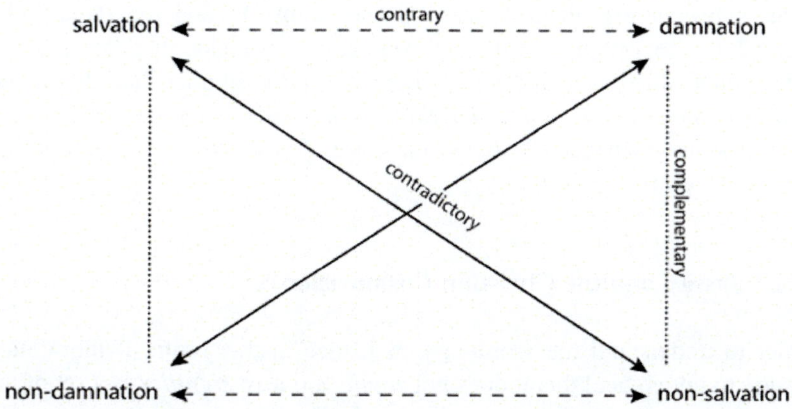

Fig. 4.14 Carré Sémiotique

reaffirm the role of *justice* has of organising all the other virtues, representing them at the centre of life in society, and directing the cycle of life to the celestial destination. The figurativisation of the *semiotic square* implies (Fig. 4.14), therefore:

4.1.6 Affreschi *in the* Stanza della Segnatura *of the Vatican*

The *Stanza della Segnatura* contains an excellent specimen of renaissance art from a religious agenda, found in the *Musei Vaticani* (Rome, Italy),[222] painted by Raffaello Sanzio, between 1508 and 1511, using the *affresco* technique. It can be said that, in the history of the iconology of justice, in the Western world, this is one of the two most beautiful representatives of the figuration of *justice*, in a theological-platonic vision.[223] The inspiring cosmovision of the whole of the movement of the room is inserted into the *Christian vision* of the world, but the evocation is aimed completely at the enhancement of the *virtues* coming from the old classic world, *Truth*, *Beauty*, *Good* and *Justice*, according to the more relevant comments by Portuguese jurist Paulo Ferreira da Cunha.[224] Only on the wall *Scuola di Atene,* are found represented Socrates, Plato, Aristotle, Epicurus, Diogenes, Averróes, Zoroaster, Ptolomeo, Heraclitus, and this perhaps is the most beautiful representation of *philosophy* and the *philosophy schools* ever collected in Western iconology. It should be highlighted that, in this small environment, where an ecclesiastical tribunal operated, and that

---

[222] http://www.museivaticani.va/content/museivaticani/it/collezioni/musei/stanze-di-raffaello/stanza-della-segnatura.html. Accessed 14.01.2020.

[223] "Qui, sul fondamento della teologia cattolica e della filosofia platonica, siamo al vertice della cultura d'Occidente fatta propria dalla Chiesa di Roma nel suo momento senitale" ("Here, on the foundation of Catholic theology and Platonic philosophy, we are at the top of the Western culture made proper by the Church of Rome in her senital moment"—*translation*) (Paolucci 2013, p. 151).

[224] *Cf.* da Cunha (2004), p. 131.

became, subsequently, the Library of Pope Julius II—and the Pope had himself conceived the iconography of the environment—,[225] inside the Vatican,[226] a whole wall is dedicated to *justice*; it is true that this wall is smaller than that dedicated to *Scuola di Atene* and *Disputa del Sacramento,* but even so *justice* occupies a considerable and symbolically balanced space of any other pictorial representations in the whole room.

4.1.6.1 Justice and the Christian Cosmovision

In order to understand the iconology of justice in this room of the Vatican, it is necessary to understand that it does not *signify* alone, it *signifies* as a set of the whole construction of the environment of frescos. From the semiotic point of view, it *encrypts significances* through *images* that were not decodified with attention and care, they lead us on wrongful tracks about the *meanings* produced by the work. Indeed, this is the nature of the *complex works*, the example of which made by Michelangelo and Raffaello Sanzio, in the Vatican.[227]

The *pictorial context* provides cohesion to the *visual text*. And this because it is part of a *system of understanding* of the world, for which a *symbolic system* is engineered here, in a way which each thematic framing is reported and indicates the other. The environment is marked by four walls (*Scuola di Atene; Disputa del Sacramento; Santi e Dottori; Parnaso*) that correspond to four medallions of the ceiling (*La Filosofia,* on the east wall, connected to the element water*; La Teologia,* on the west wall, connected to the element fire*; La Giustizia,* on the south wall, connected to the element earth*; La Poesia,* on the north wall, connected to the element air). The writings that go along with the figures of the medallions of the ceiling are to send their most direct messages, namely, through the images associated to *written verbal signs*: *La Filosofia* (*Causarum Cognitio*); *La Teologia* (*Divinarum Rerum Notitia*); *La Giustizia* (*Unicuique suum*);[228] *La Poesia* (*Numine Afflatur*). See Fig. 4.15.

In a complex and holistic *narrative message*, which involves the *theological-Christian* and *philosophical-platonic vision* of the world, and comes to life through *decorative pictorial images*, interconnected between themselves, it is clear that the codification shines through the official vision of the Church, and the force of the classic images of renaissance hue, achieving maximum aesthetic excellence (with live colours and classic shapes), capable of forming a *system-of-significances* and *symboligies* reported reciprocally, about the things of the spirit that help man to connect with himself, of his worldliness, with divine things, through the tasks of the spirit, that involve the *virtues*. The human effort, the human fight, to lift itself in

[225] *Vide* Paolucci (2013), p. 150.

[226] *Cf.* da Cunha (2004), p. 51.

[227] *Cf.* Calabrese (2015), p. 93.

[228] *Cf.* da Cunha (2004), p. 88.

Fig. 4.15 Raffaello Sanzio (1483–1520) *La Giustizia—Medaglione della volta* (1508–1511) Stanza della Segnatura The Vatican, Italy Personal Archive: Photography: © pyo

one's condition, seems to be what commands the *general significance* of the most complete vision of the environment.

And it is exactly the *movement-of-reading* of the whole room. Man seeks through *human reason* to understand the world (objective of the *School of Athens*). Next, exerting his power of free choice, he goes on to coexist and reconcile himself with the creation through revelation (objective of the *Disputa del Sacramento*). Next, one can only perceive the completeness of life, with the ability that the Arts and Poetry are capable of providing beauty to the senses, just as Justice is able to embody itself in what life in common possible, in other words, in Laws.[229]

4.1.6.2 Justice As an Idea and Cardinal Virtue

The two smaller walls are found face to face, the *Parnassus*, with the representation of various poets (Homer, Virgil, Dante, Petrarch, Boccaccio, Sannazzaro, Ariost, Horace, Sappho), and the *Parete della Giustizia*. *Justice* represented in the form of a Greek Goddess,[230] in one of the signs of the ceiling—and the ceiling here wishes to signify that justice is an *idea* in the platonic meaning—[231] observed by four angels,

[229] *Cf.* Paolucci (2013), p. 252.
[230] *Cf.* da Cunha (2004), p. 87.
[231] *Cf.* da Cunha (2004), p. 120.

with eyes open, serene facial stance, carrying a sword with the right hand, and scales with the left hand,[232] and looking directly at the scene painted in the *Parete della Giustizia*. As can be seen in Fig. 4.15, the medallion on the ceiling of the room makes the Goddess of *justice* a Greek style representation, which looks down from above the *Parete della Giustizia*:

At the *Parete della Giustizia,* it is there that *justice* does not only appear as one of the objects of knowledge, in this case, as an object of knowledge of Law, but appears, above all, as an idea that is achieved as *virtue*, amongst the other *cardinal* and *theological virtues.*[233]

Therefore, *justice* is strongly present in the *Stanza della Segnatura,* and keeps its strength there where it is supported and inspired by various other *virtues* that accompany it. Right at the top of the *Parete della Giustizia* is the tympanum *Le virtù cardinali e teologali,* where three of the *cardinal virtues* (*Strength,* supported on a horse and carries clothes with features of strength, is accompanied by the natural strength of the lion animal; *Prudence¸* looks at itself in the mirror held by an winged angel and *Temperance,* holds the reins of horses), and which should inspire *justice*, are represented there. In addition, the angels also painted there represent the *theological virtues* (*Faith*: angel with finger pointing above; *Hope,* angel with lighted torch in hand; *Charity,* angel that collects something from a horse), which should equally inspire *justice*.[234] *Justice* itself is not represented in the *Timpano,* because it is already represented on the ceiling.[235]

From the higher inspiration of justice in the *virtues*, on the lower part of the same wall, one goes on to notice that *justice* is achieved among men by means of Law, in the way as it is known at the time, in other words, by way of the book of *Corpus Iuris* by Justinian and of the book of the *Decretais canônicas de Graciano*,[236] conferring clear guidance that all Law is found in *Roman Law* and *Canon Law*, the two main *sources of Law* reputed in the period of *Cinquecento* to *Seicento*.[237] Yet, in the *Stanza della Segnatura,* a biblical scene of the *Judgement of Solomon* is represented,

[232] *Cf.* da Cunha (2004), p. 86.

[233] *See* Paolucci (2013), p. 152.

[234] "L'altra parete breve è insieme la glorificazione del Diritto e delle Virtù che devono ispirarlo. Ed ecco, nella lunetta rappresentate tre delle quattro Virtù cardinali (*Fortezza, Prudenza, Temperanza)* che sono potenzialmente presenti in ogni uomo, e le Virtù teologali (*Fede, Speranza, Carità*) che vengono da Dio" ("The other short wall is at the same time the glorification of the Law and the Virtues that must inspire it. And here, in the lunette you represent three of the four cardinal Virtues (Fortitude, Prudence, Temperance) that are potentially present in every man, and the theological Virtues (Faith, Hope, Charity) that come from God"—*translation*) (Paolucci 2013, p. 153).

[235] "La Giustizia - la quarta Virtù cardinale - non compare in questo assembramento perché è già presente con il cartiglio esplicativo ("*unicuique suum*") e con i simboli iconografici della bilancia e della spada, nella corrispondente porzione di volta" ("Justice - the fourth cardinal virtue - does not appear in this assembly because it is already present with the explanatory scroll ("unicuique suum") and with the iconographic symbols of the scales and the sword, in the corresponding portion of the vault"—*translation*) (Paolucci 2013, p. 153).

[236] *Cf.* Paolucci (2013), p. 153.

[237] *Vide* da Cunha (2004), pp. 132–133.

something that should inspire each and every person who endeavours to achieve justice, or has by profession *justice*.[238]

4.1.6.3 Justice As an Idea and Positive Law

In a general view, one notices that *justice* is an ideal archetype,[239] which depends centrally on *Prudentia,* which, among the virtues, is that which is decidedly at the centre of the pictorial construction by Raffaello.[240] The other *virtues* are found on a lower plane, in relation to this virtue. This is explained by how much the notion of *Prudentia,* in the platonic-Aristotelian-ancient tradition, and also, in the Thomistic-medieval tradition, is decisive for the achievement of *justice.* With this, on the whole, one notices that *justice* is something that takes part in the general *balance* of things in the world, which depends vividly on the *virtues* to be achieved, and which are materialised by means of Positive Law (Roman Law; Canon Law).[241]

Positive Law arises from *justice*, it is based on *justice,* for this reason, its materialisation between men is only the imperfect apparition (or, the most perfect possible, in the order of earthly things) of a universal, constant and eternal idea.[242] Furthermore, in the whole of the *Stanza* it is clear that without the effort of knowledge, there would be *ignorance,* without the effort of faith, there would be *incredulity,* without the effort of poetry, there would not be more subtle arts of the *spirit*, and without the effort of justice, it would not be in the kingdom of *injustice.*

4.1.6.4 The Semiotic Square and Pictorial Text

In the case of the *Affreschi* in the *Stanza della Segnatura* of the Vatican, there is an effort on Raffaello's part to make sure that the *complete cycle* of *Affreschi* points towards the classical structures of *Good, Beauty, Truth* and *Justice* as a kaleidoscope of elements that should inspire the Christian to the general balance of life. But, not only this; in fact, all *Good*, all *Beauty,* all *Truth* should rush to support *Justice*.[243] In this system of theological-Christian understanding, the room holds a complete cycle, which expresses a philosophical-platonic vision, and which, if travelled in its entirety, passes on the *message* to its interpreter that *justice* participates in the general balance of mundane life.

[238] *Cf.* Paolucci (2013), p. 153.

[239] *Cf.* da Cunha (2004), pp. 87–88.

[240] *Cf.* da Cunha (2004), p. 120.

[241] *Cf.* da Cunha (2004), p. 111.

[242] *Vide* da Cunha (2004), p. 85.

[243] "She could also be seen as dominating the disciplines – Poetry, Theology, and Philosophy – through a reading of the room as depicting the ideal Christian world, in which "all branches of knowledge unite in the service of Justice"" (Resnik and Curtris 2011, p. 76).

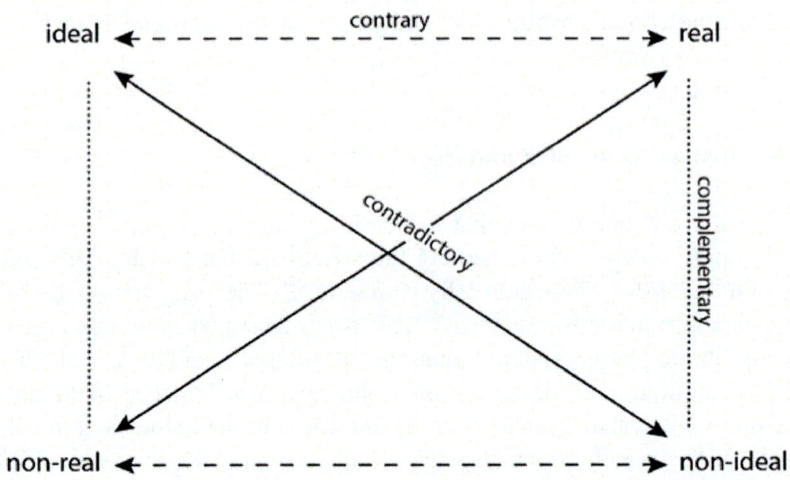

Fig. 4.16 Carré Sémiotique

But, if focus is given on the *figure of justice* (*La Giustizia*), it is characterised by certain traits: *eidetic classes* (*Suum cuique tribuere*), *topological classes* (ceiling v ground), which reaffirm the role of *justice* as an *idea* (in the platonic sense) that points to the *Virtues* and to the *Laws* (Positive Law), that are found on the wall (on the lower plane), which should guide *human action* on a mundane plane, aiming for general balance. If emphasis is given to the *symbol of justice*, it can be seen that it is drastically opposed to the place where the observer is, that is, on the ground, so that the opposition between *ceiling v ground* is achieved in the relation between *high* and *low*, between *divine* and *human*, between *Justice* and *justice*, that pulls to a relation of gradual *narrative transcendence*, where the movement of the believer to observe the virtues and the laws is present, in order to achieve justice, or, in hindsight, from leaving the idea of justice, to reach the materialisation in laws, and, from there, affecting *human action.* In this way, the semiotic square gives a figuration and exhibits the tension between ideal and real (Fig. 4.16—*Carré Sémiotique*).

4.1.7 *Alegoria in the* **Grand'Chambre de Justice** *in the Parliament of Flanders*

In the Parliament of Flanders (Brussels, Douai), it is installed in 1714, the *Grand'Chambre de Justice* is fully executed in 1768–1769, to hold the parliamentary discussions, containing paintings done by the painter of the Royal Academy, Nicolas-Guy Brenet, at the dawn of the eighteenth century, given that these constitute a sample of the notorious quality in the attempt of comprehension of the records of artistic works of *allegoric* nature[244] in respect of justice in the period of the *Old Regime*.[245] It is testimony of the art of *Enlightenment*, but it is also the testimony of an *iconography* aimed at the enhancement of the growth of power and influence of the magistrates.[246] As a whole, the *alegorias* painted in the *Gran'Chambre* are not the pure repetition of tradition, containing *artistic* and *symbolic innovations*, which refer to Nicolas-Guy Brenet's own dictionary and its context.

In correspondence to the growth of the power of magistrates, in which was celebrated as being the capital of justice, Douai, is in the centre of the city where the *Palais de Justice* is situated, and it is in the chamber of judgements that the *alegoria* is installed with the function of exercising a double role: (1) on the one hand, the celebration of justice as a central virtue, in relation to other virtues; (2) on the other hand, aesthetic pedagogy which functions as a warning to magistrates about the fact that the growth of its powers should be associated to the fulfilment of its task, with a higher degree of study, competence, rationality, virtues and justice.[247] It is a memorial warning and, at the same time, an indication of paths towards its meaning and, for this reason, has little arbitrary and a lot of intentional-contextual, either in the context of the artistic work of its author, or with regard to its public-recipient.

4.1.7.1 The Centrality of Real Power

But, here, at the heart of the *Old Regime*, *justice* is represented under the power of the king, in the case of Louis the 14th, who is present in a central form in various allegories of the Palace,[248] especially in the painting done by Nicolas-Guy Brenet, which is a copy of the work by Hyacinthe Rigaud that is in the Louvre, done in 1768.[249] This measures, in the main figuration of the *Palais, justice* in the bottom painting in abyss just below the royal sceptre on which Louis the 14th supports

[244]"L'allégorie est une représentation d'une idée, exactement comme peut l'être un mot dans l'ordre lexical. Si la syntaxe dispose les mots dans un certain ordre pour produire du sens, le programme de Brenet assemble ces vertus pour faire percevoir le sens du jugement, l'essence de l'acte de juger" ("Allegory is a representation of an idea, just like a word in the lexical order. If syntax arranges words in a certain order to produce meaning, Brenet's program assembles these virtues to make us perceive the meaning of judgment, the essence of the act of judging"—*translation*) (Hayaert and Garapon 2014, p. 23).

[245]http://www.douaitourisme.fr/index.php/. Accessed 11/05/2020.

[246]*Cf.* Hayaert and Garapon (2014), p. 31.

[247]"La peinture est une poésie muette et vice versa. La suprématie de l'allégorie à l'âge classique correspond à un âge d'or e la peinture. Placée au sommet de la hiérarchie des genres, l'allégorie a pour dessein de vanter les vertus des Grands, du Souverain comme des Princes. De leur rappeler leurs devoirs également" ("Painting is silent poetry and vice versa. The supremacy of allegory in the classical age corresponds to a golden age of painting. Placed at the top of the hierarchy of genres, allegory has the purpose of extolling the virtues of Greats, Sovereigns and Princes. To remind them of their duties as well"—*translation*) (Hayaert and Garapon 2014, p. 16).

[248]*Cf.* Hayaert and Garapon (2014), p. 35.

[249]*Cf.* Hayaert and Garapon (2014), p. 50.

himself with his right hand, indicating that the king is fair. On the other side, the left hand of Louis the 14th is supported by the sword, which is sheathed and hanging from his waist, as a delicate potential energy directed at the possibility of the use of *force*. In other words, only in a *pictorial image, justice* and *force* are circling and surrounding the central figure of the king, which demonstrates that the *History of Law* seeks to identify with the exact trait of the period.[250] On its own, this image is self-saying of the expression of *power* in the *Old Regime*, and of its concentration on the figure of Absolute Monarch.

The magistrates perform their function under the watchful eye of the Monarch, and the rational clarification should guide, through the exercise of the virtues, the allocation and the distribution of justice in society. Before the plurality of magistrates and parliamentarians, *justice* is thus a concession, a *power-acting-in-place-of,* whilst the *unit* of power is maintained in the hands of the Monarch. For this reason, the triumph of justice turns into the central allegory of the period of *Enlightenment,* clarifying the action of magistrates and parliamentarians.[251]

4.1.7.2 The Triumph of Justice: Justice and Ancillary Allegories

The *Grand'Chambre* has the characteristic of a *theatre,* where political and legal disputes can encounter a *noble* accent. And it is in this space that the décor rejoices. In its setting, around the Monarch, there is a *parade* of virtues that inspire various motives. In its totality, the *cycle of allegories* of the *Gran'Chambre* of Flanders is the exaltation of virtues, such as, Prudence, Religion, Justice and Force.[252] Despite these individual pictures were done not at one time, but in steps of the execution of the work, the meaning of the room should be seen in a circular and intertextual form, where one *aesthetic text* remits another *aesthetic text.*[253] But, the diverse virtues *iconized* here are only *ancillary* figures in the Chamber of Justice to the great Triumph of Justice, the only one of the crowned *virtues*, and whose figuration allows it to be represented in the form of a very fair skinned maiden, young, with one breast showing, enveloped by the clouds, shielded by three *putti*, with a sword carried in the right hand, with the attitude of one who looks at the figure of the king, and points with the left hand to her kingdom, or, to the infinity of the kingdom of justice, where a *putto* exercises the role of the *transcription* of the *sayings of justice*, revealing the passage of the oral to the written in the *modus* of the exercise of the sentences and judgements.[254] Here, it should be highlighted that this *image of justice* does not refer

[250]*Cf.* Lopes et al. (2009), p. 110.

[251]"Au XVIIe et XVIIIe siècles, un thème prédomine: celui du "Triomphe de la Justice". L'allégorie perdure au siècle suivant, elle devient le mode privilégié du décor judiciaire" ("At XVIIe and XVIIIe centuries, one theme predominates: that of the "Triumph of Justice". The allegory persists in the following century, it becomes the privileged mode of the judicial décor"—*translation*) (Hayaert and Garapon 2014, p. 36).

[252]*Cf.* Hayaert and Garapon (2014), p. 32.

[253]*Cf.* Hayaert and Garapon (2014), p. 49.

[254]*Cf.* Hayaert and Garapon (2014), p. 60.

to the use of the *scales*, and it is shown with *eyes open*, and not blindfolded. To the contrary of tradition in which its body is covered, here, *justice* has its cleavage exposed in nakedness, perhaps evoking the *nursing* nature of *justice*.[255]

The other virtues of the room are hiding the primordial task of *justice*. Its ancillary role, however, does not reduce its *symbolic force,* nor the imagination with which the allegories were coated with attributes to be able to give the meaning correlated to its functions. For this reason, with the other virtues, numerous elements are present in the *totality* of the *Chambre* that invoke ancillary ideas for the exercise of *justice.* Alongside the *allegory of religion* are the *Holy Scriptures* in the form of a book and the crucifix;[256] alongside the *allegory of prudence* are the snake and the mirror;[257] alongside the *allegory of force,* a masculine figure, the *bridle* can be found (used to hold the animals, a usual feature of the *allegory of temperance,* here merged with the *allegory of force*);[258] alongside the *allegory of study* are *light,* the *ruler* and the *set square,* the *owl,* the *hourglass,* the *book;* alongside the *allegory of truth,* a standing feminine figure, there is a sheet with *geometric* figures extracted from the *Elements* of *Euclid* and the *ouroboros* (serpent which eats its own tail, and which indicates the cyclic and infinite nature of time).[259]

This is the complete cycle, with *figures, images, icons* and *symbols* that stir the conscience, and call the magistrates to the exercise of judicial vocation, by means of a *cathartic-aesthetic* process[260] of a pedagogic and highly moral nature.[261] Here, the cathartic-aesthetic nature, as well as, pedagogic and instructive are forms of convincing and remembrance of the judicial functions and its responsibilities, subtly woven through the exaltation of virtues. This form of aesthetics of persuasion, used here, reinforces something which the *medieval painting* already did by recalling that the corruption of the judge can lead to *severe punishment*, such as the figure of the judges with hands cut off (*Les juges aux mains coupées*),[262] a figure from the fifteenth century, much more *dramatic, shocking* and *convocation* of the duties of the function of the judicature by the threat—as Robert Jacob reminds us—[263] constant in the *Hotel de Ville de Genève* (Switzerland). The figures invoked here by Nicolas-Guy Brenet have something of ethereal, angelic, divine, giving an air of

[255] *See* Hayaert and Garapon (2014), p. 30.

[256] *Cf.* Hayaert and Garapon (2014), p. 60.

[257] "Le serpent et le miroir sont des attributs anciens de *Prudence*. Selon l'écriture sainte, le serpent est l'animal prudent par excellence '*Estote prudentes sicut serpente*'" ("The serpent and the mirror are ancient attributes of Prudence. According to scripture, the serpent is the prudent animal by excellence 'Estote prudentes sicut serpente'"—*translation*) (Hayaert and Garapon 2014, p. 67).

[258] *Cf.* Hayaert and Garapon (2014), p. 70.

[259] *Cf.* Hayaert and Garapon (2014), pp. 84–85.

[260] *Cf.* Hayaert and Garapon (2014), p. 23.

[261] *Cf.* Hayaert and Garapon (2014), p. 89.

[262] "*Les juges aux mains Coupées* (The Judges with Hand Cut Off), a late fifteenth/early sixteenth century fresco from the Geneva Town Hall, is another startling image" (Resnik and Curtis 1987, p. 1750).

[263] *Vide* Jacob (1994), p. 74.

suspension in the whole room, and which summons to duty by *inspiration,* and not by *fear,* as until the end of the Middle Ages it sought to do either in the churches, or in the rooms of justice. Therefore, if this *iconography* is a continuation of the tradition of evocation of the responsibilities of the act of judging,[264] it is also disruptive in the capacity of alluring the recipient of the messages, by the *force* contained in the *lightness* and *subtlety* of the representation of the virtues.

4.1.7.3 The Semiotic Square and Pictorial Text

In the case of the Allegory of the *Grand'Chambre de Justice*, in the Parliament of Flanders, the work by Guy Brenet contains various pictorial choices that are connected to the general ambience of the *Grand'Chambre,* pointing to the royal nature of power and justice. Even so, the figure of justice is represented in a way that it is considered a *central virtue,* in relation to all the others, which are coadjutants (study; prudence; faith; force; truth) to the role that it performs in a room of justice.

But, if focus is given to the *figure of justice* it is found characterised by certain traits capable of inspiring the magistrates, namely, that of a feminine figure, with snow-white skin, where the light colours prevail: *eidetic classes* (spiritual v material),[265] *topological classes* (centre v lateral), that reaffirm the role of *justice* as a virtue that, in the room, is the only one crowned. *Justice* is the *Virtue* of all *virtues.* Hence, the *Triumph of Justice* is a *divinising construction* of Justice, with the function of inspiring the magistrates to fulfil their duty by force of the aesthetic elements present, all appealing and enticing of the *summons to the duty of justice by inspiration,* and not by fear, in a way that the *chromatic classes* evoke the spiritual (white v black; blue v red), the lightness and subtlety of the fundamental virtues of the spirit, with the objective of alluring the soul of the magistrates (angel; crown; cloud; whiteness), in order to inspire them towards the task of justice. Therefore, the semiotic square compares spiritual and material (Fig. 4.17—*Carré Sémiotique*):

4.1.8 The Drawing Iustitia *by Victor Hugo*

Through an enigmatic image, it is during the nineteenth century, that we find in the work of a French poet, the poet-drawer who manifests his love for the arts from very early on,[266] Victor Hugo, a legacy of impacting significance for the history of the iconography of *justice.* And this already due to this first characteristic of pulling out of the *drawing*, and not from a *painting*, a work about *justice,* capable of transferring

[264]*See* Deonna (1950), p. 144.

[265]*Cf.* Calabrese (2015), p. 109.

[266]"Cette tendance à laisser s'immiscer la reverie dans ses feuilles, écrites ou déssinées, esta habituelle à Hugo" ("This tendency to let the reverie creep into his papers, written or drawn, is common to Hugo"—*translation*) (Molinari 2010, p. 09).

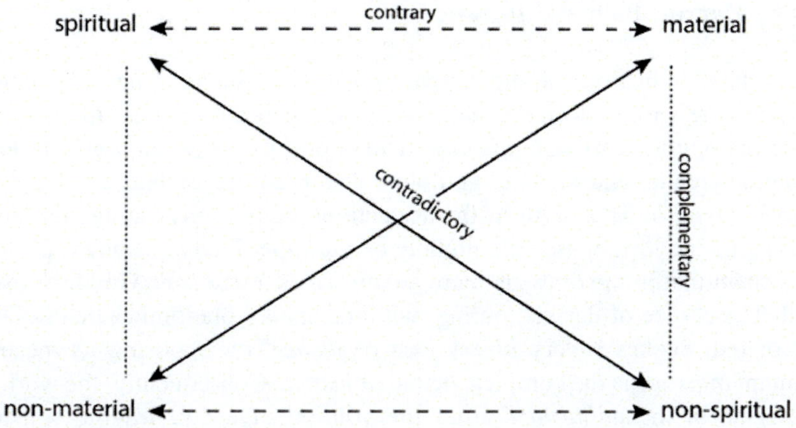

Fig. 4.17 Carré Sémiotique

paramount force to the idea of *justice.* Also, for the second characteristic of referring to all four thousand drawings left by the author of *Les Misérables* and the *Nôtre Dame de Paris.* Furthermore, by the context of disturbing transformation of the known world, by new trends of art and painting of the nineteenth century.

The work consists of a drawing, done in *graphite crayon*, black paint and done on paper, currently found framed and displayed by the exhibition in the *Maison Victor Hugo*, in the *Place des Voges*, that once was the residence of the poet in the period from 1832 until 1848, in the neighbourhood *Le Maris,* in Paris (France). Its title reports directly to what it seeks to designate, with clarity and objectivity: *Justitita* (1857, Paris).[267] This is not the only time that Victor Hugo reports the social, legal and justice issues, and it is not the only time that he draws something related to the theme of capital punishment.[268] For this reason, a central theme is reported—whatever, the capital punishment—, which is repudiated by various previous texts by Victor Hugo, the example of the poem *Les quatre Vents de l'ésprit,* contained in *La Révolution* (1857):

> Ô terreur! Au milieu de la place déserte, [. . .]
> Apparaissaient, hideux et debout dans le vide,
> Deux poteaux noirs portant un triangle livide; [. . .]
> Une tête passa dans l'ombre formidable.
> Cette tête étati blême; il en tombait du sang [. . .][269]

[267] http://parismuseescollections.paris.fr/. Accessed 11.05.2020.

[268] *Cf.* Molinari (2010), pp. 52–53.

[269] "Jean Massin a rapproché ce dessin d'un passage de 'La Révolution' (*Les quatre vents de l'esprit*)" ("Jean Massin likened this drawing to a passage from 'The Revolution'"—*translation*) (Molinari 2010, p. 56).

4.1.8.1 Horror, Pain and Injustice

The work is indicative of the humanist spirit of Victor Hugo, to whom they repudiated the various forms of *injustice,* and, deep down, what *Iustitia* evokes is exactly the opposite, that is, *injustice.* The opposition between high and low, light and dark, screams and silence, guillotine and head are of *intense* and *disturbing symbolic strength.* The depth of the aesthetic work is asphyxiating, and despite its title evoking the idea of *Justitia,* nothing of *traditional iconography* is present here, to the extent that in the drawing there are no scales, there is no Goddess, there is no sword. The choice of dark colouring, with the smoky predominance of black, with mark of red, evokes a very *blurry* idea of *justice*, by opposing its meaning: the maximum *injustice* is the complete denial of *justice.* Consequently, the work appears to navigate in the *unfinished*, from the volition of a cut, leaving something in *suspension* something that civilisation had not still (at that time) decided to abolish: capital punishment. A staring head looks at the infinity of the sky, from there receiving some tint of light, and, reproducing the last scream of pain, it wonders in the left hand space of the paper, leaving at the bottom of the guillotine, the ash and the mist. The void cannot stop occupying the rest of the work, spreading *astonishment, bitterness* and *mourning*.

This is not meant as an attempt to *signify Justice*, to *crown justice*, to *praise* the virtue of *justice*, much more than to cry for it, and to alarm where and when it is not present. This is an *aesthetic work* criticism and accusation, in so far as its force is placed in this *suspension of death and pain*, which evokes by *written verbal signs* the direct evocation of the notion not present among the humans of *justice*. The word *Iustitia* is written in spilled blood and embedded in the cracks of the asphalt bricks that cover the empty, gloomy, arid, abandoned urban space and forgotten in the shadows and the mist.[270] With such little colour, with such little figurative composition, and, among the smoky formations of colour, it is possible for the poet to *say so much* and *say so deeply* about the terrible world of *torture* and *terror,* which he himself seeks to repudiate, accuse and condemn.

But, Victor Hugo is a character of his time, understood as a member of French romanticism. Romanticism is a movement of the nineteenth century, and is placed in

---

[270] "Trois ans après la série des quatre pendus, Victor Hugo revient sur le thème de l'exécution capitale, maintes fois dénoncée dans ses écrits, avec um nouveau dessin saisissant. Il montre une tête tranchée flottant, hagarde, dans l'espace. Le regard du supplicié reflète encore la terreur des derniers instants, tandis que la bouche grimace toujours dans un ultime cri d'effroi. Dans la nuit noir comme l'encre, cette âme s'élève symboliquement vers le ciel. Au sol, le sang verse trace entre les paves les lettres de l'éternelle supplique de l'auteur pour la clémence et le respect de la vie: JUSTITIA" ("Three years after the series of the four hanged men, Victor Hugo returns to the theme of the capital execution, often denounced in his writings, with a striking new drawing. He shows a severed head floating, haggardly, in space. The gaze of the tortured still reflects the terror of the last moments, while the mouth still grims in a final cry of fear. In the ink-black night, this soul symbolically rises to the sky. On the ground, blood is shed, tracing between the paving stones the letters of the author's eternal plea for mercy and respect for life: JUSTITIA"—*translation*) (Molinari 2010, p. 56).

the bowl of great tensions of the century, a century marked by the repercussions and echoes of the French Revolution of 1789, by the rise of Napoleon, by the disputes about republicanism, and, moreover by the Paris Commune (1848). The engagement of the work by Victor Hugo, the example of *Les Misérables* (1862), is huge and testimony to the great political activity that has involved him his whole life. Since romanticism, by the way, the *aesthetic work* does not evoke only and exclusively the beautiful, but, now, also, the ugly, grotesque, shapeless, misery, pain, death, suffering.[271] But, in the *History of Art*, the moment is that of post-impressionism, where painters and artists like Paul Cézanne (1839–1906), Vincent Van-Gogh (1853–1890) and Henri de Toulouse-Lautrec (1864–1901) stand out. In this respect, the *scream of pain* held in the drawing by Victor Hugo (despite Victor Hugo having died before Edvard Munch) echoes, resembles and aspires to the same atmosphere of *The Scream*, by Norwegian painter Edvard Munch (1893),[272] or even, holds the same *despair* contained in the work of the Spanish neo-baroque painter Francisco Goya (1746–1828), with special reference to *The Third of May* (1808).[273]

4.1.8.2 The Semiotic Square and the Drawing

In the case of the Drawing *Iustitia* by Victor Hugo, the tension placed in the drawing in *black crayon* is that which opposes *life v death.*[274] There it echoes the scream of horror from the head which volitates high, and which is only briefly illuminated by white tones, against an immense background of darkness, silence and asphalt grey. The small contrasts of red that impregnate the word *Iustitia* only reaffirm its absence among men. Therefore, on the plane of expression, in the composition of this *pictorial text,* one notices *eidetic classes* (justice v injustice; life v death; blood v light), *topological classes* (high v low; head v body) and *chromatic classes* (black v white; black v red; light v shade; light v dark).

In the work by Victor Hugo, true life is outside the human world, which is obscure and remains impregnated with death and blood flowing through the land, where capital punishment is still a common practice. Therefore, there is a parallelism between true life, where there is light and justice is projected, and worldly death, where there is shadow and justice is written in blood, which collaborates to reinforce the *pictorial tension* provoked by the drawing. And it is structured around the opposition that, in the semiotic square, enables to compare *life v death* (Fig. 4.18—*Carré Sémiotique*):

[271] *Cf.* Tore (2011), p. 06.
[272] *Cf.* Janson (1992), p. 657.
[273] *Cf.* Janson (1992), p. 603.
[274] *Cf.* Calabrese (2015), p. 82.

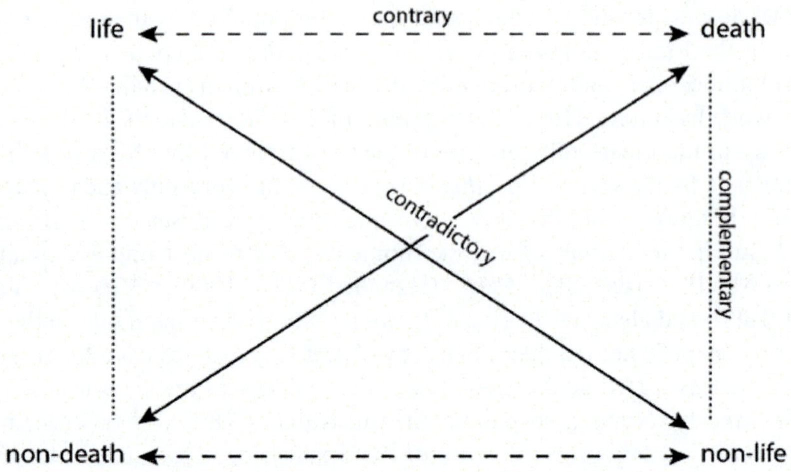

Fig. 4.18 Carré Sémiotique

4.1.9 The Painting Guernica *by Pablo Picasso*

The history of modern and contemporary art completely disrupts the previous conceptions about the relation between image and reality. The *surrealism* had exactly this capability of rupture, with the relation to artistic tradition of the preceding schools.[275] If until then the notion of *representation* was up to adequately translating the symbolic power of art, now there is a strong migration of painting towards something increasingly abstract, disconnected from the *mimesis* and the capability of evoking real figures. The world of *images without references*,[276] or referring to *imaginary references,* become the new form of expression of art. The images without references can be called—as Santaella and Nöth do—*plastic signs.*[277] More and more contemporary art is manifested—especially through abstract art, as John Dewey notes—,[278] the more painting loses in real external references and gains in plastic, imagetic and non-iconic projections.[279]

Within the tradition of contemporary art, the oil painting entitled *Guernica* (1937), by Pablo Picasso (1881–1973)—who lived, for intertwined periods, *cubism* and the split between form and content in aesthetic work—,[280] has *stentorian force*. The picture was painted in Paris, where Pablo Picasso lived at the time, but refers to past events in Spain, during the scenario of the civil war,[281] portraying the cruelty of

[275] *Cf.* Santaella and Nöth (1998), p. 196.
[276] *Cf.* Santaella and Nöth (1998), p. 37.
[277] *Cf.* Santaella and Nöth (1998), p. 38.
[278] *Cf.* Dewey (2010), p. 196.
[279] *Cf.* Santaella and Nöth (1998), p. 196.
[280] *Cf.* Janson (1992), p. 658.
[281] *Cf.* Proença (1990), p. 156.

the power of General Franco who, supported by the German bombers Adolf Hitler and Italian airplanes, provoked a massacre by bombing the Basque community of *Guernica,* on the 26th of April in 1937, having caused more estimated hundreds and thousands deaths, having mainly affected the civil population. The celebrity Pablo Picasso already made him an established artistic name, and he had been selected to paint a work that would represent the presence of Spain in the *National Exhibition of Arts and Techniques*, to take place in Paris. Throughout this period, the disturbing events in Guernica came to the knowledge of the artist, who resolved to take them as an *object* of his *work*, for that occasion. The immense work is now in Spain, after its repatriation in 1981, at the *Museo Nacional Centro de Arte Reina Sofia.*[282]

4.1.9.1 War, Violence, Horror and Injustice

The power of grievance of the work of art is one of its potential characteristics, and this work is pinpointed as one the great works of art in the *History of art,* which is placed at the *front* of grievance in the face of war, horror and injustice. This is the *power of the aesthetic sign*, which is, of *narrating* the *indescribable.*[283] This *aesthetic text* is a *world symbol* of the fights against war, oppression and violence, and not by chance, but for having given *shape* to pain, to suffering, and making *imagetic figures* that are placed in a scene speak, at the time of the *impressionist* construction of the work. Its *symbolic codification* is given by a *tragic and Baroque artistic language* that establishes a paradoxical round-circuit in its composition.

This work is an omen of the horrors of the Second World War, and, its response to a *localised* event, it is also a response to a *pattern of events*, which will dominate the scene of the twentieth century. For this reason, there is no other work of art of the twentieth century with such force, as this, with the capability that it brings together in presenting the *shattering*, *split, pain, death* and the *inhumane* results of the war, in addition to the power of *victimisation of civilians,* in the endless nature of the *screams* that were perpetually heard, by the *figures* contained in the picture. This is how this work is a *grievance of the barbarities* of the twentieth century. Perhaps it is the *pictorial text* that better identifies—by its flying and dismembered shapes—the *necrophiliac* nature of human destructiveness, just as pointed out in *The anatomy of Human Destructiveness* (1973), the *philosophical text* by Erich Fromm.[284]

The picture contains deformed figures, broken bodies, in addition to presenting mutilations, fragmentations, and the fight for life in the last efforts of the characters that appear in the *aesthetic work* to survive. Here, the whole force of the surrealist tracing of Pablo Picasso finds conditions to gain meaning, exactly there where a shape of *découpage* of bodies, people, houses and animals is made. It represents a

[282] http://www.museoreinasofia.es/en/collection/artwork/guernica. Accessed: 14.01.2020.

[283] *Cf.* Santaella (2016a, b), p. 146.

[284] *Cf.* Fromm (1987a, b), pp. 483 and ss.

positioning of the artist before *history*, especially, being able to *condemn* the *violence of the war.*[285]

In the work by Picasso there are many figures of women present, since the women signify life, and its suffering is the suffering of life. There is no sign of the physical presence of bombs in the picture, but only the effect which they could cause, by the systematic bombing experienced by the city, in Spain, and captured from a distance by the images of the newspapers, in France, by the artist. The painting also constantly evokes, the light of electricity and the presence of the candlestick, which alternate in the ability to lighten the darkness. As a monochromatic work, and in the language of light-dark, and its opposition, what it means. Therefore, they are observed in the composition of the work: a woman with a child on her lap; a woman with arms up high; a woman who screams; a chicken in flight, to indicate that the bombing had occurred on normal days of market, having dispersed the animals; a dismembered soldier, divided and left on the ground, indicating the fight for the republic and the anti-Franco resistance established during the civil war; the horse that screams, given that it signifies the Spanish people themselves; the bull, which also points to the very symbolic unity of the Spanish people, dismembered and destroyed by political division.

4.1.9.2 The Semiotic Square and Pictorial Text

In the case of the Painting *Guernica* by Pablo Picasso, where the shattering of bodies prevails in all angles of the work, the *rupture of human bodies and animals* occupies the whole possible configuration of the work. Therefore, in the composition of this *pictorial text,* one notices *eidetic classes* (life v death; war v peace; construction v destruction; whole v piece), *topological classes* (high v low) and *chromatic classes* (black v white; light v dark).

The interpretation of this picture is complex, since it involves many variables, but it is the biggest symbol of repudiation to the war, and, in this sense, a protest for peace. Inside, there is a parallelism between light and life, and dark and death, since the whole *paradox* embedded in the picture by Picasso points to the failure of the *modern* idea of *Lights,* represented in the figure of the *lit lamp* in the setting. It is worth reinforcing the cubist nature of the representation allowing us to see with force the tension between whole v piece, and the idea of *shattering* (of life; of life; of market; of animals) across the whole composition. Even so, the *semiotic square* can be seen in the most evident relation between *war v peace*, the main object in the pictorial narrative (Fig. 4.19—*Carré Sémiotique*).

[285] *Cf.* Plaza (2010), p. 07.

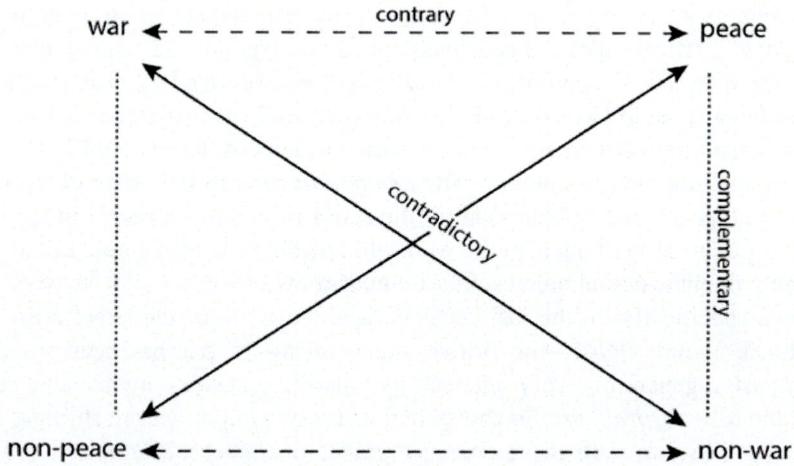

Fig. 4.19 Carré Sémiotique

4.1.10 Street Art *by Banksy*

Street Art is a form of current artistic protest, arising from the suburban culture of the 1970s in the USA, based on the culture of *spray,* marked by its young and urban, rebellious and transgressing nature. Its importance is due precisely to the fact that it is a profile of non-museumified work of art, inscribed in the open air, in constant dialogue with the *urban cloth*. Therefore, it is without a doubt, a form of *contemporary art,* an art *of the streets,* which, moreover, portrays themes of daily life on the streets, a form of *free art,* untied from academic ties, of suburban nature, multi-thematic and which is part of the *urban cloth* of the big contemporary major cities.[286] By its own ephemeral attitude, it escapes the conventions, and places itself in *urban life* from its appearance as an *aesthetic sign,* there where *urbanity* is used to placing only grey, asphalt and concrete. In order to escape the traditional shapes, in the modern world, of *framing* the work of art, in formal cultural spaces, it places itself as a *work* subject to the conditions of the urban environment, which ranges from pictorial degradation, to vandalism, and, from this, to the simple incomprehension of the public authorities about its meaning.

Spray is, however, part of an *urban culture* and in this sense a *young and artistic language,* which speaks about the contemporary city it wants to silence. There, where it is given an urban appearance, the texture of *graffiti,* it is conceived in contrast, of colour in the face of urban grey, of the artistic presence in face of the

[286]"El arte contemporâneo, libre de las ataduras que la originalidad le imponía a los artistas modernos, abre possibilidades de alcances no solo icónicos, indexicálicos y simbólicos, sino también contextuales, meramente sensitivos o experimentales y experienciales" ("Contemporary art, free from the ties that originality imposed on modern artists, opens up possibilities of scopes that are not only iconic, indexical and symbolic, but also contextual, merely sensitive or experimental and experiential"—*translation*) (Rendon 2014, p. 138).

impersonality of contemporary cities, as sensitive language where everything was reduced to verticalisation, speed, passage, massification and degradation. In this point, there are not few, but many, Brazilian cities portrayed by *graffiti* (Sao Paulo; Rio de Janeiro; Belo Horizonte; Porto Alegre; Recife; Brasilia), and which possess internationally renown artists (Speto; Kobra; OsGemeos; Criola; DMS),[287] showing the power of arts on the street.[288] The *dehumanisation* of the urban environment is denounced by art that is expressed, in the sense of making it *reveal* in the city, the creative potential contained in its walls. In *graffiti,* social themes, urban themes, everyday themes, casual themes are of constant evocation.

More specifically, in the last decades, it is the work of the street artist Banksy (Bristol, England, 1974)—the British street artist—[289] that has been standing out enormously, generating very interesting polemics, besides myths and criticism, about the role of *spray*, *graffiti* and stencil. Banksy's initiatives are strongly inspired by social criticism, and the themes of power, war, peace, authority, politicians, environmental destruction, the race for money are always present in his urban interventions. The ironic tone, the artistic quality, the irreverence, the capacity to put the last topic of public debate on the public agenda, the ingenuity, anonymity, anti-system language and the reflexive power of Banksy's interventions have been making him a world renowned artist, attracting the interest of art galleries, and activating the observation interest of an increasingly mobilized public. For no other reason, it is so instigating and important, for the purposes of this iconographic journey, to include Banksy's work as a path to understanding the challenges of contemporary life

4.1.10.1 Justice, Injustice and Violence of the State

In particular, it is worth considering the work entitled *There is No Justice, There's Just Us,* by Banksy, a work inscribed on the walls of Dublin (Ireland, 2013).[290] It is an aesthetic work painted on the a street wall, with broad significance for the universe of street artists, but which explores this dimension, to deal with the subject of justice associating two crucial themes for the big urban centres of the world: the police violence; the aim for justice. For this reason, the double tension of *justice* and *violence* will organise the work, giving it a unique and singular character: *justice being beaten by a police officer*. Indeed, they are many street artists that like to continually portray issues connected to the police universe—the example of the work by Banksy entitled *Law and Order* (Toronto, Canada, 2010)—as the *streets* are

[287] https://streetartbrasil.wordpress.com/. Accessed 11.05.2020.

[288] *See* Malland (2012).

[289] http://banksy.co.uk/faq.asp. Accessed 11.03.2020.

[290] *See* Ket (2014), p. 76.

occupied by the permanent task of patrol and security on behalf of the police forces, throughout the world.[291]

Here one notices that the *symbolic of justice,* in contemporary times, receives the same treatment as *contemporary art.* This means that as contemporary art becomes increasingly more *indefinable,* retracing the relation between *shape* and *content,* the representation of justice will multiply, diversify, pluralise and accuse specific, situational and local problems, concerning issues of justice/injustice. The *painting,* in the form of *graffiti,* is constituted on the street, speaks to the street, and originates from the street. This is, therefore a *pictorial text* of high social density, with an *accusatory, revealing* and *denouncing* nature, the abuse of power in the exercise of the *monopoly of force*, by the state authorities, as a violation of justice.

The force of the *figure* of *justice* is in the aggressiveness of its ideation, in so far as the vigorous *iconographical representation* precedent in the history of the *symbol of justice*—of a Goddess, crowned, on the rise, full of attributes of force and balance—is now substituted by this *disruptive* figure, where the evocation of its *symbolic* is found in the form of a *youngster*, placed in a position of infantile and sexual fragility, it is in a horizontal position and back turned, and is beaten by a policeman. Nothing hides what *street art* wants to denounce: the shield of the police rests next to the sword (now, broken), just as the uniform that depersonalises the personal nature of the police officer, dressed in an absolute black, which appears as a bigger figure, contrasting with the feminine figure, fragile, that still holds the *scales* in an *awkward* and *unbalanced* way, kept *blindfolded,* but manifesting her horror her lips half-open in *astonishment.* The whole composition is based on *contrast*: the opposition between the black of the garments of the police and the white of the clothes of justice; the man who exerts brute force, before the woman with tones of light skin; the truncheon in aggressive use pointed to the body of justice, and the scales disproportionate and hanging, in wait of an act of brutality; the fragility, in the face of force; the energetic concentration of the police officer, in the face of the astonishment of justice; this anonymous place in the city, in the face of inhabited and glamorous places, where all is in order. The composition transmits the *scandal, astonishment, bewilderment,* and is rich in meaning, since it deals with a *scream of the streets,* about a reality of *arbitrariness,* evoked by art, about the *excessive use of the application of force.*[292]

[291]"A favourite target for man street artists is the police and other authority figures. It goes without saying that the two groups are diametrically opposed, with police and government normally targeting street artists for arrest" (Ket 2014, p. 73).

[292]*Vide* Ket (2014), p. 76.

4.1.10.2 The Semiotic Square and Pictorial Text

In the case of *Street Art* by Banksy, in *There is no Justice, There's Just Us,* there is a clear opposition between justice and violence. It is explicit in a way so clear, at first sight, it does not reveal the whole set of *micro-meanings* that are internalised in this complex work of *street art.*

The *Narrative Programme* held in the work is a paradoxical victory of *brute force* over *justice,* in a way which, after an action of confrontation between *police* (force) and *justice* (scales), the first wins, and leaves the sword of justice, broken next to the shield, to make use of the stool, where it performs the action (suspended in the work) of thrashing *justice.* Before thrashing the symbol of *justice,* applying an unfailing correction to it (since, there is no blood, and there is no pain, there are no cuts and there is no death), it is possible to listen to the *character* of the police whispering in a cynical and demeaning way, even challenging and inaudible, through his mask of protection, which is also hidden at the level of the title of the work: *There is no Justice, There's Just Us*, where *Justice* and *Just Us* possess a confusing relation of phonetic proximity to being pronounced in English. This aesthetic-phonetic provocation is absolutely *constitutive* of the work, and necessary for its understanding and interpretation.

The *eidetic classes* (justice v injustice; force v balance), the *topological classes* (vertical v horizontal), the *chromatic classes* (white v black) reaffirm the contrasts between the plane of violence (black; vertical; force; man; truncheon) and the plane of justice (white; horizontal; scales; woman; unarmed), in a way of creating an astonishing and shocking nature disruptive to *street art*, in its capacity of *grievance of police violence* and *arbitrariness of the use of state force*. Furthermore, it should be noted that the work functions as—in its representation of a state of non-justice—a radical opposition between the *balance* expected of the *scales,* and the *unbalance* in which it is, and this *unbalance* of the scales is caused by the *lack of control* of the use of force. Therefore, there is an *internal and opposite semiotic connection* between the opposite poles of the truncheon (high; erect; vertical; black) and the scales (low; unbalanced; sideways), where the *lack of control* points to the *unbalance*. One notes, therefore, the inversion of polarities between *force* and *balance*, *balance* prevails through the *scales*; where there is the *lack of control* of *force*, unbalance prevails through the truncheon.

Therefore, in the tessitura of this work there is something stronger and more alive than the mere opposition between justice and injustice, since the discussion about justice is implied in it, is a discussion from the point of view of life in the streets, implying the idea that violence against justice is an injustice. Therefore beyond the more naïve reading of this work, which has several sub-overlaps of meaning, the semiotic square appears to point to the tension between *arbitrary v control*, in a way it can be figuratised in the following form (Fig. 4.20—*Carré Sémiotique*):

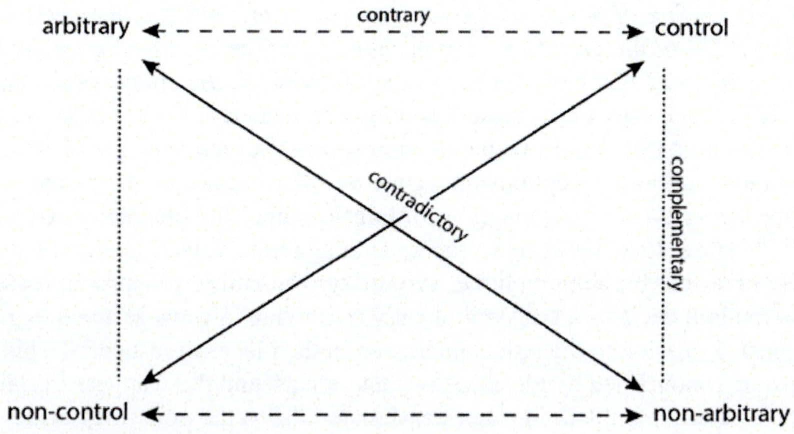

Fig. 4.20 Carré Sémiotique

4.2 Semiotics, Law and Architecture: The Ritual of Justice

The *Semiotics of Art* also encompasses a *Semiotics of Architecture*.[293] In the *Semiotics of Architecture* are at stake the space, the use of space and the tensional relation between the *functionality of the work* (real relation of man with the world) and the *aestheticity of the work* (ideal relation of man with the world).[294] Through its functional aspect, the work of architecture places itself in the world at the service of functions, and, through aesthetics, the work is based on symbols, urban meanings, and it is not rare that it is an *index* of *power, status, condition of class,* or even, in its absence or deficiency, signifies its opposite, that is, *index* of *sub-citizenship, marginality* and *exclusion.* Here one does not speak of a representative role of architecture,[295] but of *functional* and *aesthetic roles* of architecture, given that architecture is structured on the basis of the *architectural sign,* which in turn, evokes man and his conditions (technical, social, political, economic, cultural, religious, historical) in the relation of occupation and constitution of spaces.[296]

Architecture manipulates *material* and *symbolic*, drawing on technical and artistic resources, in order to create solutions between the functional and the aesthetic, occupying and giving *meaning* to space. And this reveals the deep connection between the use of space, society and historical condition.[297] Hence, the possibility

[293] *Vide* Courtés (1979), p. 42.
[294] *Cf.* Puls (2006), p. 29.
[295] *Vide* Dewey (2010), p. 392.
[296] *Cf.* Puls (2006), p. 21.
[297] *Cf.* Branco (2015), p. 02.

of the *architecture of power*, of the *architecture of prison*,[298] of the *architecture of punishment*,[299] of the *architecture of memory*,[300] of the *architecture of justice*.[301]

It is in this way that one wishes to check how much the buildings are *filled with meanings*,[302] and how much these *meanings* are related to the *symbolic universe of justice*, as far as the *choices* made in *architectural language* define visions, frameworks and translate conceptions about justice. The studies of the *Semiotics of the Architecture of Justice*—or even, according to some, the studies of *Architectural Law*—[303] show that the *design*, décor, architectural project, choice of materials, conception of the building, volume, symmetry, verticality, proportion, localisation, are not random decisions, but symbolically referred to, always destined to give faith and elevated mission to the tasks undertaken in the places of justice.[304] This implies that *justice* is nourished by ideas, visions and ideals, and these appear to claim to be materialised and moulded, in shapes and materials, to the point they achieve a real and concrete dimension, existential, finally.

And, in architecture, *art* is summoned to the temples, palaces, houses, squares, because its *power-to-make-speak-to-material,*[305] which is a *power-to-make-know,* is capable of constituting and investing in *human culture,* that which is *pure material* (stone; clay; brick; plaster; sand; gypsum; cement; glass; iron), converting it into an object full of significance at the service of culture, religion, government, economy, commerce, institutions, mobilising the prestige, intelligence, usefulness, symbology, vanity, pride, terror, wealth, ideology, faith, the ideological convictions in favour of intentional or non-intentional objects, but in any case, present in the relation of human occupation of spaces. The *architectural form* is, therefore, capable of materialising ideas and conceptions, and giving *concrete existence* to what it wishes to implement in the world, to the extent that the *form* that leaves traces of *significance,* the example of the capability to transmit *force* of an Egyptian temple or

---

[298] *Vide* Foucault (1995), p. 207.

[299] *Cf.* Gonzáles (2016), pp. 72–73.

[300] *Vide* Felman (2014).

[301] "Qu'il s'agisse de maisons ou de palais de justice, ils sont toujours des témoins irremplaçables, qu'il faut savoir interroger sans relâche. L'architecture constitue une composante essentielle de l'image de la justice" ("Whether they are houses or courthouses, they are always irreplaceable witnesses, who must be questioned relentlessly. Architecture is an essential component of the image of justice"—*translation*) (Jacob 1994, p. 11).

[302] *Vide* Branco (2015), p. 02.

[303] "Lo que llamo Derecho arquitectónico resultaría de la aglomeración de ambos, de su trama sellada y compacta, pero interactiva" ("What I call architectural law would result from the agglomeration of both, from its sealed and compact, but interactive, fabric"—*translation*) (Gonzáles 2016, p. 72).

[304] "The law has always been, and continues to be, structurally dependet upon aesthetics, upon the rhetoric of the ornament, to elicit faith in its ideals and principles. And this can be reconstructed through an analysis of the tropes and figures of the design of court buildings" (Haldar 1999, p. 135).

[305] *Cf.* Puls (2006), p. 22.

transmit the *balance* of a Greek temple.[306] Architecture, in a certain way, names the world in the ways of living, and takes from humanity the possible fields of space and its relation with other elements from the surroundings and environment.

4.2.1 The Architecture of Justice

The *buildings of justice* are loaded with significance for the field of the state of justice.[307] This underlines very specifically the relation between *Law & Art*.[308] Furthermore, this initial finding is of important relevance, but should be essentially accompanied by the historical vision around *justice,* without which the finding loses its meaning. For this reason, the importance of analysing the history of the *architecture of justice* is highlighted. And, in this sense, the history of the *architecture of justice* involves,[309] fundamentally, two great periods, namely: (1) the period of the absence of buildings (until the twelfth century A.D.); (2) the period of the construction of buildings (medieval, from the twelfth century to the fourteenth century A.D.; modern, from the thirteenth century to the sixteenth century A.D.; modern-regal, from the sixteenth century to the seventeenth century A.D.; classic, from the eighteenth century to the twentieth).[310]

In the period of the absence of temples, or of judicial spaces, since the farthest periods, it has been reported that it became a habit to form a *space* socially representative for the community, where the questions of *justice* were treated separately from common life, constituted in a diverse space of ordinary life, and thus, on one hand, protected from violence and, on the other hand, invested in a ritualistic form.[311] They are, above all, executed in the open, under the shade of *trees* (ash, oak) or around *stones*,[312] whose *symbolic community* investment made nature assume new functions. Throughout the centuries, until there were spaces of justice formed for this (twelfth century A.D.),[313] the meetings around a *tree of justice*—or,

---

[306] *Cf.* Argan (2013), p. 78.

[307] *Cf.* Branco (2015), p. 03.

[308] "Whether symbolic or historical, the link between the beautiful and the just is evident in the various representations and statues of Justitia that adorn the courts of law and other public buildings of the great European cities. Justice is presented as a beautiful Greco-Roman figure with her scales, sword, and – form the sixteenth century on – blindfold, wich, according to art historians, represent respectively the balance and harmony of law, its force, and its impartiality" (Douzinas 1999, p. 53).

[309] *Cf.* Puls (2006), p. 32.

[310] *Vide* Garapon (1999), p. 26.

[311] *Cf.* Garapon (1999), p. 28.

[312] *Cf.* Branco (2015), p. 04.

[313] "Toute incursion dans l'univers des représentations judiciaires commence donc par les manuscrits à peintures" ("Any incursion into the world of judicial representations begins with the manuscript paintings"—*translation*) (Jacob 1994, p. 21).

its equivalent, namely, a *column of stone*[314] (e.g.: the column of stone in the market square of Trier)-,[315] performed the founding role of representation of a *special place.* Now, the *tree of justice* represents the *ancestral tree*[316] that operates as an *axial pillar,* which regulates and orders the world, at the foot of which it is given the administration of justice by the authorities, generally, in the name of the divinity (ies). *Wood* (or *stone*), *ancestry,* the *authority of nature,* the *ceremonial locality,* the *solemn nature of the act,* the *presence of the authorities of the community,* the *expertise of the space* in relation to common life, are the main traits that mark and identify the *birth* of the *ritual of justice.*

The period of the construction of temples, or judicial spaces, in turn, extend from Antiquity, Middle Ages, and Modernity.[317]

In classic Antiquity, the *ágora* is elected as the most notorious and most common public place, for the achievement of the *ritual de justice,* something with deep community meaning, since the *ágora* is the place of commerce, religion, government and laws.[318] Once the old world was eroded—both the *Roman civitas*, and the Greek *pólis*—, now under the influence of the barbaric people, the idea of conducting the *ritual de justice* in a *special place* (removed or central) will persist. For some time, until the twelfth century, it will take place in castles, churches,[319] in guilds, and, even, in taverns.[320] From then, it will establish a tradition of *medieval architecture of justice*, enshrined by auditoriums, by the houses of petition and by the first apparitions of civil buildings aimed at justice.[321] In these medieval buildings, the functional and aesthetic structuring of the architecture of justice on two levels will be common, with the jail below the level of circulation, and the level of the court on the floor above, in a true representation of the *symbolic reading* that one had of the *universe* as a whole, divided between good and bad, of justice and injustice.[322]

It is there that it was announced, in the medieval period, alongside the economy of the rising market, in the centre of the market *square* (E.g.: the *Pallazzo della Ragione,* in Padova, Italy). According to the observation of Robert Jacob, it is possible to notice that the medieval period has something of relevance in the sense

---

[314]*See* Jacob (1994), pp. 44–45.

[315]*Cf.* Jacob (1994), p. 43.

[316]"Aquel árbol, producido por la naturaleza y al que se otorgaban poderes mágicos, fue el primer cobijo del Derecho. Un derecho probablemente tan natural como el mismo árbol" ("That tree, produced by nature and given magical powers, was the first shelter of the Law. A right probably as natural as the tree itself"—*translation*) (Gonzáles 2016, p. 59).

[317]*Cf.* Garapon (1999), p. 26.

[318]*Cf.* Gonzáles (2016), p. 60.

[319]*Cf.* Gonzáles (2016), p. 64.

[320]*Cf.* Branco (2015), p. 04.

[321]"Dès la fin du XIIe siècle apparaissent des bâtiments appelés "auditoires" ou "maisons des plaids", dont la fonction était d'abriter l'exercice de la justice" ("As early as the end of the XIIe century, buildings called "audiences" or "court houses" appeared whose function was to house the exercise of justice"—*translation*) (Jacob 1994, p. 96).

[322]*Vide* Jacob (1994), p. 102.

of the affirmation and consolidation of the *symbol of justice* in a way as it has been known since then in the imagination of the West.[323] It is in this period that the appearance of the houses of justice in the centre of the cities is clearly noticed, as Judith Resnik and Dennis Curtis state.[324] Now, this way of conducting the *ritual de justice* is, however, ancestral,[325] given that is dates back to periods prior to the classic Greek-Roman world, and is perpetuated, in some places, in Europe, until the period of the *French Revolution,* in the eighteenth century.[326] In medieval and modern architecture, it is possible to see that, as the *Palaces of justice* started to emerge, the figure of the *tree of justice* and the *central columns* of the building began to represent and evoke what is deep-rooted in the *ancestry* of this long-lived history of the *ritual of justice,* as historian Robert Jacob demonstrates.[327]

From the moment the *architecture of justice* was institutionalised in the *modern courts*—considering the history of the strengthening of the autonomy of judges as a professional class, the independent revolutions and the three-way split of powers—architectural space soon became not only a civil conventional building, but a planned reflection of the echo of a *civilizatory conquest*. What is seen in it is more than the set of its stones, for it in its arch-history that one finds—in a spectral way—its *proto-type-founder*. The architectural traits of the *Greek temple* or the *Roman temple* are constantly invoked by the tradition of the architectural spaces of justice, included in the modern world, especially from the *Palaces of Justice,* or *Temples of Justice,* between the sixteenth, seventeenth, eighteenth and nineteenth centuries,[328] when they multiplied and gained full autonomy.[329]

This *prototype-founder* functions as a species of *code-symbolic-architectural* historical founder of the legitimacy of the decisions of justice. As can be seen from Fig. 4.21, the *Supreme Court of Justice* building (Washington D.C., USA), as a building from the beginning of the twentieth century, manifests in all its splendour, perfection, clarity and style what this tradition of the *Temples of Justice* ended up consecrating.

Architectural language allows the conferral of *dignity* and solemnity to the decisions of justice.[330] For this reason, generally, *architectural language* relies on the *adornment, solemnity* and *plaster,* in addition to an ostentatious decoration to

[323]*Cf.* Jacob (1994), p. 18.

[324]"Civic halls, providing "the stage for the ceremonial display of power" come to mark city centers" (Resnik and Curtris 2011, p. 134).

[325]*Vide* Jacob (1994), p. 17.

[326]*Cf.* Jacob (1994), p. 44.

[327]"L'essentiel est d'observer que colonnes et arbres de justice ont perpétué, avec une constance et une force remarquable, la fixation de la scène judiciaire autour d'une réplique symbolique du pilier de l'univers" ("he main thing is to observe that columns and trees of justice have perpetuated, with remarkable constancy and strength, the fixation of the judicial scene around a symbolic replica of the pillar of the universe"—*translation*) (Jacob 1994, p. 45).

[328]*Vide* Jacob (1994), p. 203.

[329]*Cf.* Garapon (1999), p. 31.

[330]*Cf.* Branco (2015), p. 11.

Fig. 4.21 Supreme Court of Justice Feature of the Main and Front Façade Washington, D.C., The United States Personal Archive: Photography: © poyola

demonstrate the *solemnity* and *selectivity* of the ambience of justice, as the essay by Piyel Haldar points out in the work entitled *Law and the image,* by Costas Douzinas.[331] Now, what is done in a *Palace of Justice* is not arbitrary, it has a story and gives continuity to the course of civilisation, from its *prototype-founder.* It is there that the *Palace of Justice* reveals a strong symbolic investiture, which translates, as French sociologist Antoine Garapon states, three fundamental experiences: that of a separated space, that of a sacred space, that of a initiatory path.[332]

And this is done because these send 'messages', for centuries and centuries—considering the temporal permanency of the *architectural sign,* for its durability, publicity and persistence in time -, about the characteristics that mark and evoke the *deep symbology* of this culture and this tradition, namely: measure; order; proportion; mathematics; symmetry; accuracy; harmony; technique; balance; force; reason; stability; culture; origin; foundation; power; authority. The formation of the *modern temple of justice* of the classic period will deepen even more this *ordination* of space

[331]"The elegance of legal architecture provides the background against wich justice I seen to be done; it advertises itself as a select and exclusive space in wich a monopoly over the administration of justice according to rational precepts is supposed to reigns" (Haldar 1999, p. 135).

[332]*Cf.* Garapon (1999), p. 34.

in a rational way.[333] But, its function is clear: to echo, it sings along, and to sing along, it recalls, rekindles and keep alive a millenary tradition of *cultivation* and *search* of *justice* through the values that seem constitutive to it, considered the very high and relevant *symbolic-social function* of justice.

4.2.2 The Architecture of Justice and the Symbolic Investiture

The whole architectural space goes through a *symbolic investiture*. The *symbolic of justice* corresponds to the set of the very *semiotic, aesthetic* and *symbolic* stimuli to the dimension of justice and which are, normally, charged in the architecture of justice to *remember, recall, admonish, instruct, intimidate, praise, evoke* and *inspire*. And, in fact, Judith Resnik and Dennis Curtis highlight the idea that building is itself an act of power, which imposes the capacity of designating state power and importance of the judicative function, so that the *architecture of justice* constrains and imposes.[334]

The *symbolic* does not act at the level of rational, for this reason, it has strong power of stimulus as it affects a number of senses—especially, touch, vision and hearing—of those who circulate through *judiciary spaces.* To be immersed in the *experience* of a *Court House*, explicit messages and subliminal messages are incorporated in the universe of the recipients of the messages. And the reactions are several: admiration; reverence; wonder; fear; embarrassment; pettiness; terror; respect; imposition. The principle, the huge *symbolic load* of the judiciary spaces is oriented to its more recurring frequenter: the judge. However, it is intended for all those for whom the judiciary space is destined: clerks of justice; judges;[335] defendants, lawyers and justice prosecutors; procedural parties; citizens. In order to strengthen the *symbolic of justice*, various elements of mythological, religious, historical elements are reunited, the example of which occurs in the *Palace of Justice of Paris*.[336]

Figure 4.22, which shows the main entrance of the *Palace of Justice of Paris* (Île de la Cité, Paris), demonstrates very well how the structure of the building is classic, is levelled with stairs above of the public thoroughfare, and is topped with verbal signs that evoke the traditions after the *French Revolution* (1789), *Freedom* (*Liberté*), *Equality* (Égalité), *Fraternity* (*Fraternité*).

For this reason, it should be well understood that the *symbolic investiture,* which corresponds to the work of the architects in the aesthetic dimension of the architectural work, does not enter into the constitution of the building as a plain *ornament*, since it enters, in this case, as synonyms of *reinstatement*, *memory*, *regeneration of*

[333] *See* Jacob (1994), p. 207.

[334] "Building serve not only as stages but also as constraints" (Resnik and Curtris 2011, p. 134).

[335] *Vide* Garapon (1999), p. 30.

[336] *Cf.* Garapon (1999), p. 27.

Fig. 4.22 *Palais de Justice* (1857–1868) Île de la Cité Paris, France Personal Archive: Photography: © ecbittar

social order and, at the same time, *expression of power*. The modern State will make *statehood* a *label* that confuses *legality* and *legitimacy*. Also, the power of the judiciary is structured in such a way to constitute itself symbolically in the speciality of discourse and in the distance from society.[337] Therefore, the whole *symbolic* of the *architectural sign* is not limited to the *symbol of justice*, but will bring together other diverse elements, such as: symbol of justice;[338] architecture of justice; rational architectural project; dungeon and room of judgement;[339] judicial ritual; sound signals from the judiciary space; internal divisions of the space of the room of hearings; garments; ordination of the time of process; hammer and scales. From the historical point of view, the *symbolic of justice* has vividly referred to elements of nature, evoking them to the satiety, to Christianise itself, in the medieval period, and, thereafter, in the modern period, to gain its autonomy in the figure of justice as virtue.[340]

It is interesting to note that the *architectural elements* of the *judiciary space* are, often, invested in *much symbolic force,* either on the external side (i), or on the

[337]"Il n'est nullement fortuit que la distance entre la justice et la société se soit introduite, symboliquement, dans les premières décennies du XVIIe siècle" ("It's no coincidence that the distance between justice and society was symbolically introduced in the early decades of the XVII century"—*translation*) (Jacob 1994, pp. 211–212).

[338]*Vide* Jacob (1994), p. 238.

[339]*Cf.* Garapon (1999), p. 29.

[340]*Cf.* Garapon (1999), p. 27.

Fig. 4.23 Enrico Quattrini *Corte di Cassazione—Palazzo di Giustizia View: Justice, between Force and Law* 1889 Rome, Italy Personal Archive: Photography: © ecbittar

internal side (ii), of architectural construction. In the dimension of its external ornamentation (i): the lions, the mouthpieces,[341] the swords, the lances, the high gates, the fences, the separation from the external world,[342] the big architectural plaster in stone, the gantries, the solidity of the construction, the raised stairs of numerous steps above the level of the street,[343] the magnificent door above the level of the ground,[344] a gantry with the symbol of justice, the Goddess of justice or Latin inscriptions.[345] All these elements are barriers and symbolic figures that impede *disorder* (and injustice) from entering into the space of *order* (and justice).

Now, on the outside the scandals, facts, conflicts, disorder, injustices, screams, acts of cruelty, and, above all, the whole dimension of violence, which it attains in the natural icons semiotic evocations of the forces of the elements that they are performing in the *counter-march* in the kingdom of violence, should be retained.[346] By way of example, as Fig. 4.23 shows, on the external façade, next to the street, in *Corte di Cassazione—Palazzo di Giustizia* (Rome, Italy), is this lion's head, that is, the evocation of the strength of the animal world, as a warning to the universe of violence, force and disorder regarding the place that *justice* occupies in the world, when entering the House of Justice.

---

[341] *Cf.* Garapon (1998), p. 207.

[342] *Cf.* Jacob (1994), p. 245.

[343] *Cf.* Garapon (1999), p. 32.

[344] *Cf.* Garapon (1999), p. 35.

[345] *Cf.* Garapon (1999), p. 35.

[346] *Cf.* Garapon (1998), p. 207.

In the dimension of internal symbolic investiture (ii): the hearing room has its subdivisions, the adoption of grand and wide spaces, with high ceilings,[347] the decoration with the symbol of justice, the big structural pillars[348] and the vertical and thick columns[349] that evoke ancestral trees,[350] the stained-glass windows, tapestries, the closed and controlled space, among other elements. Furthermore, the ornaments of the judicature, such as the court robe[351]—or, the toga—, the sounds of the judiciary space—the example of the ring, the bell[352] and the hammer[353]—, the atmosphere of suspense and concentration, expectation and reverence, of sobriety, silence and order, end up completing the *architecture of justice*, through an *architecture of the ritual of justice*.

All the symbolic 'marks'—separately, and different from other social spaces—make the judiciary space this *place special for the things of justice.* And, this means a *special place for the things of justice* to the extent that its opposite is the kingdom of violence, barbarism and disorder, in a way of establishing order, peace, reason and measure lacks a *symbolic investment* that justifies the *aesthetic-symbolic* level the whole social effort contained in this undertaking. With this, the *power of decision of the judge* is authorised to act and be imposed over the external worldliness of the facts; it is from within the Palaces, Courts and Tribunals that the *orders of justice* come out, in order to be fulfilled in the exterior surrounding space, in a way that the *communication of the architecture of justice* with the exterior is made by means of its *proclaims of justice.*[354] For no other reason, in the view of French sociologist Antoine Garapon, the *architecture of justice* and the *judiciary ritual* serve precisely for:

> Here the function of the judicial ritual: to mobilise, however many times necessary, the symbols of justice (Garapon, *The keeper of promises,* 1998, p. 205).

[347] *Vide* Garapon (1999), p. 42.

[348] *Cf.* Puls (2006), p. 21.

[349] "Les colonnes figurant le temple signifient toute la symbolique religieuse attachée à la justice qui se place hors des hommes: une fois ces colonnes passées, le justiciable entre dans le sanctuaire du juge" ("The columns representing the temple signify all the religious symbolism attached to justice which is placed outside of men: once these columns are passed, the litigant enters the sanctuary of the judge"—*translation*) (Goedert and Maillardi 2015, p. 294).

[350] *Cf.* Garapon (1999), p. 44.

[351] *Cf.* Garapon (1999), p. 80.

[352] *Cf.* Garapon (1999), p. 54.

[353] *Cf.* Garapon (1999), p. 78.

[354] *Cf.* Garapon (1998), p. 205.

4.2.3 *The* Corte di Cassazione di Roma*: The Classic Architecture of Justice*

The *Corte di Cassacione,* or, *Palazzo di Giustizia di Roma* (Rome, Italy), situated in the *Piazza Cavour,* next to the Vatican and the Castel Sant'Angelo, nominated *il Palazzaccio,* is a model of a Tribunal in the form of a temple with big dimensions (170 × 171 m), finished entirely in Travertine marble, by architect Guglielmo Calderini, with clear Greek-Roman evocations, with the date of the period of its construction at the end of the nineteenth century (1889–1911), being, therefore, under the strong influence of European tradition that covers the arch of architectural buildings of the seventeenth,[355] eighteenth, nineteenth and twentieth centuries, in classic style. The style used is Roman eclectic, and, thus, of very clear classic evocations, responding to the tendency to seek to synthesise the Roman tradition of art.[356]

What is amazing in this *Palazzo* is the *monumentality* of the building and the disposition of the functional and aesthetic elements.[357] The *monumentality* implies *distance* and *verticality*,[358] in so far as the building represents a huge *architectural mass*, heavily loaded with *aesthetic elements,* strongly linked to the notion of a temple, and filled with labels of representation of everything that concerns the universe of *Law, Legislation* and *Justice*. Here, in the image below, one can see clearly the monumentality of the building, and the ample investment in architectural mass, in addition to symbolic mass, of which it is revised (see Fig. 4.24):

The *architectural mass* is still accentuated, considering the small entrance of light, the presence of few windows,[359] and the formality of the ornaments that put up and structure the construction of the *House of Justice*. In the Palazzo—as in so many other examples—the separation between the *plane of the street* and the *plane of the tribunal* is clear, which separates and *establishes* the place differentiated from justice, something common in construction of the seventeenth to twentieth centuries, and which were missing from the medieval house of justice.[360] Furthermore, the *verticality* of the linear structure of the building leaves no doubt as to how much the

---

[355] *Vide* Jacob (1994), pp. 205–206.

[356] http://www.cortedicassazione.it/corte-di-cassazione/it/storia_palazzo.page. Accessed 11.05.2020.

[357] *See* Garapon (1998), p. 203.

[358] *Vide* Jacob (1994), pp. 210–211.

[359] *Cf.* Goedert and Maillard (2015), p. 293.

[360] "Mais ce faisant, le palais développe un nouveau symbolisme dont le trait le plus apparent est la hauteur et la distance. La maison de justice médiévale, on l'a vu, ne suggérait rien de tel" ("But in doing so, the palace develops a new symbolism whose most apparent feature is height and distance. The medieval house of justice, as we have seen, suggested nothing of the sort"—*translation*) (Jacob 1994, p. 210).

Fig. 4.24 Enrico Quattrini *Corte di Cassazione—Palazzo di Giustizia View: Justice, between Force and Law* 1889 Rome, Italy Personal Archive: Photography: © ecbittar

tendency of inspiration and notions about the *balance*, the *symmetric*,[361] the *correct,* the *proportional*, the *just* and the *measure*, already by the very message held in the architectural language of the building.[362]

The building ends up being, in itself, the revelation of an *aesthetic pedagogy of justice*,[363] founded in three fundamental lessons: (1) a lesson of the *History of Law*, when observed by specialists and those interested; (2) a lesson of *Morality*, to those who enter into it with functions typical of justice; (3) and, also, a lesson and a warning in respect to laws, to other bystanders and citizens. In the phase of the *monumentality* of the architecture of justice, it is clear that the *ornamentation* is loaded, corresponding to the discursive form that prevails, in its interior, of the *rhetorical adornment*, as the study by Piyel Haldar demonstrated.[364]

Conferring *dignity*, *social force*, *respectability* and *power* to the functions of justice means not confusing, in the urban landscape, the building of justice with any other. *Architectural language* should be able to encrypt meanings, either by the

[361]"Les formes de la justice se fondent ainsi dans une symbolique de l'équilibre infini des mesures égales. Images de stabilité, reproduction illimitée, en miroir, des pesanteurs équivalentes des plateaux de la balance" ("The forms of justice thus merge into a symbolism of the infinite balance of equal measures. Images of stability, unlimited, mirrored reproduction of the equivalent weights of the scales"—*translation*) (Jacob 1994, p. 207).

[362]*Vide* Branco (2015), p. 05.

[363]*Cf.* Jacob (1994), pp. 215–216.

[364]"The persistent dependency of law upon rhetoric is, in effect, manifest in the physical architecture of law and can be reconstructed through the analysis of the tropes and figures of court-room design" (Haldar 1999, p. 121).

choice of materials, or by the selection of *décor* applied, or by the totality of architectural investment produced around the building. Consequently the *monumentality* of the constructions of the period is common mark, between the eighteenth, nineteenth and twentieth centuries. In particular, the *monumentality* of this building expresses many things, but it may highlight its *architectural force*—of overwhelming nature, to use the words of Antoine Garapon—[365] to rival other buildings of huge *symbolic power*, as the *Vatican* and the *Castel Sant'Ângelo*, its neighbours on the same riverbanks of the river *Tevere*.

For no other reasons, if not by these already presented, this model competes in grandeur with the *Supreme Court Building* of the United States of America, located on *One First Street* (Washington DC, United States of America),[366] whose work is attributed to architects Cass Gilbert, Jr., and John R. Rockart, the work carried out between 1932 and 1935, highlighting the 16 Greek columns in a Corinthian style and the huge central chapiter with themes of justice.[367] Furthermore, holding up the staircase, the two statues attributed to James Earle Fraser, *Contemplation of Justice,* a statue of a woman seated in a meditative posture, holding a statue of justice blindfolded in her right hand (on the left hand side of the entrance), and, *Authority of Law,* a statue of a young and muscly man, seated, holding the tablet of law with his two hands, and, simultaneously, the sword (in the background) in his left hand (on the right hand side of the entrance).

In it, also, is housed the same orientation and conception of the *Palais de Justice of Paris,* situated on the île de la Cité (Paris, France), whose main façade is in neo-classic style, in the *Cour du Mai*, dated 1783–1786.[368] The *Palais de Justice of Paris* is located on the île de France, a traditional space of power of the French Monarchy of the *Old Regime*, and, for this reason, it is installed there, sending messages to the French historical past and the city of Paris.[369] The work is done in layers—that respond to the various historical stages of the building—operating as a true *symbolic palimpsest* of the social and historical processes lived in France, between the eighteenth and twentieth centuries.[370] Here, the four statues that hold up the main entrance of the building: abundance; justice; prudence; force can be highlighted.[371]

Furthermore, it should be remembered, the *Palazzo di Giustizia di Roma* inspired the construction in magnificence and monumentality of the *Palace of Justice,* of the *Tribunal of Justice of Sao Paulo* (*Tribunal de Justiça*—Sao Paulo, Brazil), whose

---

[365] *Cf.* Garapon (1999), p. 47.

[366] "In many parts of Europe and in the United States, Justice stands as the lone virtue depicted. Several courthouses built in the United States during the ninetheenth and, to a lesser extent, the twentieth centuries include Justice as part of the decor" (Resnik and Curtis 2011, p. 1747).

[367] https://www.supremecourt.gov/about/photos.aspx. Acessed 11/03/2020.

[368] *Vide* Goedert and Maillard (2015), p. 293.

[369] *See* Taylor (1999), p. 139.

[370] *See* Taylor (1999), pp. 171 and ss.

[371] https://www.cours-appel.justice.fr/paris/histoire-du-palais#01. Accessed 11/03/2020.

work was attributed to the architect Ramos de Azevedo, work installed at the centre of the City of Sao Paulo, at the Praça da Sé, a place of habit and frequency of professionals of Law and the main public authorities of the City, in what can be called the quadrilateral of power:[372] Secretary of Public Security; College of Law of USP; Public Ministry of Sao Paulo; Town Hall of Sao Paulo: OAB-SP. The building conforms to a neo-classic style, given that its inauguration, definitively, took place in 1943, having been listed by the CONDEPHAAT since 1981 as the historical patrimony of the City of Sao Paulo.[373] Inside the building, in the main *hall*, the so called *Sala dos Passos Perdidos* stands out, a massive ensemble of Carrara marble and granite of wide span and strength, surrounded by 16 columns (yellow granite), with chapiters in bronze, and, on the fifth floor, the *Sala Ministro Manuel da Costa Manso*, containing stained-glass windows by Conrado Sergenicht Filho, who exalted the *virtues of justice*.[374]

The structure is in a rectangular format, and the rectangular shape is not something accidental, but—in architectural language—something *significant* for the idea of the perpetuity and perfection of *justice.*[375] Indeed, this tradition in *architectural language* has been installed from the sixteenth century, filled with meaning.[376] The façade of the building is entirely decorated, on all sides of the architectural rectangle—in a rectangle of the streets named after jurists, the front square being the *Piazza dei Tribunali*—with lions, medals, heads of warriors, columns, windows with gantries, floral ornaments, knobs, being adorned with the words *Lex* e *Ius,* on the side, and, just above the main staircases, at the entrance of the *Corte,* is the statue of the *Giustizia.* Here, justice is without a blindfold, has a serene expression, and is revealed to the eyes of the bystander in an enthroned and vigilant manner; it has at its side, a masculine figure holding the head of a lion—representing strength—and, on the other side, a feminine figure holding the books of law. The *Giustizia* looks forward and with the left hand holds a book and with the right hand holds a sword. It follows the tradition of justice divinized and enthroned from the Palaces of Justice of

[372]"In the United States, as in Europe, a court also marked the seat of local power" (Resnik and Curtris 2011, p. 135).

[373]http://www.tjsp.jus.br/Museu/PalacioDaJustica. Accessed 11.03.2020.

[374]*Vide* http://www.tjsp.jus.br/Museu/PalacioDaJustica.

[375]"Autre trait commun: la forme rectangulaire du bâtiment. Les palais de justice construits au XIXe siècle tendent à s'approcher de la forme cubique car "la forme d'un cube est le symbole de l'immutabilité". "Et Claude-Nicolas Ledoux d'ajouter que "la forme d'un cube est le symbole de la justice". Cette architecture produit ainsi un effet d'intemporalité: en n'intégrant pas le palais de justice au tissu urbain, l'architecte signifie que la justice ne doit pas être traitée comme une simple affaire quotidienne" ("Another common feature is the rectangular shape of the building... The courthouses built in the XIXe century tend to approach the cubic shape because "the shape of a cube is the symbol of immutability". "And Claude-Nicolas Ledoux adds that "the shape of a cube is the symbol of justice". This architecture thus produces an effect of timelessness: by not integrating the courthouse into the urban fabric, the architect means that justice should not be treated as a simple everyday affair"—*translation*) (Goedert and Maillard 2015, p. 293).

[376]*Vide* Jacob (1994), p. 207.

the period,[377] and it is a constant, perhaps not with so much symbolic presence and force in front of a *Palazzo,* as in this case.

But, in this case, justice is not alone, as it is anticipated by numerous figures of eminent jurists who are lined up, surrounding the door of the entrance of the *Corte di Cassazione,* and arranged in the front of the *Palazzo* facing the *Piazza dei Tribunali.* There they are juxtaposed numerous legal consultants, jurists and speakers, from the long-lived Roman and Western tradition, including Vico Giambattista (jurist, eighteenth century A.D.), De Luca Giambattista (jurist, seventeenth century A.D.), Cicerone Marco Tullio (speaker, second-first century B.C.), Papiniano Emilio (jurist, second century A.D.), Bartolo da Sassoferrato (medieval jurist, fourteenth century A.D.), Romagnosi Gian Domenico (illuminist jurist, eighteenth century A.D.) the statues standing, and, in turn, Modestino Erennio (Roman jurist, third century A.D.), Gaio (Roman jurist, second century A.D.), Paolo Giulio (Roman jurist, third century A.D.), Ortensio Ortalo Quinto (Roman speaker, second A.D.—first B.C.). Ulpiano Eneo Domizio (Roman legal consultant, second/third century A.D.), Marco Antistio Labeone (legal consultant and black Roman, first B. C./ first A.D.), Crasso Lucio Licinio (speaker and Roman jurist, second B.C.-first B.C.), Giuliano Salvio (Roman jurist, first and second A.D) are the statues in seated positions.[378]

4.2.4 The Palace of Justice of Lisbon: The Contemporary Architecture of Justice

The *Palace of Justice of Lisbon* (Lisbon, Portugal) is a model of *contemporary judicial architecture*. This is a complex infrastructure that had its inauguration in 1970, a work and conception of 1962, elaborated by Portuguese architects Januário Godinho de Almeida and João Henrique de Mello Breynen Andresen.[379] The conception of the architecture is *modernist,* highlighting the straight lines, the dimension and the volume, the infrastructure *monumentality*, as well as a privileged location in the urban design of the city of Lisbon. The location of the *architecture of justice,* normally centralised, is substituted here by another posture, which is *campus* of justice, in a position of broad land, but also high, in relation to the whole city and the port area, revealing at once the importance and significance of justice for all, as its common situation of targeting of the decisions of justice to the whole city.[380]

[377]"On le voit, le palais de justice avait une véritable fonction sociale de représentation d'une justice divinisée, représentée en majesté" ("As you can see, the courthouse had a true social function of representing a divinized justice, represented in majesty"—*translation*) (Goedert and Maillard 2015, p. 294).

[378]*Cf.* Garapon (1998), p. 204.

[379]*See* http://www.trienaldelisboa.com/ohl2017/places/palacio-da-justica/. Acesso em 11.05.2020.

[380]*Cf.* Branco (2015), p. 08.

Fig. 4.25 Palace of Justice of Lisbon (1970) Marquês de Fronteira Street Lisbon, Portugal Personal Archive: Photography: © pyo

In this architectural work, the decoration has not yet disappeared.[381] On the contrary, the decoration of the *Palace of Justice of Lisbon* (see Fig. 4.25) favoured ceramic and the use of modern materials, where the evocation of traditional Portuguese art in bricks and tiles is highlighted, having been attributed to Portuguese ceramicist Jorge Barradas. He was responsible for the execution of four big panels, where they appear works from 1969 that represent themes of *justice* and of *Law*, namely, *The Scales, the Code, the Outside judge, Justice*. In addition to these, the Palace also houses other ceramic panels, attributed to Portuguese painter Júlio Resende, who made six panels, namely, *Wisdom*, *Serenity*, *Strength*, *Truth*, *Temperance* and *Prudence*. In addition to these, six other panels are presented, these last ones attributed to visual artist Querubim Lapa, entitled *Adam and Eve cast from Eden*, *The Law that enables Peace among men*, *Creation of a Code*, *The practice of justice based on Law*, *Spirit of Order* and, even, *Temperance*.

From what we can see, this building manifests a very peculiar *symbolic-architectural posture*. From one side, it seeks to break the *palatial tradition*, and with the view of the architecture of justice in a Greek-Roman temple style, adopting a *modernist* vision, at the end of the twentieth century, with straight lines and favouring the functionality of spaces. From the other side, it does not let go, in some way, of a *symbolic of justice,* reconciling *modernity* with tradition, in the evocation of *legal signs* of huge traditional importance, indeed, incorporating classic themes in the evocation, either of the notion of *justice,* or of the notion of Law. To the extent that the *Scales* represented here, despite the *modernist cut* in the history of

[381] *Vide* Branco (2015), p. 10.

the judiciary architecture, it attempts to re-establish the connection with tradition, evoking a *symbol* that has been consolidated in the tradition from the Egyptians, Greeks and Romans, up to medieval and modern tradition. To recall *Adam and Eve*, one sees the principles of civilisation—in the Christian sense—the *original sin* as founder of a tradition where guilt and error are associated with the evils of the world.

In this building, therefore, a specific *situation of transition* of times, in the use of *architectural language*, is gathered. It is for this reason that the Palace of Justice of Lisbon is studied and interpreted by Patrícia Branco as being a model that favours *functionality*,[382] and not *ornamentality*, without stripping down *traditional symbolic evocation*. The Portuguese building goes along with the trend of other contemporary judicial spaces, all marked by the breadth, emptiness and glass structures. By the period of its dating (1970), it is clear that it is a work of architecture of *transition*, between the time of the temples of justice and the time of the contemporary and digitalised buildings, in the sense of the big *contemporary Tribunals*, that now consider themselves for their *democracy, efficiency, transparency* and *digitality*. In this sense, a good example is the *Supreme Court* of Israel, in Jerusalem.[383] In this work, studied from the semiotic perspective, the conciliation between *modernity* and *tradition* is also clear, as far as the *symbolic of the city* (the wall and door of the City),[384] the fundamental national references of the State of Israel, and the more constants calls of tradition there are clearly preserved.[385] It is represented, for many interpreters, particularly in the reading of Piyel Haldar, a *symbol of democratisation* of justice.[386]

The *architecture of contemporary justice* sends a message to society, that it adapts, is flexible and updated to the demands of modern time. This means that from the *classic conception* of *Temple of Justice* to the contemporary conception of *Modern Building*, important change are taking place in democratic times, to contemporary demands and the challenges of the last generation. In *contemporary judicial architecture,* the passage of *architecture-monumental* (classic of Greek-Roman inspiration; solemn; far-fetched; closed; heavy; big architectural mass;

[382] *Cf.* Branco (2015), p. 15.

[383] http://elyon1.court.gov.il/eng/siyur/index.html. Accessed 11.05.2020.

[384] *Cf.* Garapon (1999), p. 35.

[385] "As Clare Melhuish has pointed out, the semiotics of the *Supreme Court* building in Jerusalem derive from an understanding of tradition and articulate a sense of national and legal identity as well a profound need for order. Modern court architecture, however, does not eradicate the need for ornament in order to articulate these ideals of rationality, order, and identity. All recent buildings have, with varying degrees of success, made use of the rhetorical ornamentation in order to capture and celebrate 'one of the most fundamental set of principles upon wich our society is based'" (Haldar 1999, p. 131).

[386] "The Suprem Court of the State of Israel, situated in Jerusalem, is one example of the many new-style courts. The building, it is suggested, attempts to 'calibrate the relationship between the individual and the collective through mutual agreement'. As is often the case in contemporary court architecture, the court tries to democracize the law, to flatten the hierarchical structure, and to disguise the alienating atmosphere of 'superordination' in the courtroom. Members of the judiciary and the public, for example, approach the courtroom at the same level" (Haldar 1999, p. 130).

formal; higher; grand; aloof; palatial) to *architecture-transparency* (open; fluid; transparent; accessible; informal; light; fast; efficient; clear; digital; democratic)[387] is significative of what it regards the change of the prioritisation of the meanings of justice.

Therefore, in a clear approach of the disconnection of the adornments of buildings from the previous period, and its overload of symbols, the structures of concrete, steel and glass—exploring the dimensions of *smooth* and *polished* as characteristics of *beautiful digital,* as Byung-Chul Han analyses—[388] they tend to mark their *mission* and *task,* to the extent that they are placed before the construction of justice in the *democratic, transparent* and *digital* era. This implies a split, in the universe of more traditional architectural representations, a factor that implies a certain reservation by some jurists, who accuse the *contemporary vacuum* of echoing the dimension of the *absence*, *hollow*, *without-meaning*, *undefined and lack of reference*,[389] characteristic of post-modern condition.[390] Here, the very project of Enlightenment, and the symbolic of Enlightenment, indicates how much the *dismantling* of the era of great certainties, great truths and meta-narratives, are diluted in the dimension of what is liquid, empty and amorphous. It is evident that the architect goes through wondering and doubt, about what to juxtapose, during conception of justice for these times.[391]

But, there are terms of *architecture of contemporary justice,* prioritised in a place of *secrecy*, *transparency*,[392] instead of weight, lightness, given that *architectural language* can do this by means of the use of glass and steel.[393] After all, the quality of what is vitreous, is proper to what values *visibility*, *lightness*, *modernity*, *transparency*, *rectitude*, *perpetuity*, *translucent*, the disposition to natural illumination. These are the semiotic traits of the notion of *transparency*, and of what it evokes.[394] It is there that one finds meaning of the *architectural discourse* of the twenty-first century.[395]

In face of the *tension* between *tradition* and *modernity,* it is clear that the tendency for the contemporary *option*—in judiciary architecture—for modernity, as it is a crucial public service for society.[396] This indicates that *justice* is not enclosed in its walls, or even, that it does not coat itself in tradition to shrink itself to the level of the

[387]"Governments explain their decisions to case their courts in glass and to bathe them in light as representing the values – transparency, accessibility, and accountability – that undergird the exercise of force" (Resnik and Curtris 2011, p. 15).

[388]*Vide* Han (2015), p. 37.

[389]*Cf.* Garapon (1999), p. 270.

[390]*Cf.* de Souza (2005), p. 87.

[391]*See* Garapon (1999), p. 207.

[392]*Cf.* Goedert and Maillard (2015), p. 295.

[393]*Cf.* Goedert and Maillard (2015), p. 295.

[394]*Cf.* Goedert and Maillard (2015), p. 292.

[395]*Cf.* Goedert and Maillard (2015), p. 296.

[396]*See* Branco (2015), p. 12.

decorated ornaments and the distant palatial visions, but alters itself to house the demands of the citizenship and justice of the twenty-first century. And this is not by chance, but intentional and on purpose, from the part of the State, before the citizens.[397] From the study on investments and the association between lawyers, judges and architects,[398] one notices the growing importance that these *architectural signs* possess in *public space* and represent in terms of society.[399]

Its rupture is not only at the level of *architectural symbolic,* since its true rupture is given at the level of the *conception of justice* that it houses inside, responding to the complaints of change, alteration, updating, transparency,[400] democracy,[401] accessibility, productivity and speed that come before the questions of the decisions of justice. This has implied, on the part of the architectural solutions, conceptions of projects and tendencies of reform and selection of buildings to house official installations of the State, in the field of justice, the prioritisation for other elements, such as: *functionality; efficiency; accessibility; sustainability; location; ergonomy; information.*[402] The organisation of justice and the administration of justice become relevant issues in serving the professionals of the system of justice, and in the quality of the public service provided,[403] that, finally, these traits are above whatever other characteristics that mark the traditions and preceding historical periods, given that the belief in justice does not depend as much on the ostentation of its symbols,[404] as the capability of offering solutions to a complex, globalised and interdependent world, there where the faith in justice is placed, in the materiality of the results of the judicial proceedings. This is the revelation of the intimate relation between the

---

[397] "L'architecture contemporaine des palais de justice ne doit aucunement être regardée comme un hasard. En effet, il convient de constater cependant que l'État entend attacher une réelle symbolique, renouvelée, à la justice" ("Contemporary courthouse architecture should not be viewed as a coincidence in any way. It should be noted, however, that the State intends to attach a real, renewed symbolic value to justice"—*translation*) (Goedert and Maillard 2015, p. 297).

[398] "Committed to monumentality when resources permitted, communities deployed prominent architects to showcase their corporate identities and their legal authority.

The deployment of courthouses to signify government was not simply an outgrowth of the expansion of political and economic power. Rather, this special form of building reflects the intersecting interest of three professions – lawyers, judges, and architects – that generated the building type now known as a courthouse" (Resnik and Curtris 2011, pp. 135 and 136).

[399] "Before 9/11, the building had 890,000 visitors a year" (Resnik and Curtris 2011, p. 151).

[400] "L'architecture des palais de justice tend à s'inscrire dans cette logique de transparence. Rompant avec la monumentalité du passé, les nouvelles réalisations entendent laisser voir et donner à voir" ("The architecture of courthouses tends to be in line with this logic of transparency. Breaking with the monumentality of the past, the new buildings are intended to let people see and be seen"—*translation*) (Goedert and Maillard 2015, p. 292).

[401] *See* Goedert and Maillard (2015), p. 292.

[402] *Cf.* Branco (2015), p. 05.

[403] *Cf.* Branco (2015), p. 19.

[404] "If justice needs to be seen to be done, if it has to be ostentatious, it is because law continues to demand faith. Law needs to stand out from the mundanity of other institutions and therefore needs an ornate architecture" (Haldar 1999, p. 135).

Fig. 4.26 Faculty of Law—University of São Paulo Central Facade, 1938 Largo de São Francisco, São Paulo, Brasil, Personal Archives: Photography: © pyo

architecture of justice and the practical conception of justice existing at the historical time.

4.2.5 The Faculty of Law in Largo of Sao Francisco: Architecture of Education and Architecture of Justice

If up to now the models of architecture connected to the *architecture of justice* were analysed, when examining the *Faculty of Law in Largo of Sao Francisco*, in Sao Paulo (Brazil), one starts to analyse an architecture connected to the *teaching of Law*. The *architecture of education* is not less important than the *architecture of justice,* and there are consistent historical studies in this respect, and one is able to see how much the *architecture of education* stems from the *architecture of justice*.[405]

Figure 4.26, which registers the main façade of the building of the *Faculty of Law of São Francisco* (*Faculdade de Direito do Largo de São Francisco,* São Paulo, Brazil), is quite characteristic in the sense of establishing a clear connection between the *architecture of teaching* and the *architecture of justice.* The building as a whole is rather interesting to be analysed, in addition to its external façade, because the layout of the classrooms, interior decoration, stained glass windows, the painting

[405] *Vide* Garapon (1999), p. 42.

scattered throughout the building, bring very interesting evocations to the study of architecture that is at the service of the ideas of justice.

And, in particular, the *architecture of education* of the *Faculty of Law in Largo of Sao Francisco*, similar to that of the *Faculty of Law of the University of Coimbra*, in Portugal, established in 1290,[406] and later installed in the whole infrastructure of the *Paço Real*—renamed to *Paço das Escolas* in 1597—,[407] showing the closeness of the *Laws, Law, Justice,* in relation to the *Power* and the *State.*

Indeed, it was Coimbra that used the students of Law of Brazil, during the whole colonial period, and, in part, during the imperial period, until came the initiative of the creation of two courses of Law to be laid down in Brazil, and which they could confer autonomy to legal studies after Independence, with the advent of the Law of the 11th of August of 1827.

It is, before, the legal act of creating the courses is the emancipation that enables the intellectual tear and the untying of the colonial cultural dependence with relation to the *University of Coimbra*,[408] which had been the cradle of formation of jurists in the colonial period, an important step and that enables the graduation of bachelors graduated in Brazil itself, in an autonomous nature,[409] and that form the cultural, political and administrative elite of the country from then on.[410]

The current *architecture* of the building that houses the *Faculty of Law in Largo of Sao Francisco* does not correspond to the original structure where it was installed, initially, the course of Law in Sao Paulo, from the Law of the 11th of August of 1827, which was responsible for the officialisation of the creation of legal courses in Brazil by Emperor Dom Pedro the 1st, who also created the course of Law in Olinda. This last one to be installed on the premises of the Sao Bento Monastery, from the 15th of May in 1828, while the course of Law in of Sao Paulo, after searches among the various Monasteries of Sao Paulo, namely, Carmo, Sao Bento and Sao Francisco, it was decided to install it in what would be the most spacious and favourable structure for education, namely, the *Convent of the Franciscans*, adjoining the Church of Sao Francisco.[411] However, both installations, both in Olinda and in Sao Paulo, denote the frank approximation between *Church* and *State,* in the period of Brazil-Colony to Brazil-Empire, as well as being born in provisional instalments granted by the Church to house the students and the teachers soon after the Law of creation of Juridical Courses.

The current buildings of the *Faculty of Law in Largo of Sao Francisco* (University of Sao Paulo) and the *Faculty of Law of Recife* (Federal University of Pernambuco) are very beautiful constructions of the twentieth century. In the case of Recife, a construction that was finalised only after the works carried out between 1906 and

---

[406] *Vide* Marcos (2016), p. 09.

[407] *Cf.* Queirós (2018).

[408] *Cf.* Adorno (1988), p. 81.

[409] http://www.direito.usp.br/ Accessed 11.03.2020.

[410] *Vide* Adorno (1988), p. 163.

[411] *Cf.* Martins and Barbuy (1999), p. 21.

Fig. 4.27 Faculty of Law—University of São Paulo Arcades, 1938 Largo de São Francisco, São Paulo, Brasil Personal Archives: Photography: © pyo

1911, in the neighbourhood of Boa Vista, in Recife, settled in a new building of neo-classic style and eclectic nature, the project was assigned by French architect Gustave Varin, and the work carried out by engineer José Antônio de Almeida Pernambuco.

In the case of Sao Paulo, from the project of the famous Portuguese architect rooted in Sao Paulo and the successor of Ramos of Azevedo, Ricardo Severo,[412] a work that was finished after the period of construction from 1933 until 1938,[413] being furnished with a portico of entrance, in eclectic neo-classic style,[414] with ornaments of Luso-Brazilian Baroque style,[415] on a monumental scale, recalling the *Portico* of entrance of the *Paço Real of Coimbra*. The *Portico* has a front terraced façade, counting six wide and solid external vertical columns, all in Greek-Roman style, all tall and with Corinthian ornaments, which affirm a *building-monument,* evoking it also a traditional notion—similar to the configuration of a *Court of Justice*—of a space of *Greek-Roman memorial* influence, reproducing the archetype of all Western ancestral history of justice (see Fig. 4.27).

Therefore, it was what went from a simple structure accommodated in the space of the Franciscan Convent, at the beginning of the twentieth century, in a provincial context, at the time in a City of more than twenty thousand inhabitants, and that had

[412] *Cf.* Von Martin (1998), p. 163.

[413] *Cf.* Reale (1996), p. 40.

[414] *Cf.* Von Martin (1998), p. 184.

[415] *Cf.* Von Martin (1998), p. 188; Reale (1996), p. 44.

become insufficient to house the Faculty of Law,[416] to a *Faculty-monument*, now at the beginning of the twentieth century, being revealed as a *symbol of the cosmopolitan capital*, since it started to be bordered by skyscrapers similar to New-Yorkers. Not without tears, doubts, critics, was that a *Faculty-monument*—the example of the *Paço Real of Coimbra*, and of the co-sister of Recife—is erected, with modifications, to the *original project*,[417] on the debris of demolition of the old Convent of Sao Francisco, making a living memory in the already consolidated and well-trodden space of the *Largo of Sao Francisco*—from Bohemia to theatre, from arts to studies—,[418] sedimented since the nineteenth century as being the space for excellence of the students of Law in Sao Paulo. And they are exactly the students of Law that make the Faculty of Law an environment so plural, so diversified, so reactive to contexts, so changing with time, having seen how much exists of *official life* and how much exists of *parallel life* (the example of 'Bucha')[419] to the academic curriculum.[420]

Its topographical situation is, therefore, central in the City of Sao Paulo, since the provincial times, and exerts either a *historical-memorial role*—always occupying the place of the origins of the installation of the legal courses in the country, on the 11th of August of 1827—, or a *symbolic-strategic role*—by concentrating close to the old administrative-political headquarters of the City, thus considered the old configuration of the Pátio do Colégio, and, also, considered the current geographical circuit of the power of the City and the State of Sao Paulo (Tribunal of Justice of Sao Paulo; Secretary of Public Security of the State of Sao Paulo; Town Hall of Sao Paulo; João Mendes Júnior Forum; among others). Furthermore, in terms of cultural patrimony, the building is composed of other monumental buildings, such as, the *Municipal Theatre* and the *Tribunal of Justice of Sao Paulo*.

The aspect of the *architectural sign*, wedged in the heart of the City of Sao Paulo, constructed in grey stone of large investment of *architectural mass* sends clear messages of solidity, force, structuring, pointing to something compact, in a square geometric way; the *architectural sign* reveals its vocation to *serve* in power, revealing a commitment between *shape* and *content,* in which it points to the formation of the elites turned towards the objectives of a legalist, bureaucratic, impersonal, strong, robust, inexpugnable, stable State. From the outside, the impression that the *building construction* gives is; from the inside, as if one considers the beautiful nature of the Arches, which recall the cloisters of monks, in addition to the group of stature defined by the high ceiling on all the floors, to reduce the human scale in all the ambiances (classrooms; meeting rooms; jury rooms; teachers rooms; grand hall),[421] a state of affectation of human conduct is created in which, by the architectural scale

[416] *Cf.* Reale (1996), p. 44.

[417] *Vide* Von Martin (1998), p. 183.

[418] *Cf.* Von Martin (1998), p. 45.

[419] *Cf.* Von Martin (1998), p. 40.

[420] *Vide* Von Martin (1998), p. 63.

[421] *Cf.* Von Martin (1998), p. 185.

used, *respect*, *sobriety* and *reverence* are imposed,[422] just for the fact of entering or just being in the building. Internally, the building became comfortable and very appropriate for education at the beginning of the twentieth century,[423] but it was very quickly out-dated, as a historical-building, in the capacity of accommodating sufficient installations for administrative services, didactic services and other functions that it exercises, considered necessities at the end of the twentieth century and the beginning of the twenty-first century, when an annex building was constructed for it.

From the *semiotic* point of view, the building as a whole evokes the idea of the conciliation between *modernity* (a demand of the twentieth century) and *tradition* (an evocation of the origins in the nineteenth century), in the fights and disputes for the final configuration of architecture of the building.[424] The construction preserves, by its choices, the traits of *solemnity, officiality* and the foundational aspect of the *ritual of justice*,[425] keeping in everything the *labels of power* (classrooms; grand hall; symbols; coats; pillars; statuary; stained-glass windows; busts; plaques; tombs; speaker garments; memories; strict academic protocols; imperial palm trees), especially in a place so crossed by real and symbolic disputes, finally, a space for the formation of the Brazilian political elite.

From the *symbolic* point of view, it speaks of an institutional *hyper-demarcated* space, a striking building in the memory of the students of numerous generations, in addition to being a place laden with meaning, historical records, tombs and memorably crossed by the political and general history of the country itself. Being declared historical patrimony by the CONDEPHAAT, since 2002,[426] and considering the number of plaques, historical objects, pictures, original installations, sculptures (twenty of seven),[427] it ends up functioning as a *symbolically disputed* space, among didactic, museological, cultural, national memory, archive of documentation and library functions, in addition to being a space of academic memory,[428] of celebration of official acts. It is, therefore, an *urban place* of historical crossings, comings and goings, and which has always represented a space of fermentation of ideas, fights, ideologies and debates of extreme relevance for Brazilian *public life*.[429] Lessons, seminars, conferences, celebrations, contests, social projects, debates, disputes, extension activities, formations, protests pass through that space. It is, in this sense, a barn of jurists, writers, ideologists, philosophers, businessmen, artists and governors, of various generations. It is also a *House of Education* that cultivates a type of *encyclopaedic, eclectic and multi-centric knowing,* since it is sprawled by legal, political, philosophical, literary, artistic and journalistic questions.

---

[422] *Vide* Garapon (1999), p. 42.
[423] *Cf.* Von Martin (1998), p. 189.
[424] *Cf.* Von Martin (1998), p. 189.
[425] *Cf.* Garapon (1999), p. 43.
[426] *Vide* Vidigal (2017), p. 25.
[427] *Cf.* Barbuy (2017), p. 17.
[428] *Vide* Telles Junior (1999), p. 27.
[429] *Cf.* Adorno (1988), p. 158.

From the sociological point of view, one notices that it was never exactly a *House* exclusively aimed at education, but indeed, the creation of the bureaucratic elite of the country, since its foundation, until present day. Historically, this always creates a tension between the *quality of education*[430] and the *imperial mandarinate* of bachelors in politics and public life, as Sergio Adorno states.[431] In the nineteenth century it was already notable the lack of scientific-academic spirit,[432] something that has only been modified from the end of the twentieth century to the beginning of the twenty-first century, according to new circumstances and demands of education and research, which are currently in effect. This was how, with vocation aimed at *public life,*[433] the Faculty of Law, in the same was as that in Coimbra,[434] it has a history that crosses the twentieth century and is confused with the history of Brazil.[435]

It is evident that, in this sense, one cannot dissociate the *function* of the building, the *function* of education of Law, and the symbolic *function,* since these three dimensions are intrinsically associated. And it is this way that the building as a whole can be interpreted as an *arch-architectural-sign*. It is an *arch-sign,* since it is laden with *symbols* inside, representing a form *structural celebration* and, at the same time, a form of becoming a *sign-icon* of the history of the country. This is how the composition as a whole is a celebration of bachelorism as constitutive of the affirmation of the Brazilian State.[436] Indeed, the pillars of the *Portico* evoke the pillars of political history, either of the Empire, or the Republic, and the narrowness of the bachelors with the political-administrative exercise of constitution of the Brazilian State. And this makes the building translate, from the point of view of *nonverbal signs*, the idea of a *semiotics of power*. It portrays the direct association between *power* and *knowledge,* through the *legal technique* and access of knowledge of the *laws*. This is an environment where the *mixing* between *knowledge* and *power* takes place through a complex and electric fusion, of all of its aspects. Here, form the semiotic point of view, the *know-how* becomes a *can-say,* so that the theory is converted into practice, and the practice is confused with the exercise of *power-of-saying-the-law*. The *architecture of education* houses the process of conversion from *knowledge* into *power,* and this is how the *architectural sign* serves in its double primordial function, namely, as much *ideological,* as *practical*.

And, to translate the imbricated dynamics of the *function* of the building, of the *function* of education and of the symbolic *function,* it ends up representing a synthesis of ambiguities of history and Brazilian political life, with its qualities and defects. Up to now, the two ambiances of more social and ceremonial nature, the Congregation and the Grand Hall, are marked by the presence of two pictures, of

430 *Cf.* Adorno (1988), p. 103.

431 *Cf.* Adorno (1988), p. 79.

432 *Cf.* Adorno (1988), p. 121.

433 *Cf.* Von Martin (1998), p. 93.

434 *Cf.* Marcos (2016), p. 126.

435 *Cf.* Von Martin (1998), p. 118.

436 *Cf.* Adorno (1988), p. 92.

Dom Pedro the first and of Dom Pedro the second, which centralise the rooms, to mark this as the *House of Politics,* under the *sceptre of power.* In front of the symbolic fight for autonomy of the Colony, in face of the Metropolis, the attempt of emancipation of the cultural yoke and legacy left by the colonizer, in the ambiguous condition of the symbolic consecration of the colonizer. On one hand, modern monument, on the other hand, cult to tradition, revealing with clarity the *dialectic* that constitutes the history of the country, according to the keys of comprehension of the *History of Brazil*[437] and, also, of *Anthropology.*[438] A place of *freedom*, but, at the same time, a place of *control.* A place of ordination of *national,* but, at the same time, an attempt in the search of that which is *universal.* In all, its grey stones evoke parts of the history of the nation, functioning as a true *symbolic archive* of national life.

Lastly, when highlighting the analysis of the *symbol of justice,* it can be seen that it is present in numerous internal spaces of the historical building of the Faculty of Law, often added to the doors of glass, to the partitions of the ambiances and to the light fixtures and railings. For this reason, the internal decoration in an *art deco* style is evocative in all the spaces of the building, either of the *symbol of Law,* or of the *symbol of Justice.* But, in addition to these more discrete and specific reasons, in the central *hall* of the atrium of the *Faculty of Law*, from where the staircases part to the three upper floors, one notices a set of stained-glass windows—whose backs are illuminated from the patio where the tomb of Júlio Frank is located -, which is evocative, as an allegory, of a *History of Brasil,*[439] surrounded by universal values, such as *Philosophy, Justice, Force and Temperance.*[440]

In one view that goes from the ground floor towards the third floor of the building, the historical succession involves stained-glass windows that copy pictures of the Paulista History Museum, resembling classic themes of Brazilian painting, this history only occurred under the watchful eye of Law and Justice, resembling the idea of the mission that the Faculty and its bachelors had and have in the *public life* of the nation.[441] Therefore, from the ground floor to the first floor, one sees the stained-glass windows of the Largo of Sao Francisco, lined to the right by *Justice*, and to the left by *Philosophy.*[442] From the first floor to the second floor, the *Foundation of Sao Paulo*, hedged by the *Pátio do Colégio* and by the *Partida das Monções*. From the second floor to the third floor, the *Scream of Ipiranga,*[443] lined from the right side by *Temperance* and from the left side by *Force.* On the third floor, *there* is the *Law of the XII Tables*. In all of this set, the allegories of *Justice, Philosophy, Temperance* and *Force* are inspired in the figures used Raffaello Sanzio,

[437] *Vide* Schwarcz (2017), p. 599.

[438] *Cf.* DaMatta (1986), p. 19.

[439] *Cf.* Von Martin (1998), p. 190.

[440] *Cf.* Von Martin (1998), p. 190.

[441] *Vide* Von Martin (1998), p. 190.

[442] *Vide* Von Martin (1998), p. 191.

[443] *Cf.* Von Martin (1998), p. 191.

Fig. 4.28 Faculty of Law—University of São Paulo Symbol of Justice, Vitral, 1938 Largo de São Francisco, São Paulo, Brasil, Personal Archives: Photography: © pyo

in the *Stanza della Segnatura*, in the Vatican.[444] It should, however, be noted that in the *Parete della Giustizia,* by Raffaello in the Vatican, in the tympanum *Le virtù cardinali e teologale,* they state three cardinal virtues, such as St*rength, Prudence* and *Temperance,* and in the stained-glass windows of the Largo of Sao Francisco, *Prudence* is not represented. This is clear, since there was no pretence of reproducing the *Stanza,* in its entirety in the stained-glass windows, but only of inspiring the models of some of them in Renaissance, humanist and universally famous conceptions in the history of art, within the worldly knowledge about it. Anyway, *Justice* and *Philosophy* are the perfect reproduction of the constant frameworks of the ceiling of the *Stanza,* given that the notion of *Justice* that was painted by Raffaello evoked the theological-platonic conception a *Universal Idea of Justice,* in other words, of an *ideal* that only reaches its material achievement through the *laws.*

Therefore, the whole composition of the stained-glass windows leads to a *pictorial narrative,* in a stained-glass way, that places the foundation of the course of Law, way below, in the episodes of the *History of Brazil,* culminating in the ultimate victory of Law, or even, in contemporary times of the *Democratic State of Law,* which encounters its expression in the last stained-glass window, on the third floor (at the apex, at the peak, on the highest floor), in which the symbolic association is noted between the *Arches,* the *Law of the Twelve Tables* and the *Symbol of the Scales*.[445] In Fig. 4.28, from the bottom to the surface, on the first level, there are the

[444] *Cf.* Reale (1996), p. 61.

[445] *Cf.* Von Martin (1998), p. 191.

Arches, on the second level, the book of the *XII Tables* is inscribed, and, on the third level, the *symbol of scales* stylised where the loyal is substituted by the erect sword.

It is important to note the singularity of the *symbol of justice,* in this representation, where the central rod of the scales, is the blade of the sword, along with two side plates, in a unique joining between sword and scales (perhaps the attempt to unite the two more constant elements of the iconography of justice in a single symbolic synthesis)—very uncommon from the point of view of Western *iconographical tradition,* which is used to arranging *sword* and *scales* in opposite equinoxes in the hands of the Goddess of justice (just as it appears in the stained-glass window on the ground floor)—in a way which is made possible to understand that, in this *symbol*: (1) force is the centre of justice; (2) scales express balance in the use and application of force. There is, still, in an unequivocal way, the connection of the tradition of Brazilian Law to its Roman-Germanic origins.[446] Also, in the background of all Law, in Brazil, they are the Arches, to spread the knowledge that makes the exercise of the *Law* and of *Justice* possible, in the country. But, in the end, the whole *narrative* in a stained-glass form merges to affirm that, inspired in the ideas of *Philosophy*—as *Causarum Cognitio*—and of *Justice*—as a platonic idea—, in connection to *Strength* and *Temperance*, history should unravel itself until achieving and performing in the form of exercise of the moderate force by measure of the scales, and performing in the form of the *Law,* of *Justice* and of the *Right.*

4.3 Semiotics, Law and Theatre: The Theatre of Justice

The *Semiotics of Art* also unfolds into a *Semiotics of Theatre.*[447] Already in principle, it is important to emphasise that Algirdas Julien Greimas already recognised, in the *Dictionnaire*, the existence of a *Semiotics of Theatre,* identifying it to a part of Semiotics that deals with *theatrical discourse.*[448] And here, the approach is useful and important, in so far as the *Theory of Theatre* is very much connected to the *Theory of Law,* there where is can make us think the practices of Law.

And, here, when one questions in the respect of a *Semiotics of Theatre,*[449] and its relation to the *Semiotics of Law,* it is so that the relation of constitution of the *theatre*

---

[446] *Vide* Von Martin (1998), p. 191.

[447] *Cf.* Volli (2015), p. 283.

[448] "Dans un sens restrictif - celui qu'adopte actuellement la *Sémiologie du théâtre* - le discours théâtral est d'abord le texte, sorte de partition oferte à des exécutions variées; c'est ainsi un discours à plusieurs voix, une succession de dialogues, érigée en genre littéraire. Dans cette perspective, la *Sémiotique théâtrale* fait partie de la sémiotique littérarie dont elle partage les préoccupations" ("In a restrictive sense - the one currently adopted by the Semiology of the Theatre - the theatrical discourse is first of all the text, a kind of score oferte to various performances; it is thus a discourse with several voices, a succession of dialogues, erected as a literary genre. In this perspective, theatrical semiotics is part of the semiotics of literature, whose concerns it shares"—*translation*) (Greimas and Courtés 1993, p. 392, *Théâtrale Sémiotique*).

[449] *See* Mounin (1970), pp. 92–93.

of justice is clear. This conception according to which one would be, in trials and legal proceedings, before a *theatre of justice,* is not in any way of arbitrary new or unusual approximation. Much to the contrary, it is a solidly established approximation in various studies in this respect, within or outside of studies and research of *Semiotics*, as Alexandre Flückiger points out.[450] Indeed, in the area of the studies of the *Semiotics of Law*, this type of approximation has been made since the 1990s, in the midst of affirmation and expansion of the semiotic-juridical studies, as witnessed in *Linguistique Juridique,* by Gérard Cornu.[451]

4.3.1 The Theatre of Justice and the Performance of Justice

The *language of theatre,* in its origin, is associated to language of religious rites, and is to do with the necessity of pedagogy of the city and the constitution of the space reserved for the re-enactment of the common rites.[452] The *theatrical performance* is to do with life in common, and maintains roots in the logic of the *common symbolic* constitution, of the unit of *pólis*.[453] Furthermore, the *semiotic universe of theatre* is the universe of *syncretic language,* in the sense of Greimasian semiotics.[454] A huge variety of sensorial stimuli rush to the *universe of theatrical performance,* where the *dramaturgical action* occurs, from the performance of *actors,* who represent *characters,* vested with roles conferred by *aesthetic text.* Now, the notion of what the *theatrical scene* is organised around unity and plurality is what it confers the possibility of dealing with the *theatrical performance.* The *theatrical performance* is possible thanks to the confluence of various *verbal* languages (discourses; text) and *nonverbal* (scenography; music; illumination; images) that take place in the *scenic space,* and that compete for the success of the aesthetic work.

But, from here, one intends to see beyond the *theatrical performance,* moving towards the study of the *performance of justice.* Just like the *theatrical performance,* the *performance of justice* is not made up of only *discursive language* used by the parties involved in a social conflict that is target of a legal process. Indeed, for the purpose of this analysis, it should be emphasised that the term performance starts to

---

[450] *Vide* Flückiger (2001), p. 02.

[451] "Sous cette lumière, le *tribunal redevient un théatre et le procès la pièce qui y a été donnée*. Dans son énoncé même, le jugement publie le nom des acteurs dans la distribution des rôles. Tout jugement contient l'équivalent d'un programme de théâtre ou d'un générique de film. Il contient, en cette partie double si familière, la double indication des personnages et des interprètes" ("In this light, the court becomes a theater again and the trial the play that was given there. In its very wording, the judgment publishes the names of the actors in the cast. Every judgment contains the equivalent of a theater program or a film credits. It contains, in that familiar double part, the double indication of the characters and the interpreters"—*translation*) (Cornu 1990, p. 356).

[452] *Cf.* Argan (2013), p. 74.

[453] *Cf.* Guénoun (2014), p. 18.

[454] *Cf.* Fiorin (2009), p. 37.

be used not in its vulgar sense, associated to the idea of spectularisation, but in its semiotic sense of *performance*[455] as something which points to the *symbolic complexity* of a determined phenomenon—in the way it sought to use it, in the previous study, entitled *Legal language*: semiotics, law and discourse.[456] In the case of the *performance of justice*, it accentuates what there is, in the circumstances of the acting of the *legal actors* in legal processes, in the area of the *theatre of justice,* a complex contest of *languages, texts* and *rites* that reinforce the *legal scene* so that it is filled with meanings. More than this, it is the meeting of languages that makes the *performance of justice,* and not of *written or spoken textuality,* extracted only from *arguments* (legal and non-legal) in parts. And, finally, the performance of justice is articulated in the form of the performance that *lays bare*—that sees and is seen, just as in the *theatrical performance*—,[457] and under the observation of all the legal actors and others involved—the situation of justice/injustice *sub judice*.

And, in fact, if one takes the elements that are under analysis, in their entirety, the *legal scene* maintains similarities to the *theatrical scene*. This parallelism, despite having limits, is an important path for the comprehension of what the Democratic State of Law depends upon this *game* established in the *procedural arena,* where rights and duties are exercised aiming to achieve the best appreciation possible for the cause, and the evaluation possible of *legal texts* applicable to the situation *sub judice*. It is to this extent that the approximation is valuable, and the importance of the *ritual of justice* for the achievement of rights is noted, and the *justice performance* should be considered a diversion from this process.[458] This parallel between theatre and law also brings some important contributions for the analysis undertaken by the *Semiotics of Law*, which can be identified, in a more analytical way, in ten parts, in the way set out below:

1. the *legal actors*, vested in roles, executing actions to which they are proper, drawing on the *power-of-saying-the-Law,* in other words, on the *power of discursive representation* of the characters, society, the State and of public interest, act in the *legal scene*;

---

[455] *Cf.* Greimas (1981), pp. 82–83.

[456] *Vide* Bittar (2015), p. 311.

[457] *Cf.* Guénoun (2014), p. 26.

[458] "L'example de ces procès evoque plutôt un théâtre de l'absurde. La réflexion precedente montre pourtant que l'exercice de la justice formalisée et représentée dans un procès au cours duquel différents rôles sont attribués et qui laisse un 'jeu' aux différents acteurs est la condition de l'existence d'une société démocratique veillant au respect des droits fondamentaux de ses citoyens. Si la justice exclusivement spectacle est une déviance, la justice sans scène est bel et bien une illusion" ("The example of these trials rather evokes a theatre of the absurd. However, the preceding reflection shows that the exercise of justice formalised and represented in a trial during which different roles are assigned and which leaves a 'play' for the different actors is the condition for the existence of a democratic society that ensures respect for the fundamental rights of its citizens. If justice exclusively based on spectacle is a deviation, justice without a stage is indeed an illusion"—*translation*) (Flückiger 2001, p. 07).

2. the *characters represented* (author(s); victim(s)), from its actions in the *theatre of life,* considering the possible *positions of social action* (criminal; defaulting; contractor; victim; contributor; worker; employer; etc.), whose *dramas, actions* and *situations* are represented in court, for evaluation, legal framework and verification of responsibilities;
3. the *third parties,* external to the *legal scene,* they are tornados before the legal process, the spectators of the *legal result* (identifying themselves or not with the procedural poles and with the legal results);
4. the *place of enactment*, which operates as *counter-background* legal therapy, is found on the stage and through scenic elements, and the ways in which they interfere in the *quality of the interaction* of the *legal scene,* in so far as it defines the ways of justice, rituals of justice, the ways of practice of the word, the orchestration of the procedural steps, the forms and positions of the actors in scene (virtual model; circular-mediation model; jury model; audience-model);
5. the *narrative plot,* which describes the existential plot (always historical, cultural and socially placed) in which the characters are involved, preliminary to the *legal scene*;
6. the elements of *narrative strategy,* of the theatrical scene, the I-discursive adopted (I-lyrical; I-heroic; I-dramatic, of theatrical generations),[459] tornado elements of the *legal strategy* (procedural strategy; dramaturgic strategy; argumentative strategy), in the *legal scene,* where the *person,* the *facts* or the *conflict* are emphasised, in a way coupled to the game with the elements of the legal system and its sources (loophole; conflict of norms; interpretation of the norms; ambiguity of legal language; weighting of principles);
7. the *cathartic process* (*káthursis*),[460] in which the actor(s) involve themselves in the legal scene, rechanging *attention positions,* reviving the facts and social past actions, re-enacting the *existential drama* and, often, with various affections involved (tears, lies, disguising, suffering, confession, regret, irritation, anger, revenge, perversity, forgiveness, resignation), rechanging the perspectives of the legal outcome, by means of the agreement, giving up, abandonment, condemnation, absolution, reconsideration, appeal;
8. the *aesthetic power* (the exercise of art and the search of cultural realisation) of representation and awareness of the auditorium in the reproduction/representation/interpretation of the *aesthetic work,* something which in the *legal scene* is translated into *legal power* (instituition of the duty) of determining the *legal outcome* of the *judicialised narrative*;
9. the *aesthetic finality* of producing affection, replaced in the *legal scene* by the finality of the resolution of conflicts, accountability and decisive stabilisation of social relations, considered the social function of Law;
10. a *conclusive field,* which exerts the role of *counter-weight* to the unreality of legal discourse, seeking to solder again the *mask of the character* and the *face of*

[459] *Vide* Candeias (2012), p. 18.

[460] *Cf.* Guénoun (2014), p. 37.

the person, the *represented facts* and the *effective reality,* the *symbolic vestiges* and the *real relations,* the *scenic-legal reality* and the *socio-legal reality.*

For no other reason, Alexandre Flückiger affirms:

Des acteurs, un texte, des spectateurs. L'analogie entre justice et théâtre est troublante.[461]

4.3.2 The Theatre of Justice and the Symbolic Space of the Heuristic

The *theatre of justice,* as a constitutional expression, indicates the *space separately* destined specifically for the *practices of justice.* Its existence dates back to the ancestral practice of the *ritual of justice,* and is confused with the long-life history of the *architecture of justice,* in its phase of absence of constructions and buildings. Therefore, the idea of that shade to a tree, or around a stone, but, in any case in the open air,[462] destined for a *special place,* to collect the deliberations of the community about the *just* and the *unjust,* is ancestral. The very idea of a *park*—surrounded by wood—from where the *square* differentiated from the world is set up where the *scene of justice* should be developed, is an indicator of the idea that even the modern tribunals maintain in a certain way. That is why it derives the name *parquet* (*parc*; *parquet*; *barre*; *barreau*), until present day associated to the name of the Public Ministry. This is the mounting of the *fictitious space of justice,* this is the mounting of the *theatre of justice,* as Robert Jacob points out.[463] Often, the modern idea[464] of square or rectangular buildings recalls this initial and founding stage of the tradition about the practices of judgement and the public deliberation about justice.[465]

The *space of justice* is the *space of the heuristic,*[466] in other words, there where the *legal debate*—the contradictory dialogue of positions—[467] unfolds, and where the activity of constitution of arguments, the presentation of versions of the facts, the

[461] *Cf.* Flückiger (2001), p. 02.

[462] "Longtemps, on l'a dit, les plaids se tirent en plein air et cette justice à ciel ouvert survécut parfois jusqu'à la fin de l'Ancien Régime" ("For a long time, it's been said, the pleadings are fired in the open air and this open-air justice sometimes survived until the end of the Ancient Regime"—*translation*) (Jacob 1994, p. 93).

[463] *Cf.* Jacob (1994), p. 94.

[464] *Cf.* Jacob (1994), p. 94.

[465] *Cf.* Jacob (1994), p. 93.

[466] *Cf.* Carneiro (2002), p. 27.

[467] "C'est un dialogue contradictoire. Le débat judiciarie en est le modele. Ils se définit par deux traits: 1°. Les interlocuteurs sont des adversaires; 2°. Les interlocuteurs sont des plaideurs" ("It's a contradictory dialogue. The judicial debate is the model for it. It is defined by two features: 1st. The interlocutors are adversaries; 2nd. The interlocutors are litigants"—*translation*) (Cornu 1990, pp. 219–220).

production of tests and the purge of doubts constituted over a process will earn the possibility of being clarified and arriving at decisions of justice. Now, as it is well known how much the heuristic involves the capability of production of persuasion, convincing, combat and dispute about the best arguments.[468] This is a social conflict that gains the coloured of discursive conflict—where the oratory and the techniques of discursive persuasion are present, as Gérard Cornu highlights—[469] in a form of legal argumentation, within the ethical-procedural conditions, which invalidate the acting of *discursive actors*. For this reason, it can be said that the *legal actor,* to perform his role, acts in an interesting position, which is between the strategist and the comedian.[470] This is developed, both in the *space of justice*—and, also, in the *parliamentary space*—, where the debate, the confrontation of views, the oratory strategies and the dispute for hegemony and seduction of the opinions are in play.[471]

4.3.3 The Theatre of Justice, Rite of the Process and Symbolisation of Conflict

The *rite of the process* makes up the *symbolic space* within which the procedural acts are practised,[472] constituting, on one hand, the *procedural routine,* and, on the other, the *opportunities of speech and proof.* In the diverse legal steps of a legal process, they open up the conditions for which the *legal actors,* while exercisers of *actantial roles*,[473] mobilise *legal texts* and *discourses* about facts, values, rights and tests, towards the *legal decision.*

In this sense, the *characters* do not act in the vacuum, but they act properly within the rite, in other words, in a *procedural space* defined, regimented, constituted and delimited for the exercise of the *power-of-saying-the-law*, this being its stage.[474] More than this, what one bears in mind is that the *rite* allows a transfer from the universe of violence to the universe of language,[475] where the *symbolic* takes charge of the primordial task that ensures *rationality* and constitutes a second *reality* about the *reality of the events*. And, in fact, this second *reality*, is the *symbolic-procedural reality*, within which it acts by means of the *legal representation,* field for the exercise of *legal actors.*

Therefore, the *theatre of justice* is not only the enactment, the game, the representation. It is, above all, the form of replacing *violence,* symbolising the conflicts.

[468] *Cf.* Cornu (1990), p. 353.
[469] *Cf.* Cornu (1990), p. 229.
[470] *Cf.* Flückiger (2001), p. 09.
[471] *Vide* Flückiger (2001), p. 02.
[472] *Vide* Garapon (1999), p. 70.
[473] *Cf.* Fontanille (2015a, b), p. 147.
[474] *Cf.* Guénoun (2014), p. 130.
[475] *Cf.* Garapon (1999), p. 147.

Here it is clear that the *theatre of justice*—in the perspective of study of the *Semiotics of Law*—points to something much deeper, complex and important than the mere *surface* of *verbal* and *nonverbal* expressions that make up the narrative plots of the legal causes in dispute. The *theatre of justice* involves the *social actors* on the basis of involvement by the law.[476] The *constitution* of the narrative structure through which the conflicts are processed is the condition for the re-enactment of the facts and for the *domestication of violence,* closely followed by the writing of French sociologist Antoine Garapon.[477]

4.3.4 The Theatre of Justice, Process and Roles of the Legal Actors

The *process* is still surrounded by the *legal space,* where it attains existence (opening of the files), where the procedural acts are executed (procedural rite), where it is closed and archived (archiving), rarely being able to be taken away from this space (on an exceptional basis). The place of process, as *symbolic space* made up around conflict, is the *legal space.* For this reason, the characters of the process should act, vested in certain roles, with certain rights and duties, within the delimited fields of *legal space.* For this reason, the *legal space* is the *architectural surrounding* that *meta-symbolises* conflict. It is an *over-language* (architectural language), with triple semiotic overload, in so far as it refers to *legal language* of the files of the process (symbolisation of the conflict), and this, in turn, refers to the *natural language* on the basis of which the characteristics of social conflict are marked.

The legal space houses the *conflict* now already *symbolised;* it is a conflict *redefined, institutionalised, baptised* by *legal language.* For this reason, to give rise to the process inside, the conditions are formed for what the legal space constitutes a separation in relation to the surrounding world.[478] This implies that the procedural parties, now, are promptly *convened* to an audience, they are accompanied by its *representatives*, they speak to the *registrar,* they can drive the files *in the place,* in a way that this *new symbolic-architectural universe*—the provisional house of conflict and, at the same time, the permanent house of the process—a whole new dynamic and new rites are in play for the search of the legal decision.

The *legal space*—depending on the instance, procedural phase, competence, profile of the conflict—are characterised by diverse *architectural marks* (the wall; the railings; the waiting room; the registry; the court room; the *cancel*; the jury room)[479] that help to circumscribe the acting of the *legal actors* in the representation

[476] *Cf.* Garapon (1999), p. 229.

[477] *Cf.* Garapon (1999), p. 283.

[478] *Vide* Garapon (1999), p. 41.

[479] *Vide* Garapon (1999), p. 46.

of the interested in the outcome of the conflict through the legal decision. The legal space and its subdivisions confer the *right destination* of the role to be exercised by each one within the *ritual of justice*, given that the *cancella* is the most central place of the legal ritual.[480] Including, in the *legal space,* the judge represents the invested authority of *power-of-saying-the-law* that represents the axial pivot of culture, tradition and preservation of civilisation, in the face of disorder, violence and injustice.[481]

4.3.5 The Theatre of Justice, Actantial Investiture and Discursive Roles

The *legal actors* act in the *legal scene,* some in the face of others, each one having its *discursive place*, and the actantial *semiotic-narrative position* of its role.[482] The role is something of the order of the law, institution, ethics and profession. Each *legal actor* develops a *role*, in so far as it is *programmed* to exercise certain procedural tasks, within the *narrative programs,* making his vested role predictable, in so far as it is essential to justice (defence; prosecution; ritualization; *amicus curiae*; decision), as Jacques Fontanille draws to our attention.[483] For this reason, the *legal arena* is characterised by the *inter-action* of *legal actors*, vested in *actantial roles*,[484] given that they act in the *legal narrative*, in a *game* of constant permutation of arguments, in a dispute that considers technical, moral and legal aspects boiling in the framework of the search for the *truth* of legal decisions.[485] The action of *legal actors*[486] is performed through the mobilisation of *discourses* and *tests,* and the *discourses* are the *opportunities of speech* in a *narrative structure* semioticly constituent of the conditions of which it is able to arrive at the legal decision.[487] Therefore, the *narrative predication* of each *legal actor* is carried out according to an *actantial role*.[488]

---

480 *Cf.* Garapon (1999), p. 37.

481 *Vide* Jacob (1994), p. 46.

482 "L'indication des rôles e des acteurs unit l'aspect institutionnel et l'aspect personnel du discours juridictionnel" ("The indication of the roles of the actors unites the institutional aspect and the personal aspect of the jurisdictional discourse"—*translation*) (Cornu 1990, p. 356).

483 *Cf.* Fontanille (2015a, b), p. 151.

484 *Cf.* de Barros (1988), p. 80.

485 Greimas (1981), p. 81.

486 "...l'acteur juridique a pour rôle de *diriger une action*" ("...the role of the legal actor is to direct an action"—*translation*) (Flückiger 2001, p. 08).

487 *Cf.* de Barros (1988), p. 03.

488 *Cf.* Fontanille (2015a, b), p. 149.

For the exercise of each one of the institutionally relevant *roles* (prosecution; defence; ritual; judging), in the process, Law invests in—through legal norms—*legal actors,* as François Ost notes.[489] There are various *actors* of the *theatre of justice*.[490] There they are the judge, the prosecutor, the lawyer, the defendant, the victim, the popular jury, the police, the delegate, the witness, the bailiff, the registrar, the public.[491] These various *actors* see and are seen, in the course of procedural narrative,[492] as generally happens in the *theatre.*[493] Above all, to enter the *legal scene* it is necessary for the *legal actor* to be dressed in the *mask*, that is, to be made up in *persona*—from where the *character* acts in a *fictional role* that is attributed to him by law occupying a *place-of-discourse*—[494] by which he can perform his role in a way of *dramaturgical acting*—using the nomenclature established by Jürgen Habermas, in *Theory of communicative acting*—[495] in defence of a *position of world* in face of a *conflict* in dispute. And, in *dramaturgical acting,* the achievement of the *performance* in the enunciation of discourses[496] by each legal actor depends on his abilities and competences, strategies and forms of acting that claim, more or less, the same schemes of theatrical acting.[497] And, even in this, the differentiation is made between actor, actant and character, from the semiotic point of view.[498] In this point, the Polish director of theatre and cinema Richard Boleslavski, through one of the characters of the book *The art of the actor,* states:

> – The actor creates the whole extension of the life of a human soul on the stage, each time he creates a role. This human soul should be visible in all its aspects, physical, mental and emotional. In addition to which, it should be unique. It should be *the soul.*[499]

From there—as Algirdas Julien Greimas notes—the importance of studying, from the narrative point of view—and the *procedural narrative* is a species among the diverse narratives—the *discursive actants*. The *actants* are situated before discursive arrangements previously established in the *narrative structure* of the process.[500] The *legal actors* act in a way of *representing* them (interests, people, institutions, values,

[489] *See* Ost (2001), p. 93.
[490] *Cf.* Garapon (1999), p. 95.
[491] *Cf.* Garapon (1999), p. 187.
[492] *Vide* Fontanille (2015a, b), p. 147.
[493] *Cf.* Guénoun (2014), p. 14.
[494] *See* Candeias (2012), p. 19.
[495] *Vide* Habermas (2012), p. 165.
[496] *Cf.* de Barros (1988), p. 36.
[497] *Cf.* Ferracini (2013), pp. 118–119.
[498] *Cf.* Fontanille (2015a, b), p. 148.
[499] *Cf.* Boleslavski (2015), p. 77.
[500] *Cf.* de Barros (1988), p. 80.

results),[501] and therefore they establish relations between the *masks* with which they act in the legal scene.[502] Therefore as in the theatre, in one of the characters of Richard Boleslavski in *The art of the actor*, the art of representing points to:

> – To represent is *the life of the human soul receiving its birth through art.* In a creative theatre the object of concentration of an actor is the *human soul.* In the first period of his work– the exploratory – the object of concentration is the very soul of the actor and of men and women who surround him. In the second– the constructive– only its own soul.[503]

4.3.6 The Theatre of Justice, Court Attire and Discursive Roles

The investiture of the character, for the acting in the *legal scene,* is done by means of *court attire,* which *constitutes* the possibility of *acting in name of something relevant to social life.*[504] It is already common to note that the professionals of Law dress in a formal manner, differentiating them from other profiles of professionals. But, on top of the formal attire regularly used in the area of Law, the *court attire* is a *plus.* In this sense, the *court attire* has the function of *purification of the character*, in some kind of *rite of investiture in the power-of-saying-the-Law*, for its entrance in 'scene' for which it exercises its 'functional' role, considering the actantial position of discourse in which he is vested. In the analysis of Antonine Garapon, the use of court attire equals the professionals of Law in the condition of belonging to a community of rules, before which the power of exercising a role around justice and the laws is recognised, and, therefore, in the face of crime and violence.[505]

The toga for the judge symbolises the *responsibility* in which he is placed, in so far as he is placed in a relevant *social function,* and which, before the scene of justice, *justice* is something that despite being signposted as an attribution of his person, overcomes all his subjectivity; he who exercises it, does so on behalf of the community to which he is destined, not only before the parties, not as interested in the cause, but as a social investment that reproduces a civilisation discovery and has to do with the measure, balance, peace, order and social regulation.[506] The toga distances the *judge* himself from the *person-judge,* and therefore makes him, by the act of carrying him, what he institutionally has the *duty* and *obligation* of preserving.[507]

---

[501] *Cf.* Ferracini (2013), p. 57.

[502] *See* Garapon (1999), p. 92.

[503] *Cf.* Boleslavski (2015), p. 27.

[504] *Cf.* Garapon (1999), p. 85.

[505] *See* Garapon (1999), p. 88.

[506] *Cf.* Garapon (1999), p. 85.

[507] *Cf.* Garapon (1999), p. 86.

4.4 Semiotics, Law and Literature: The Process and the Legal Decision

The *Semiotics of Art* can be unfolded, also, in a *Semiotics of Literature.* It should become clear, as of now, that the field of the *Semiotics of Literature* is one of the deeper, traditional and well set fields of work of *Semiotic Theory,* with numerous applications and studies, highlighting the very work developed by Algirdas Julien Greimas—and, also, the record contained in the *Dictionnaire,* by Algirdas Julien Greimas and Joseph Courtés—[508] in the comprehension of the *literary narratives,* from the *narrative modelisation* founded in the division between *manipulation, competence, performance* and *sanction*. And, at his time, Algirdas Julien Greimas was very inspired by the conception of Russian theorist of *narratology,* Vladimir Propp,[509] from where it gave rise gradually to *narrative Semiotics*,[510] aimed at the comprehension of *literary texts* and *narrative structures*.[511] And, finally, this was constituted as being the part of *Semiotics* that is concerned with *aesthetic-literary discourse*—the notion of narrative is here considered a central notion for the *Semiotics of Literature*—,[512] understanding the *narrative mesh* of literary texts as what is most closely researched in this area of applied studies.

In this point, the approximation of fields of study is relevant, to the extent that the *Theory of Law* has been using the approximation between *Law and Literature*[513] to exactly count for the practical dimension of the construction of *narratives* in the universe of the *legal process.* And, this approximation between *Law & Literature* is not only made to *affirm* the proximity between *legal text* and *literary text,* but also—and, often, above all—to italicise the *marking differences*[514] that exist between these two diverse fields of aesthetic knowledge (playfulness; openness of meaning; fiction; openness to interpretation; delay of the resolution about the truth) and of legal knowledge (social conflict; decision; closure of processes; certainty and security).[515] For this reason, the differences that they mark the *use* of *aesthetic texts* and the use of

[508] "La sémiotique littéraire (ou, si on la considere comme procès sémiotique, le discours littéraire) est un domaine de recherches dont les limites semblent avoir été établies plus par la tradition que par des critères objectifs, formels" ("Literary semiotics (or, if we consider it a semiotic process, literary discourse) is a field of research whose limits seem to have been established more by tradition than by objective, formal criteria"—*translation*) (Greimas and Courtés 1993, p. 213).

[509] *Cf.* Greimas (1979), p. 11.

[510] *Cf.* Greimas (1979), p. 29.

[511] *Cf.* Greimas (2014), p. 61.

[512] *Cf.* Greimas (1979), p. 19.

[513] *Vide* Vespaziani (2010), pp. 123–137.

[514] *See* Callejón (2016), p. 335.

[515] *Cf.* Callejón (2016), p. 348.

legal texts should be clear, since they exercise discursive functions very differently between them, as, indeed, Bruno Romano emphasises.[516]

And, in fact, it has already been discovered that Law is composed of an *immense mass of texts,* around which the *legal actors* circulate.[517] For this reason, today they are many influential conceptions in the *Theory of Law* that work with the idea that Law is offered to the field of relation between *Law and Literature*. In this point, they can be listed, at least, the conceptions of Paul Ricoeur and Ronald Dworkin, among others.[518] Here, it is worth recalling what they affirm, both the theorists, to start with Ronald Dworkin:

> I would like to compare the development of Law to the preparation of this, we say, romance in chains.[519]

Followed by, Paul Ricoeur:

> In the narrow limits of the process the act of judgement appears as a terminal phase of a drama with various characters: the parties or its representatives, the public ministery, judge, the popular jury, etc..[520]

Therefore, in the same wake of the two authors cited above, one can even list another, that of Spanish jurist Francisco Balague Callejón, who affirms:

> No sólo desde el punto de vista narrativo podemos encontrar similitudes, porque también el Derecho incorpora una faceta escénica que lo aproxima a este tipo de artes, lo que explica la reiterada presencia de la apelación a procedimentos judiciales en el teatro o en el cine.[521]

And, finally, this last one of French theorist, Gérard Cornu, when he applies the linguistic-discursive analysis to Law:

> Sous cette lumière, le tribunal redevient un théâtre et le procès la pièce qui y a été donnée.[522]

And, here, the *Semiotics of Literature* in its relation to the *Semiotics of Law*, can be perceived as a field of curious and relevant intersections exactly there where it comes close to the territory already duly worked by the *theatre of justice*.

---

[516]"Il *giudizio giuridico* riguarda una condotta imputabile. Il *giudizio estetico* concerne una monteplicità di fenomeni, separati ed uniti nelle qualificazioni che presentano il bello" ("The legal opinion concerns an imputable conduct. Aesthetic judgement is about a monteplicity of phenomena, separated and united in the qualifications that present beauty"—*translation*) (Romano 2013, p. 15).

[517]*Vide* da Cunha (2013), p. 209.

[518]*Cf.* Dworkin (1997), pp. 44 71.

[519]*Cf.* Dworkin (1997), pp. 44–71.

[520]*Cf.* Ricoeur (2008a, b), 177.

[521]*Cf.* Callejón (2016), p. 336.

[522]*Cf.* Cornu (1990), p. 356.

4.4.1 Social Interactions, Narrative Gramar and Modern Society

But, a little before that, and this conception is already sufficiently repeated in the field of Law, exploring the relation between *Law and Literature* as a relation between the *literary narratives* and the *situations of justice*—the task more alive and current of *Semiotics*—in a socio-semiotic line—, and the one that can most contribute to the field of the *Semiotics of Law* currently is to do with the recent incursions proposed by the French semioticist Eric Landowski, in the book *Risky interactions* (*Les interacctions risquées*, 2005), offering a semiotic point of view that comes simultaneously close to *Anthropology* and *Linguistics*.[523] Eric Landowski had already progressed the *Semiotics of Law,* where he collaborates with Algirdas Julien Greimas, in the undertaking of the comprehension of the micro-universe of meaning of *Business Law,* in *Semiotics and Social Sciences.*[524] In addition to this, it cannot be ignored that the comprehension developed by Eric Landowski not only part of the Greimasian legacy, but above all is established without dispensing of the important contribution brought especially by the work of Joseph Courtés, foreshadowed by Algirdas Julien Greimas, *Introduction to narrative and discursive semiotics,* dated in 1976.

But, here, in the more recent work, *Risky Interactions,* dated in 2005, the conceptions are already largely more complex and developed. And this because—as José Luiz Fiorin notes well—this work allows a *reading of world of the facts of life in its daily dynamic,* from the vision modelled by semiotics from four *regimes of* (schedule; chance; adjustment; manipulation), offering greater or lesser degrees of risks and expectations,[525] and which, by reaching the existential plane of human interactions, enables the finding of the position of *Semiotics* in addition to the *literary narratives,* to the *narratives of experiences* of human interactions in society. The starting point of the theoretical model is what we are 'condemned to produce meaning'.[526]

Here, what one seeks to describe is a *narrative grammar* of *social interactions,* one that already comes close to the result of these studies of conclusions clearly established in the field of *Sociology* and of *Philosophy*,[527] particularly when they deal with *social interactions* in the context of *modern society.* And, from this model, a field of new, interesting, riveting work is configured, that puts the notion of *subject* in evidence and in the centre of these reflections.[528] And this to affirm that the *modern subject,* in social interaction, is found *programmed* executing given

[523] *Vide* Landowski (2014), p. 11.

[524] *Cf.* Greimas (1981), p. 76.

[525] *Cf.* Fiorin (2009), p. 08.

[526] *Cf.* Landowski (2014), p. 15.

[527] *Cf.* Landowski (2014), p. 14.

[528] *Cf.* Landowski (2014), p. 11.

functions in *society,* in so far as the social division of work, specialisation of knowledge, legal-bureaucratic domination, laicisation and rationalisation of social interactions in the *modern world.* Between *rites, habits* and *uses,* the subjects in the *modern world* are established.[529]

Therefore, the *modern subject* is *given* the differentiated *social role,* and, in this, its *social performance* starts to be described according to a plane of strong social constraints:[530] it is expected that, in the role of *worker,* that the *subject* works; in the role of *public servant,* that it serves the public; in the role of *educator,* that it educates; in the role of *driver,* that it drives. The *social roles* they establish what Eric Landowski calls '*algorithm of behaviour,*[531] notion of that gives *social roles* their respective *degrees of risk* in social interactions established (schedule, zero degree of risk/regularity; chance, high degree of risk, unpredictable/eventuality; manipulation, controllable degree of risk, controllability/intentionality; adjustment, possible degree of risk, sensitivity).[532]

But, the roles are not static, implying *mutual exchange,* which make the *interactions* between the diverse *roles* in society, something *complex* and *risky.* This leads Landowski to not harden the comprehension and work with the idea not of *rigidity of roles,* but with the idea of *ritual regularities* of behaviour,[533] in so far as life is made of things that are expected and predicted and things that are not expected and predicted.[534] After all, the *worker,* can go on *strike*; the *public servant* can *be corrupted*; the *educator* can *give up educating*; the *driver* can cause an *accident.* Therefore, where the *degree of risk* increases or reduces, the effects of the *interactions* become more or less predictable, and, in this sense, more susceptible to receiving—through the *legal security* offered by *legal norms* in its *programmes of predictability* of socially programmed conduct to fall apart—'pre-visions' which are possible and necessary *legal consequences* of its interactions.

4.4.2 Legal Interactions, Process and Legal Discourse

Legal discourse captures the eventuality, predictability, causality of social events, to *dispose them*—as *social units*—towards legal consequences of practised actions, through the use of sanctions (rewarding or punishing). Here, foreseeably, the role of the legal system is of offering conditions to what the *procedural pre-narratives* make *procedural narratives* relatively predictable, from the *continuity* that they are capable of establishing between the *plane of social interactions* and the *plane of*

[529] *Cf.* Landowski (2014), p. 38.
[530] *Cf.* Landowski (2014), p. 24.
[531] *Cf.* Landowski (2014), pp. 22–23.
[532] *Cf.* Landowski (2014), p. 08.
[533] *Cf.* Landowski (2014), p. 28.
[534] *Cf.* Landowski (2014), p. 23.

procedural interactions. Here—to go inside this 'new world' of process—also, it can be said that it is expected that the lawyer *defends,* that the prosecutor *accuses,* that the jury *judges,* that the judge delivers the *legal decision* taken by the process. There is a much established *procedural programme* that confers *full official programming,* but, it is not in itself sufficient to *guarantee* the *certainty of the results,* since numerous variables appear to determine the *demarcation* of a procedural contest, as it searches for *justice* by means of *legality.*[535]

Before they become *parties* (active party or author; passive party or defendant) of a *process,* the subjects are entangled in *social roles,* in the *modern social divisions.* Now, life in society has already turned itself into the occupation of places in the condition of *social actants.* This is how the *social actors* entangle themselves in *pre-procedural narratives.* In wider social contexts, the diverse *narrative plots* bring legal consequences: a crisis of jealousy in a love affair that leads to a crime of passion or a divorce; the manifestation of social hate of class, that is externalised as crime against patrimony; the verbal reaction exalted, that leads to an insult/libel/defamation; the professional negligence, that leads to an accident at work. Once invested in pre-procedural narrative contexts certain social relations end up flowing into *procedural narratives.* It is here that the *social actors* start to occupy *actantial positions,* acting as *actants* and *actors*, in *procedural contexts.*[536]

This is how the *process* does not create its characters, since the conflict already joins them before the moment of *pre-procedural* narrative; the *process* does not create the facts nor the evidence of the facts, they are already given at the moment in which they are made up of the *pre-procedural* narrative; the *process* does not create the legal texts that they target as legal rules, since they already exist and target as valid and current about the facts, conditioning them by *normative programmes* to *legal consequences,* before the *legal judge* who is exercised under the *discussion, interaction* and *jurisdictional observation.*

Already in the process, the *roles* of the *legal actors* are marked by strategic interactions, which observe the logic of the *discursive positions,* taking advantage of the *place-of-discourse* to exercise the *manipulation* of evidence, documents, legal interpretations, legal theses, aiming to reach a *favourable result* of their *discursive position.* The *discursive regime* is here appropriately that of *manipulation*—something characteristic of *free and democratic interactions,* since they presuppose subjects free

[535]"*La ragione dell'ativitá del giudice non consiste nella funzionalità autoreferenziale delle operazioni processuali, né nel porre fine, qualsiasi sia la condizione, ad una situazione di conflittualità.* Si afferma così che *il processo è uno strumento istituito per garantire la ricerca della giustizia nella legalità,* non è la celebrazione di una *legalità* ostentata con indifferenza contro il desiderio universale di *giustizia*" ("The reason for the judge's activity does not consist in the self-referential functionality of procedural operations, nor in putting an end, whatever the condition, to a situation of conflict. It is thus affirmed that the trial is an instrument established to guarantee the search for justice in legality, it is not the celebration of a legality ostentatious with indifference against the universal desire for justice"—*translation*) (Romano 2013, p. 26).

[536]*Cf.* Nöth (2005), p. 158.

and capable of inducing each other by means of *do-do*—[537] where the seduction and inducement to results govern all *logic of the process,* in a controllable degree of risks, in which the *legal decision* is the *disputed object,* of whose outcome there is a relative degree of certainty in dispute, being relevant the *intention*[538] of the actors (win the dispute; conciliate the issue; avenge the opponent; defer the process; obtain pecuniary damages; defraud justice; be free from the application of sanctions; mislead the judge).[539] Therefore, the *discursive interactions* in the process are not spontaneous—they are without a doubt *risky,* since they already start from the presupposition of social and communicative ruptures previously established among the parties of the process (*social actors*)—, but based on *strategic reasons of acting,* precisely because they are considered equally rational subjects, adopted from the possibility of them exerting the *want* and the *do* that have consequences about the *sphere of the subject* interested.

While they inhabit the social world, *social actors* are part of the phenomena and conflicts that elapse in society, and there they act more or less within the beliefs, habits, memories, institutional forces, professional pressures, uses and customs.[540] But, going into the process, the *social actors* were already converted into *legal actors,* by means of procedural representation, here constituting the characteristics of this new sphere—now that of *procedural narrative*—measured by representatives, by means of *legal language,* exerting procedural roles, through the *symbolisation* of conflict. When the process reinstalls the conflict to the *symbolic level* it places an intense *textual load* of *verbal* and *nonverbal signs*, knowing that the *legal and non-legal texts* in circulation clash, contradict themselves, dispute versions of the facts, in the *heuristic* and the typical *polarity* of the *theatre of justice.*

Therefore, it is here that the *argumentation* is exercised—as art of convincing/persuasion—, knowing that it is a difficult and delicate exercise,[541] and is not marked by the *simple* rational capacity of discursive interaction, since the intentions can be *addicted, distorted, occult,* and, in this sense, where words and discursive relations are established, a complex tangle of *procedural positions, interactional expectations, possible outcomes* enter in relation of connection and/or disconnection. The Other (judge; prosecutor; lawyer; defendant; jury) with whom it *inter-acts* has two characteristics: (1) firstly, it does not act directly in front of the Other, but, *inter-acts* through texts, through the *relationship* by oblique or indirect way it does it;[542] (2) secondly, it is a subject, adopted by will, freedom, understanding, vision of world and values, and this complex plot, the *programmatic* and *mechanical predictability* is not applicable.[543] For this reason, the *Theory of Law* has been constantly turning to

[537] *Cf.* Landowski (2014), p. 32.
[538] *Cf.* Landowski (2014), p. 26.
[539] *Cf.* Landowski (2014), p. 25.
[540] *Cf.* Landowski (2014), p. 40.
[541] *Cf.* Landowski (2014), p. 29.
[542] *Cf.* Landowski (2014), p. 28.
[543] *Cf.* Landowski (2014), p. 29.

the *Theory of Argumentation* to explain the *way* the legal process is *structured,* but still without the capability of *affirming* how the procedural result can be produced, given the *relative degree of certainty* obtained in the procedural demarcations. At least, there are always *two* options of procedural demarcation, held as hypotheses of the legal decision rational and based, on deferral (total; partial) and on rejection of the cause.

4.4.3 Legal Interactions, Process and Narrative Programme

This allows us, from the semiotic point of view, to see the *legal process* as a *narrative programme,*[544] full of opportunities of speech, acting and resources, through which, formally, the arena of legalised conflict is constituted, so that there are represented the procedural steps, towards the *legal decision* and, thus, to the outcome of the *procedural narrative.* Throughout the process, the *legal actors* strive to *translate* from the text of the law and of the factual situation, to the *legal language of the proceedings*, what is in fact relevant to the outcome of the process towards the *legal decision.*[545] And, to arrive at the outcome of the *procedural narrative*—the *legal decision*—the judge acts as a mediator between the *legal text* and the public, between the *legal text* and the other *legal actors*.[546]

In the process, the *narrative programmes* (PN1; PN2; PNjudge; PNbureaucrat),[547] intersect each other, coordinated by rights and duties of *discursive actants,*[548] foreseen by *procedural legal norms,* that pre-define the steps, procedures, opportunities of speech, limits of acting.[549] And, there, in the narrative plot, the subjects (S1, S2, Sn), through their *performances,*[550] can be in a relation of conjunction (∨) with the *object-of-desire* and of disjunction (∧) with the *object-of-desire.* If the *object* is the *condemnation* of the *defendant,* the *actantial scheme* can be obtained according to which the *defence* (S1) is found in *disjunction* (∧) with the *object* and the accusation (S2) is found in *conjunction* (∨) with the *object,* in the following form:

$$\mathbf{S1 \wedge O \vee S2}$$

[544] *Cf.* Landowski (2014), pp. 22–23.
[545] *Cf.* Ferracini (2013), p. 50.
[546] *Vide* Flückiger (2001), p. 04.
[547] *Vide* Greimas (1979), p. 20.
[548] *Cf.* Nöth (2005), p. 149.
[549] *Cf.* Bittar (2015), p. 312.
[550] *Cf.* Greimas (1979), p. 23.

Or, the function of behaviour of a determined subject (S1, S2, Sn), as *Narrative Programme*, is to provoke the *state-of-things,* such that the other subject (S_2) does not obtain the *object-of-value,* in the following form:

$$\mathbf{S1 \wedge O \rightarrow S2 \vee O}$$

Or, even, the *narrative structure* can be found in a more complex form,[551] in which the *Function* (F) of each one is described in a way of manifesting what S1 intends that S2 does not obtain the condemnation of the defendant:

$$\text{F transf.}[\ \mathbf{S1} \rightarrow (\mathbf{S2} \wedge \mathbf{O})\ ]$$

Or, the contrary:

$$\text{F transf.}[\ \mathbf{S2} \rightarrow (\mathbf{S1} \vee \mathbf{O})\ ]$$

But, predictability is something that cannot be guaranteed, neither on the plane of *procedural narrativity,* nor on the *plane of semiotic narrativity.* And this finding, in the *Semiotic* respect, for this reason, does not consider the *pre-procedural interactions* and/or the *procedural interactions* subject to a pure relation of *causality,* but the fleeting, fickle, interchangeable and complex relations.[552] Therefore, the *legal interactions* leave a margin for a degree of unpredictability, and the roles can be permuted, the relations can be rechanged and the outcomes can be multiplied, even though, they cannot, in any way, alter the *programmed* and *technocratic urgency*[553] with which the mandatory outcome of the process given in the form of a *terminative decision*, even if *social conflict* has not been concluded, resolved, exhausted or overcome.

4.4.4 Legal Interactions, Process and Legal Decision

In the narrative structure of the tale, obtaining the love of the *princess* can be the *object-of-value* of the *hero* of the narrative plot, in its fictional structure.[554] In the narrative structure of the detective novel, the attainment of *prison* of the criminal can be the *object-of-value* of the whole narrative plot, in its more realistic literary structure than fictional. Now, from the point of view of the structure of the legal process, the *procedural narrative plot* involves previously qualified *legal actors,* it

[551] *Cf.* Greimas (1979), p. 20.
[552] *Cf.* Landowski (2014), pp. 33–34.
[553] *Cf.* Landowski (2014), p. 32.
[554] *Cf.* Nöth (2005), p. 157.

does not matter what they say or how they express themselves, on the *surface* of *discursive use.*

The opportunities of speech are demarcated, the terms are defined, the procedural plays are predetermined forms, and the procedural steps take care of leading all the legal actors to a terminative point about the *doubts,* vagueness, uncertainties and expectations, which rule in the initial state (Ei) of the legal case, which must find its outcome, its final term, in a final state (Ef), by means of legal sentence passed in judgement. This is the role of the *legal decision,* which is, to establish the *resolution* of social conflicts, offering *public security,* at the same time in which, in procedural conditions, it establishes the best forms to come close to the best result of justice desired by the parties.

For this reason, it can be said here, that the *legal decision* is the *object-of-value* (O)[555] to be obtained by arts, as *legal actors vested in actantial roles* (S1; S2; Sjudge), through the *performatic* exercise of their *narrative paths* (PN1; PN2; PNjudge). The *legal decision* is the *object-of-desire* of *legal actors*—as those who await a favourable jurisdictional provision to its *place-of-discourse*—that makes them involved in the *legal plot.* Indeed, it is by *wishing* the *final object* of jurisdictional provision—the terminative *legal decision*—, from which socially relevant *results* travel (divorce is authorised; the employment relationship is recognised; provision of pecuniary indemnity is given; a criminal is condemned; the child is distanced from danger; access of a service of health for a terminally ill patient is conferred)—that they are *vested* in their *roles* as *legal actants,* and the gain the condition of subjects; subject is something that refers to an *object.*[556]

4.4.5 Legal Interactions, Legal Decision and Semiotic Node

Before the *object-of-desire*—the *legal decision,* the synthesis of the act of judging, according to Paul Ricoeur—[557] and the narratives of the parties, dealing with the current legislation, responding to contextual pressures, having the task of engaging with an enormity of legal texts, documents, evidence, procedural acts, prior decisions, the procedural rite requires that the *legal decision* turns into a true *meeting-point* of various texts. Therefore, the *inter-textuality* is the standard of definition and outline of the *legal decision.* Therefore, the legal decision is far from being a *soliloquy* of the judge, or even, a *logical-deductive* process of abstract law to the concrete case. In the *legal decision*, at the end of the *ritual of justice*, forms the whole *complex plot* of *texts* formed along the procedural verification, petition of the parties, production of evidence and attempt to reach the *truth* for justice. In this point, it is worth remembering the affirmation of French sociologist Antoine Garapon:

[555] *Cf.* Greimas (1979), p. 16.
[556] *Cf.* Greimas (1979), p. 18.
[557] *See* Ricoeur (2008a, b), p. 175.

> It is then essential to think the final decision as the product of a multitude of small decisions taken by various actors who are not, indeed, all judges nor even jurists.[558]

Therefore, from the semiotic point of view, a model of *narrative grammar* of the process provides conditions to evaluate the profile of *legal-procedural interaction*, despite being able to be described by the means and ways of *semiotic narrativity*, does not comply in any way to the equivalence between the *process* and situations of *mathematical programming of zero risk.*[559] It is so that the *legal decision* involves a relative degree of predictability—within the chances of hypotheses that increase or decrease each procedural communicative *input*—, but never a degree of *absolute predictability* that would reduce the *terminative legal decision* to a *robotic act,* whose content could be *foreseen*, in the sense of being defined and contained, or in the *descriptivity of the legal rule* or in the *attitude with which the judge could lead the process*. The *legal decision* is not, for this reason, a *mechanical decision*, but *semiotic resulting* from the processes of semiotic *inter-textual* operations within the *process*, to keep alive the idea of François Rastier.[560] But even, the legal decision is not capable of revealing an *absolute truth*, but only a *legal truth*—circumscribed by the procedural conditions—, in the same way that aesthetics is not capable of leading to *absolute beauty,* but indeed to *relative beauty.*[561] Here, again, the difference between Law and Aesthetics, is, also, between Law and Literature. Indeed, literature can be open to the *infinite search* of truth, while Law seeks *legal security* and delivers *decisions* that come close to the maximum possibilities of the *just.*[562] The *legal truth* is the *formal truth.*[563]

Now this leads to the conception according to which the *legal decision* is not created *ex nihilo,* it is unfolded from the set of textual matches and mismatches held inside the process seen as *judiciary arena*; the lack of evidence can be so decisive, in terms of the indisputability of a legal thesis. The *legal decision* is therefore a *semiotic-node* in so far as it sees the various influxes of narrative strategies of the parties in a *text-legal-synthesis,* which should be included representative of the capability of taking into consideration all the arguments, all the allegations, all the evidence gathered over the *procedural narrative.* In a reflection contained in a previous study, this idea of which the *legal decision* is constituted as a *semiotic-node* can be effectively highlighted.[564] Here, it is reaffirmed that neither being *subjective invention* (subjectivity of the judge actor), nor *programmed deduction*

---

[558] *Cf.* Garapon (1998), p. 171.

[559] *See* Romano (2013), p. 84.

[560] "Touté séquence textuelle, tout signe même, est suceptible de deux types de fonctionnement: intratextuel et intertextuel (ou plus généralement, et exactement, intersémiotique)" ("Any textual sequence, even any sign, is susceptible to two types of functioning: intratextual and intertextual... or more generally and accurately, intersemiotic"—*translation*) (Rastier 1989, p. 30).

[561] *Cf.* Romano (2013), p. 47.

[562] *Cf.* Callejón (2016), p. 350.

[563] *Cf.* Callejón (2016), p. 351.

[564] *Vide* Bittar (2018), p. 492.

(normative objectivity), the *legal decision* is indeed the *result* of each *inter-semiotic* movement promoted during the *procedural steps* by the *actants* of the procedural game. They sign up for the order of things that are found, in larger or smaller doses to each case, between *subjective* and *objective*,[565] one cannot remove one face, or the other face, from the process of production of the legal decision.

The *legal reasoning*—to deal with *verbal, nonverbal* and *syncretic* signs—[566] here is to do with the task of operating with *texts,* of disputing visions and interpretations open around *normative text*,[567] dealing with the short-circuit provoked between the same ones, moving in a complex semiotic labyrinth that results in the legal decision. The *legal decision* is neither the portrait of willingness of the judge, nor same as the willingness of the legislator, but of what the *intra-textual confluence* made possible over the process, considering the set of *textual conditionings*—internal to the process and external to the process—[568] incidents about the concrete case, between them, the negative attitude of the defendant by speaking up about the facts, the state of art of *jurisprudence* (the art of deciding) in the material, the validity of the accrued legal rules, the precarity of the evidence produced in the files of the process, the clues left at the scene of the crime, the legal theses sustained by the prosecutor and by the defence, the pressure of media and public opinion about the case.

In truth, the decision gains 'form' and can be 'expressed' by *written verbal signs* by the judge, in the way of *legal text*—programmed by an actantial attribution as part of the *institutional role* of the judge—, but it is not solitarily constructed by the *complex plot*[569] formed between the actors of the *theatre of justice*. For this reason, the *legal decision* is neither a portrait of the willingness of the judge, and nor the same of the willingness of the legislator, but of what the *intra-textual confluence* made possible over the process.

[565] *See* Cananzi (2013), pp. 56–57.

[566] *Cf.* Fontanille (2015a, b), p. 35.

[567] *Cf.* González (2011), p. 18.

[568] "L'*entour* (ou contexto non linguistique, au sens large) englobe le texte, l'émetteur et le récepteur. Il contient les interprétants nécessaires à l'actualisation de contenus du text" ("Surrounding (or non-linguistic context, in the broadest sense) encompasses the text, the sender and the receiver. It contains the interpreters necessary to update the contents of the text"—*translation*) (Rastier 1989, pp. 50–51).

[569] *Cf.* Bittar (2015), pp. 327–328.

4.5 Semiotics, Law and Education: The Human Rights Education

4.5.1 The Culture of Human Rights

The term *culture* (*colere,* lat.) here, given the complexity that it surrounds, is used to signify the set of practices, attitudes, ways of life, exercise of conscience, which organise the way of living in common. In the words of Terry Eagleton, the terms are declared as being "...the complex of values, customs, beliefs and practices that make up the way of life of a specific group".[570] To the dismay that it provokes, and the ambiguity that it shelters, in any case, it can be said that the *place of symbolic* is the *place of culture.* Therefore, the term culture, full of meanings, here can be taken as a system of signs, in the view of Umberto Eco,[571] or as that *backdrop,* to which Herbert Marcuse refers, to design what is structured in society in its practices.[572]

As one notices, the term *culture* is a term disputed of its significance, being a neighbour of the term *civilisation,*[573] and for this reason precisely, falling into the term *barbarism,* which allows Theodor Adorno and Max Horkheimer to affirm the existence of an *aesthetic barbarism* in the modern world.[574] Furthermore, it is known, by Walter Benjamin's analysis, that 'all document of culture is also a document of barbarism'. And it is the essay of 1940, *About the concept of history,* that one reads: "There was never a monument of culture that was not also a monument of barbarism. And therefore as culture is not exempt form barbarism, neither is the process of transmission of culture".[575] Therefore, culture may carry barbarism, and be crossed by it, constituting a field of approximation between what is called *civilisation* and what is called *barbarism.*[576]

The arts are seen only as a *micro-cosmos* in the wide field of culture, but even so, a complex and multiple micro-cosmos is sufficient to bring contributions of reflection about the theme of justice, citizenship and rights. And it is the plane of culture that parades classes it of as *beautiful* and *ugly*, and it is well-known how much beauty is a *social good* valued by humanity since forever. It was always the aim of desire, evocation, speculation, contemplation, inspiration, love, worship, and even, of theory. And this for all civilisations and cultures, in its diverse forms, and by its diverse approaches, patterns and comprehensions. Here, the *beautiful* and the *ugly* are always antagonised, creating fields of *social significance* also the most diverse, to the extent that the *ugly* already set itself up as a *bad*, *dirty*, *grotesque*, *hateful*, *poor*,

[570] *Cf.* Eagleton (2005), p. 54.
[571] *Cf.* Eco (1990), p. 169.
[572] *Vide* Marcuse (1998), p. 69.
[573] *Vide* Elias (1994), p. 23.
[574] *Cf.* Adorno and Horkheimer (2006), p. 22.
[575] *Cf.* Benjamin (1996a, b, c, d), p. 225.
[576] *Vide* Elias (1994), p. 62.

excluded, *abnormal*, *distorted*, *morally non-compliant* place, and, for this reason, generally associated to the field of standards of beauty and ugliness, from which they derive moral, cultural, political and social attitudes that define the patterns of behaviour in face of the socially accepted *beauty* and the socially rejected *ugliness.* The example of which Umberto Eco affirms, in his famous study *History of ugliness,* at the time of the war, the *other-enemy* of war is plentifully represented as the *ugly,* the *monstrous*, the *abject.*[577] It is in this line that one notices, clearly, that the standard of beauty prevailing, certainly, influenced the standard of *moral demand,* which, in turn, contaminates the *standard of justice* prevailing.

This perception directly strikes the correlation between *Theory of Law* and *Aesthetic Theory,* connected by very moderate and subtle points of contact. And this because this question very closely touches the *philosophical dimension* of the *concept of culture* and the *anthropological dimension* of the *practices of culture*, showing henceforth the fact that *law* and *culture*—and, jointly the right to culture—closely touch social and relative human nuances to the culture of human rights. Here, in this perspective of cross-border work, acting on the challenging and complex threshold of the neighbouring fields between human sciences, law, anthropology, philosophy and the arts, one notices that *culture* is a *symbolic field* where they exhibit *disputes,* but in any case, an important field of construction as a field of work in human rights. The creation of a *culture of human rights*, that is partly facilitated by the exercise of the very right to culture, is understood as a set of efforts around practices, knowledge, affects and sensitivities in human rights, that is, on its own, an imperative for contemporary democracies.

This *culture of human rights* should be exercised as part of constitutional, fundamental and social law, of importance for the formation of the human being, in face of the simple challenge of *individuation* and *socialisation.* Its potency is in the fact of being a right for other rights, since it operates at the level of conscience and at the level of practices. It installs a field of tensions, at the border between culture as tradition/conservation and culture as transformation/change. And this because every form of culture crosses us, makes us, defines us and pervades us, at conscious and unconscious levels, and there is the awakening of the active role of *right to culture* as constitutive of proper cultures, and, more than this, as a *meeting-point* and of *convergence* of several other rights, such as: the right to the city; the freedom of thought; the right to education; the right to reunion; the right to recognition; the right to inclusion; the right to freedom of expression; the right to communication. And, through the culture of citizenship and rights, one wants to face: the culture of consumerism; the culture of the trivialisation of violence; the culture of negligence; the culture of exclusion, the culture of reification; the culture of indifference to justice; the culture of trans-lesbo-homo-phobia; the culture of xenophobia; the culture of the legitimisation of social segregation.

[577] *See* Eco (2007), p. 190.

4.5.2 *The Pedagogy of Sensitivity in the Human Rights Education*

The *look of human rights*, so that it is possible, can and should be connected to the *artistic look,* even though it is by the link of strangeness.[578] What is called the *look of human rights* is that way of seeing the world that is forged on the basis of the comprehension of *alterity*.[579] Consequently, the strength of education in the process of constitution of the *look at human rights,* or the *look at reality with the eyes of human rights.* In education, the views of the world are transformed,[580] the conceptions, wisdom, feelings, values, concepts, in a way that there is none more significative than an education by art for the *self-knowledge* and the *knowledge-of-other*.[581]

It is certain that the relation between education and art, between education and moral, and between art and moral, was not always peaceful,[582] but an important path for the development of look of human rights can be indicated in *art-education*. Art itself is already loaded with meaning, and, here, it can unite the broad *symbolic power*[583] to the broad semantic load contained in *human rights.* For this reason, it competes with the idea of a general, broad, pluralist, critical and humanist formation, which necessarily involves the dimension of *artistic experiences,* and, this formation is a somewhat better and more qualified, the bigger spectrum of *artistic experiences* and *fans of opening* in genres, modalities and fields of art can be encompassed.

The aesthetic experience allows us to access dimensions, to know, to do, to value actions, to see characteristics, to notice reality in a more subtle, full, original and refined way, taking us to the dimension of the spirit.[584] In no better words, Hermann can affirm that: "It is in the aesthetic state that man reaches it plenitude, and we should introduce beauty and art in all dimensions of our life to raise us to the moral state".[585] Education that wishes to be *ethical,*[586] also, must be *aesthetic,* so *sensitive* and *humanising.* A purified education in the universe of general, universal and abstract concepts draw us away from local and specific daily life, able to contribute to the processes of dehumanisation; hence the importance of the role of *art-education,* and, hence, the importance of the association of *art-education* with the *human rights education.*[587]

---

[578] *Cf.* Hermann (2005), p. 106.

[579] *Cf.* Hermann (2005), p. 103.

[580] *Cf.* Hermann (2005), p. 40.

[581] *Cf.* Hermann (2005), p. 62.

[582] *Vide* Lacoste (1986), p. 16.

[583] *Cf.* Smith (2013), p. 134.

[584] *Cf.* Smith (2013), p. 140.

[585] *Cf.* Hermann (2005), p. 69.

[586] *Cf.* Perissé (2004), p. 171.

[587] *Cf.* de Oliveira (2014), pp. 501–502.

The example of the power of poetry, it can be underlined that "Poetry is to fly off wing", according to what Manoel de Barros affirms, in the *Book of Ignorances* (*Livro das Ignorãças*) (1st. Part, A didactic of Invention, XIV).[588]

And, even, in *Charles Baudelaire: a lyric at the peak of capitalism*, affirms Walter Benjamin:

> The poets encounter the trash of society of the streets and in the very trash its heroic subject.[589]

From this philosophical provocation, a good debate is possible about the theme *collectors,* considering the poem *Man-traction*, by Dalila Teles Veras,[590] where one can read:

they collect
    (cans, boxes, glass, paper)
    miserable share
    in the consumerist latifundium
    brancaleonic figures
    they collect and carry
    (penalties – brutal load)
    they carry and walk
    they walk and unload
    (they them, discards)
    less-value
    not storable
    restricted feed at the time
    unsure and present

The elocutive strength of the poem *says it all radically,* when the material is to emphasise the *non-citizenship* of the reality of the legions of collectors spread throughout all the parts, and who survive the *remains* of "consumerist civilisation". In the same tune, one can read in "*Objects*", of authorship of Donizete Galvão:[591]

Now,
    men are things,
    hanging accessories
    like chickens in the economy,
    through the markets,
    with heads down
    in wait of buyers.
    Now,
    goods have a life of their own
    Knick-knacks wriggle
    in front of men-things
    who continue
    with feet tied

[588] *Cf.* Barros (2010), p. 302.
[589] *Cf.* Benjamin (2000a, b), p. 78.
[590] *Cf.* Veras (2010), p. 132, *translated.*
[591] *Cf.* Galvão (2009), p. 69, *translated.*

and greedy beaks

That is why an *human rights education* has a fertile perspective of affirming 'values of conviviality' and placing questions of 'social relationship', valuing 'forms of socialisation' of the partners of law steering looks, feelings, experiences and approximations *I-other* through paths of *aesthetics*,[592] strengthening us in our autonomy (intellectual, cultural, moral and sensitive).[593]

For this reason, the purpose of a *human rights education* through *languages of arts* is of fundamental importance for the wide dissemination of contents that directly have the capability of signifying a point of view of the citizenship, diversity and recognition of alterity. In the poem of Costa Senna, in his *Cordel Poem* entitled *Ethnicity*, in the last two verses, one can read:

There is half-cast, mamluk,
There is caboclo, sarará.
Our nation is eclectic
In customs, in thinking.
Try to act correctly,
You are part of this crowd
Which you should not despise.
From blacks, whites and Indians
Come our ethnicities.
And we all have the right
To the same sovereignty.
In the place of prejudice
Look to find a way
To exert citizenship.[594]

The also well-known poem by Thiago de Mello, entitled *The Statues of man: permanent institutional act*, is precisely explicit in respect to human rights:[595]

Article I
It is decreed now that the truth counts,
that now life counts,
and hand in hand,
we will all walk for a life that is true.
Article II
It is decreed that every day of the week,
including the greyest Tuesdays,
has the right to become Sunday mornings.
Article III
It is decreed that, from this moment now on,
there will be sunflowers in every window,
that the sunflowers will have the right
to open up in the shade;
and that the windows should stay, the whole day,

[592] *Cf.* Gorsdorf (2014), p. 65.
[593] *Cf.* Hermann (2005), p. 47.
[594] *Cf.* Senna (2012), pp. 19–20, *translated.*
[595] *Cf.* Gorsdorf (2014), p. 61, *translated.*

open to the green where hope grows.
Article IV
It is decreed that man
will never need
to doubt man.
That man will trust in man
like the palm tree trusts the wind,
like the wind trust the air,
like the air trusts the blue field of the sky.
Single paragraph:
Man, will trust in man
like a child trusts another child.
Article V
It is decreed that men
are free from the yoke of lies.
Never more need to use
the shield of silence
nor the armour of words.
Man will sit at the table
with a clean glance
because the truth will be served
before dessert.
Article VI
It is established, over ten centuries,
the practice dreamt by prophet Isaiah,
and the wolf and the sheep graze together
and the food of both shall have the same taste of aurora.
Article VII
By irrevocable decree it is established
the permanent reign of justice and clarity,
and happiness will be a generous flag
forever hoisted in the soul of the people.
Article VIII
It is decreed that the greatest pain
always was and will always be
to not be able to give love to the loved one
and to know that the water
that gives the plant the miracle of flower.
Article IX
It is permitted that the daily bread
has the mark of man's sweat.
But that above all it has
always the hot flavour of tenderness.
Article X
It is permitted that any person,
at any time of life,
dresses in white.
Article XI
It is decreed, by definition,
that man is an animal who loves
and because of this it is beautiful,
much more beautiful than the star in the morning.

Article XII
It is decreed that nothing imposed
nor prohibited,
all shall be permitted,
including playing with rhinoceros
and walking in the afternoons
with a huge begonia in the lapel.
Single paragraph:
Only one thing is forbidden:
love without love.
Article XIII
It is decreed that money
will no longer be able to buy
the morning sun to come.
Expelled from the great chest of fear,
money will transform into a fraternal sword
to defend the right to sing
the party of the day that arrived.
Final Article.
It is prohibited to use the word freedom,
to which it will be abolished from dictionaries
and from the deceitful swamp of mouths.
From this very moment
freedom will be something alive and transparent
like a fire or a river,
and its abode will always be
the heart of man.[596]

Therefore, the artist can 'speak' of human rights, and it is to this extent that this 'speech' is significant, and, often, more effective in the capacity of creating awareness, it can be mobilised as *aesthetic pedagogy of human rights.* For the field of citizenship, the arts can find enormous value, as far as *they signify, they iconify, they represent.* The multiform, multidimensional and plural reality, is difficult to capture, in its totality, but the fragments of reality captured by the lens of a photographer, by the *sprays* of streets artists, they confer new meaning to other looks than those of the artist himself, this leads to his ability to *communicate,* which reveals any strategy of work in *Human Rights Education.*

4.5.3 Political Art and Politics of Art

When the subject is the politics of art, the pressure for which the work of art carries to be engaged, or even, active from the political point of view, is enormous. For this reason precisely, the work of art, for it to be free, and express freedom, not 'have to', but simple 'can', *raising awareness* of *injustice*, *suffering*, *misery* and *exploits* experienced in the human condition. This is, clearly, the definition of *political art*,

[596] *See* http://www.dhnet.org.br/desejos/textos/thmelo.htm, Accessed 11.05.2020.

just as affirmed by Jacques Rancière.[597] Consequently, political meaning is a political option of the very freedom of the artist. In *The aesthetic dimension*, Herbert Marcuse states that: "Art cannot change the world, but it can contribute to the change of the conscience and impulses of men and women, who can change the world. The movement of the sixties lead to a radical transformation of subjectivity and nature, sensitivity, imagination and reason. It opened a new vision of things, it allowed a superstructure to enter at the base".[598]

And it is in this condition that sensitivity takes on political meaning, to reveal that the place of *sensitivity* is in *public space*,[599] and not attached and constrained to the *particular sphere.* The practical and effective practice of *sensitive reason* to address *intolerance*, *violence*, *truculence*, *perversity*, *irrationality*, *oppression*, *brutality*, *barbarism* and *barbarity* of daily life is necessary. This signifies something, which is, that art *can have the freedom of engaging itself,* but it signifies something else, also, which is, that the effectiveness of art may not have reach;[600] the science of these two faces makes, in the opinion of Jacques Rancière, that art can be identified with criticism.[601]

Even so, engaged art, or even, socially emphasised art—the example of the oil painting of 1933, entitled *Workers,* of the authorship of Tarsila do Amaral, in her modernist phase, who portrays 51 faces of workers in industry—,[602] should be taken as an experience of importance, especially for contemporary aesthetics, with the multiplicity of its channels, techniques, instruments and means of expression, before the power of talking about issues that reach the *abuse of power*, *social oppression*, *violence* and *injustice*. It is for finding in cordelism the means to affirm something about violence that the poet and artist Costa Senna, in his *Cordel Poem* entitled "Violence", in the last two verses, expresses:

The violence between us
Only helps to kill us.
Since it is at school
On the street, at home and at the bar.
The violence is such
And its consequences
Stop us from loving.
Psychological violence,
In adult and infant,
Scores of violence
Of hostile behaviour
Stop, stop a moment

[597] *Cf.* Rancière (2014), p. 52.
[598] *Cf.* Marcuse (2007), p. 36.
[599] *Cf.* Gorsdorf (2014), p. 58.
[600] *Cf.* Rancière (2014), p. 53.
[601] *Cf.* Rancière (2014), p. 81.
[602] *Vide* Zaccara (2016), p. 86.

Since the discovery
They eat away Brazil.[603]

Therefore, *political art* brings with itself the possibility of utopias, since it is critical of the reality of things, which makes other horizons, of other practices, of other forms of social interaction possible. The *artistic denial* is already, for this reason, the affirmation of something else, of this utopian moment,[604] which suspends us, launching us into possibilities of meaning.

4.5.4 Art, Photography and Image

Photography represented a disturbing revolution in the field of arts in general, and, especially, of visual arts.[605] For no other reason, it received several treatments, from *abomination*[606] the *iconisation* as a new avant-garde form of art, decisively influencing new fronts of exploration of the languages of arts,[607] it was responsible for the weight of *death of painting*,[608] and for the *de-sacralisation* of the human effigy. Either by content, or by technique and by the form of capturing of images, photography was able to make stable images from the use of technical apparatus, which, definitively, substituted the mediation of painting and drawing.[609] The example of the photograph by Sebastião Salgado, of *Genesis,* as revealer of the look attentive for what is unique in nature and culture, the photograph is capable of portraying the world for moments of capture, through the objective, dark room and lens.[610]

Consequently, especially, from 1888, its wide spread, and its easy access to people.[611] In this historical perspective, it is Walter Benjamin, especially in *The work of art in the era of its technical reproducibility*, who dedicated himself to understand the historical passage that is operating through photography,[612] for this reason, his attention to the theme is only specific. From the point of view of his object, *misery* and *violence* are now seen, as art, and art should be shown, since it is beautiful.[613] From the point of view of contact with reality, the control of the photographer is not absolute, due to the unconscious acts, regardless of its desire.[614]

---

[603] *Cf.* Senna (2012), pp. 21–22, *translated.*
[604] *Cf.* Hermann (2005), p. 39.
[605] *Cf.* Dondis (2007), p. 213.
[606] *Cf.* Rancière (2014), 104.
[607] *Cf.* Pignatari (1995), p. 35.
[608] *Cf.* Pignatari (1987), p. 23.
[609] *Cf.* Dondis (2007), p. 131.
[610] *Vide* Salgado (2014), pp. 09–14.
[611] *Cf.* Martins (2017), p. 52.
[612] *Vide* Benjamin (1996a, b, c, d), p. 174.
[613] *Vide* Benjamin (1996a, b, c, d), pp. 128–129.
[614] *Vide* Benjamin (1996a, b, c, d), p. 94.

But if seen in the perspective of its actuality, over a century of transformations and technical improvements, nowadays the photographic machine has been converted into a widely spread instrument, as far as common mobile phones now have coupled powerful camera lens, in a way that photography is part of the constitutive *modus* of interactions in social networks centred in *images,* and the spread of *self-image* captured by the *selfie* is the portrait of contemporary individualism. Here, the proximity between *sign* and *society* is clear, in the mediation that signs exert between *man* and *world.*[615] Including, in the perspective of the *Sociology of photography*, the *image* is today as much subject as object of contemporary society, and, thus, in this sense, product and producer of the conditions of interaction and socialisation in the contemporary world.[616]

4.5.4.1 Art, Photography and Human Rights

In any case, photography has great sensitive potential, when the theme is of *human rights.* Photography of the *situation of hunger* of migrant populations in refugee camps, photography of the *situation of over crowding of jail inmates,* photography of the *violation of human rights* by means of torture, photography of the *exploitation of human labour,* are only some examples that possess an *elocutive strength* very important for the *formation of human rights,* as far as they *display* the situation of *indignity* to which entire populations are exposed, serving as *photograph-record, photograph-memory, photograph-evidence, photograph-report, photograph-message, photograph-journalism.* Therefore, it cannot be of some form of writing off the value and the potential that the *image* possesses, when the theme is that of *photographic text.*

And, in this sense, the photography of Sebastião Salgado reveals not only the immense technical plight, the immense artistic-aesthetic quality, but equally the mission for the centrality of the *human being* in *photography*, which signifies the tendency to place the inhumane at the centre of the discussion about the paths and destinations of humanity. They are not only passenger clicks, but entire forays and experiences that are exposed in his photographic work,[617] that involve the mission for the production of a true *ethnological iconology.*

Of all his immense work, it can be highlighted, in the theme of work, the famous photograph entitled *Gold mine of Serra Pelada* (Sebastião Salgado, Brazil, 1986),[618] or even, in the theme of hunger, the famous photograph of the child of Mali, being weighed on scales for the dietary calculation (Sebastião Salgado, Mali, 1985), in the theme of refugees, the photograph about the Refugee Camp of Bati, in Ethiopia

[615] *Cf.* Santaella and Nöth (1998), p. 131.

[616] *Cf.* Martins (2017), pp. 22–23.

[617] *Vide* Caujolle (2011).

[618] *Cf.* Salgado (2014), p. 73.

(Sebastião Salgado, Ethiopia, 1984).[619] And the *photographic art* here assumed the militant political and activist position in respect of the human condition.[620] In the deposition of the artist himself, it can be read:

> I love Rwanda. I decided to photograph its workers and its plantations, as well as the beauty of its parks and the atrocities in which they were perpetrated, justly because I love it. And at the time of horror I photographed it with my whole heart. I thought that all should know that. Nobody has the right to protect themselves from the tragedies of its time, because we are all responsible, in a certain way, for what happens in society in which we choose to live.[621]

4.5.4.2 Semiotics, Photography and Human Rights

Among the various forms of *images*—compared to *painting, cinema, digital image*—[622] *photography* is what is placed more on the plane of debate about the *truth*.[623] Consequently, the *semiotic nature* of the *photographic image* is placed in doubt, whether *icon* or *index*. This doubt is not only of interest in a *Semiotics of image*,[624] but also, a constitutive doubt of the studies of *Sociology of Photography*, of *History of Photography* and of *Photo-Journalism*, in so far as it tends to consider that the *photo-document* is the most loyal portrait of sociological, historical and journalistic reality. For no other reason, this discussion is also of interest in the *Semiotics of Law*, to the extent that it discusses the *nature* of *photographic sign*, as *legal-evidence-document*, in the context of legal and judiciary debates, in which the evidence of facts is under discussion. Its alleged capability of *capturing, reducing* the pixels, *translating* a moment in history or of facts in the most loyal way, it performs its artistic and technical mission, something which points to the *truth*. But, it cannot be forgotten, that, in fact, *photographic image*, creates a new world, a new truth.[625]

And it is exactly there that its uniqueness resides; photography is, at the same time, *icon* and *index*, in relation to the *photographed reality*, having, thus, a semiotic nature of *indexical icon*.[626] The *object represented* is certainly contained in the *photographic image*,[627] but the photographic image does not suffice itself in only being *representation of the object*, and indeed, also, creation and aesthetic interference of reality. The photographic image assumes the role of *work of art*, and, is

[619] *See* Caujolle (2011), pp. 22 and 43.
[620] *Cf.* Caujolle (2011).
[621] *Cf.* Salgado (2014), p. 93.
[622] *Cf.* Volli (2015), p. 281.
[623] *Cf.* Volli (2015), p. 280.
[624] *Cf.* Santaella and Nöth (1998), p. 131.
[625] *Vide* Martins (2017), p. 29.
[626] *Cf.* Santaella and Nöth (1998), p. 107.
[627] *Cf.* Santaella and Nöth (1998), p. 148.

subjectivitation of the *objectivity* of reality.[628] And, in this, the conscious and unconscious of the photographer make overall differential appeal, in addition they decisively throw the determination of the quality of the image, the angle, focus, intention, appeal, lighting, artificiality, induction, further treatment of the image, to its application. The photograph is *capture* of the reality, as much as, *distortion* of reality.[629]

It is this that makes photography an *enigma,* as French art critic François Soulages states, in *Aesthetics of Photography,* in as far as it is simultaneously next to the photographer (subject) and next to the photographed (object).[630] It is a remnant of what passed, and that still requires to be worked, interpreted, known, read, associated to other facts, in so far as the totality of the story is always something of the dimension of the *uncapturable,* hence the denial of the nature of *full evidence* to *any photograph,* is however, always of value of remnant of *something about the object photographed.* Finally, photography, in use at the time,[631] introduces the *ambiguity of the image*:

> By being an enigma is what the photograph, as a haiku, asks for a poetic reception and a speech at the same time always necessary and always inadequate. Ambiguity is still much stronger because the photography can always be, in a certain way, the sphere of an enactment, of an installation and of a negotiation. Therefore, in what is richer, photographic art creates works that can only sensitise us and stir us, destabilise us and shake us, and, thus, can only enrich us. Photography is then source of surprise: it makes us think and imagine, dream and see; it can urge us to philosophise; it should invite us to meditation.[632]

It is this position of *photographic image,* as an indexical icon and as remnant, as an enigma and mediation, that it makes of tremendous power for the *nomination* of *sub-citizenship* before *citizenship,* of *indignity* before *dignity,* of *injustice* before *justice,* of *violence* before *non-violence.* For this reason, in the field of the relation between semiotics, art and justice, photography expresses tremendous potential, pointing to the *situation-of-injustice* and to the *reality-of-lack-of-rights,* and in this it is one of the most powerful instruments for the capture of fugitive fragments of the real. It is because of this that the work with justice and citizenship is able to see with such clear characteristics the huge contribution of photography and its sensitive role for the Human Rights Education.[633]

---

[628] *Cf.* Santaella and Nöth (1998), p. 109.

[629] *Vide* Soulages (2010), p. 347.

[630] *Cf.* Soulages (2010), p. 346.

[631] *Cf.* Soulages (2010), p. 347.

[632] *Cf.* Soulages (2010), p. 346.

[633] *Vide* Dietrich and Machado (2017) and Cornelsen et al. (2012).

4.5.5 Art, Short-Film and Image

If the history of photography is recent, and very short, although already plenty and rich, the history of cinema is even more recent, from where it jumped to the history of television,[634] representing nevertheless a small portion of development of the visual human culture.[635] As a sphere of art, one can take cinema as the combination of *image, sound* and *words* (oral or subtitles, or in sign language), which became the main form of *world visual art* in the twentieth century.[636] The nature of cinema, for this reason, became an object of frank discussion, even questioning the artistic structure of cinema (long-film or short-film), whether art or business,[637] especially before the progress and investment obtained by the *cultural industry*. The fact is that, over contemporary history, the seventh art became reason for vast investment, and a great reach of the mass. It is Walter Benjamin, in *The work of art at the time of its technical reproducibility,* who identified the massive love for cinema, stating: "With this, he favoured the demand for cinema, whose value of distraction is fundamentally of tactile order, this is, based on the change of places and angles, which intermittently fools the spectator".[638] The extreme attention demanded by cinema is revealing of the form of art that it constituted: a technical mirror[639] of dangers and imminence of modern society.[640]

Nonetheless the points arising from the *Critical Theory,* cinema became a vehicle of important meaning for contemporary cultural practices. The experience of *cinesofia*, by Luiz Alberto Warat,[641] points to this interesting way of union between thought and art, between philosophy and sensations, critically causing the spaces of pure cognition, opening the dimension of the image, unconscious and transformation of scientific mentalities. As a practice of ethical, humanist and critical knowledge, it has a lot to offer, in the sense of allowing access to other methodologies of knowledge,[642] opening dilated fields to the transformation of the view of the spectator, which is completely engaged by the atmosphere of cinema,[643] especially of what is found acquainted in the domain of the dark room.

---

[634] *Cf.* Pignatari (1995), p. 35.

[635] *Cf.* Dondis (2007), p. 217.

[636] *Cf.* Volli (2015), p. 286.

[637] *Cf.* Adorno and Horkheimer (2006), p. 08.

[638] *Vide* Benjamin (1996a, b, c, d), p. 192.

[639] *Cf.* Benjamin (1996a, b, c, d), p. 174.

[640] *Cf.* Benjamin (1996a, b, c, d), p. 192.

[641] *Vide* Warat (2004a, b), p. 556.

[642] *Vide* Warat (2004a, b), p. 552.

[643] *Cf.* Warat (2004a, b), p. 551.

4.5.5.1 Art, Short-Film and Human Rights

But, while cinema has its importance massively given by famous films of *long-film,* it is to *short-film* we will dedicate our attention, in particular, on account of its capability to dialogue with subjects of human rights,[644] drawing on short spaces of time, of huge pedagogical value for the construction of educational activities.[645] Well beyond the simple debate about the *instrumentalisation of art,* the discussion about *art as a method of teaching* is something that is connected in the form of a *teaching-attitude* of which art is part of the daily life of education, and not something strange or unrelated to it. Above all, before any application, the *vision* of how *art, culture and education* can and should walk together, the vision that appears in *Human Rights Education.*[646]

Here one starts from the conception of what *image* (associated to words and to sounds) is a *carrier of meaning* resource, in a way that enables the reflection, in so far as a door inside the *concept-image,* following the conception by Juli Cabrera.[647] Even though it is considered that the *power of the image* comes following from the *polysemy of the image,*[648] the mediated and formative work, from the *images* cited by short-films has stimulating pedagogical value, once adequately applied to *Human Rights Education*. This is particularly valid to be affirmed, when the subject is of Human Rights, and the challenge is of creating a *Culture of Human Rights*—considered the Latin-American socio-historical reality and, particularly, the situation in Brazil in face of the deprivation of rights—, in a way that nothing becomes more disseminating than the *power of the image in movement,* made up in the form of *filmic narrative,* to awaken a way of reflection that *sensitises, humanises* and allows the *accessible dissemination* of related question in respect to the Other.

4.5.5.2 Semiotics, Short-Film and Human Rights

The language of short-film—produced by cameras of mobile phones, produced by more or less formalised techniques and resources—is a language of cinema. And, the language of cinema is the *heterogeneous language* and *in movement*, in other words, there are lots of visual, textual and audio stimuli contained in *filmic text*, in a way which, from the semiotic point of view, the cinematographic work and makes up the *plane of expression*[649] it should always be considered *syncretic language.*[650] It

[644] *Vide* http://www.iea.usp.br/midiateca/video/videos-2018/. Accessed 11.05.2020.

[645] *See* Entretodos (2013, 2014, 2015).

[646] Arguments discussed and presented at the *9th International Conference on Human Rights Education*—ICHRE, Australia, Nov. 2018.

[647] *Cf.* Cabrera (2006), p. 20.

[648] *Cf.* Santaella and Nöth (1998), p. 53.

[649] *Cf.* Pietroforte (2016), p. 52.

[650] *Vide* Volli (2015), p. 286.

means *syncretic language* is capable of *instigating, stimulating* and *mobilising* meaning, in a way of *sensitising*, *conceptualising*, *naming*, *pointing*, *reporting*, *criticising*, *persuading*, *aestheticizing*, making it possible, to mobilise consciences, perceptions and states of the soul. The language of *filmic text* has power to affect in a very earth-shaking way the impressions that are possessed about something that is taken as an *object* of cinema. Thus it is what the *image* supports, for this reason, in processes of *teaching-learning,* in so far as it is capable of *make-to-see*, *make-to-feel*,[651] and, also, *make-to-think*.

Even more, all *filmic text* produces, from the semiotic point of view, a *narrative* framework, made up on the basis of the relation between actants and objects, allowing with this, the constitution of a narrative programme which is aesthetically developed, with greater or lesser ability and competence, technique and success.[652] Often, this effort of *inter-semiotic* translation that operates, for example, the passage from *literary text* (*verbal signs*) to the *image* (*nonverbal signs*),[653] is an aesthetic effort that creates the distinction of quality between the producers, artists and filmmakers. And this is how the users are involved by the *stories* of the films, and are attracted by the language of art it exerts a *power-to-make-to-feel*—and it is how cinema manages to *super-potentialise* sensations—something that in some way is negligible for the formative processes, especially when the themes are related to the dimension of rights. And this, particularly, because the rights are able to stop being seen as a target of technical and specialised knowledge of the jurists, and be taken as something which is of interest to all citizens. A culture of human rights, indeed, can only be constructed where a wider and more generalised knowledge of the more central rights to guarantee it of dignity of the human being exists, and cinematographic arts can decisively contribute in this sense. Indeed, the constitution of a branch of work and knowledge, in the interface between *Law & Cinema* starts to turn into a productive and interesting spindle, thanks to the efforts of some authors who are highlighted in this field of contemporary investigation.[654]

It is true that, as a montage, the cinematographic work impresses as a *narrative totality of meaning,* but, as with all the other works of art, there are techniques strategies and methodologies for the *disassembly* and analysis of *filmic text*.[655] This task is not the main concern here, but to point out this semiotic possibility. However, what is worth being better analysed is the capability of production of effects that

[651] *Cf.*Cabrera (2006), p. 21.

[652] *Cf.* Fontanille (2015a, b), p. 196.

[653] *Cf.* Plaza (2010), p. 67.

[654] *Vide* de Oliveira (2011), pp. 815–850. *See too* Warat (2004a, b).

[655] *Cf.* Volli (2015), pp. 286–287.

filmic text is able to promote, considering that *syncretic language* has a multi-sensorial nature and a highly appealing and seducing effect of meaning on the user. And this is what enables the understanding of which type of role,—as it appeals to the unconscious of the spectator—the cinematographic image can have to create sensitisation and perception for themes and issues of human rights.

And this as far in which the *image* acts like a *trigger*, like a *stimulus* and like a *motivational fuse,* to awaken the curiosity and interest about the most diverse subjects, issues, dilemmas, conceptions, views and experiences that cross the *everyday life* of *existence of the individual* and the *everyday life of the socio-human co-existence.* Among other reasons, the presence of short-films hugely favours a process of teaching-learning, and it is for this reason, that its association to the field of *human rights education* is so virtuous, since it favours:

1. an approximation of *abstract themes* through *concrete situations* of daily life, in which the audience is identified with characters and actor of short-films;
2. a deconstruction of *universality* of values of human rights, launched in absentia in *contexts of life* in the family, of use of the city, learning environment, etc.;
3. a materialisation of *images* (sounds and words) of philosophical thoughts that *shorten* the task of approximation from public-reader to public-viewer;
4. an impacting relation, *psycho-affective* and *logopathical,*[656] and, thus, not only rational or intellectual that demand pre-requisites often inexistent for the audiences, in the treatment of situations that involve *violations* of human rights;[657]
5. a disturbance of deep *convictions,*[658] through striking images, *intensifiers* of reality, moving and sensitive;[659]
6. a wide accessibility, which enables avoiding the *technical language* of rights, or, *legal language,* to access contents of rights and foster citizenship in a broad way, independent of age, social class, level of education;
7. an invitation to wear the shoes of the other, to understand the diversity of typically human issues, problems and situations, and their dilemmas;[660]
8. a playful and dialogic way of *mediation* of contents of human rights, which interests the most diverse audiences, overcoming restrictions of specialisation, age and other conditions, aimed at a normally very eclectic and varied public.

It is here that once more art proves and demonstrates its *power* and its capability of *stimulus*, acting in this sense as a huge efficiency in the process of teaching-learning. This is one of the many applications and possibilities of the arts. And as an

[656] *Cf.* Cabrera (2006), p. 22.

[657] *Cf.* Cabrera (2006), pp. 23–38.

[658] "Images are sensual and fleshy; they address the labile elements of the self, they speak to the emotions, and they organize the unconscious. They have the power to short-circuit reason and enter the soul without the interpolation or intervention of language or interpretation" (Douzinas and Nead 1999, p. 07).

[659] *Cf.* Cabrera (2006), p. 28.

[660] *Vide* Bittar (2011), p. 135.

open barrier and horizon—including the *ambiguity* of *filmic text* considered—, has uncovered a whole universe of possibilities of work and development when the themes of *social justice*, *sub-citizenship*, *indignity*, *violence*, *socio-economic inequalities*, *forms of oppression*, are placed and exposed on the screens, and the formative processes mobilised. Here, again, as already illustrated in the previous chapter, it is also clear how powerful *short-film* is for the development of a culture of human rights, especially considering the environment of intolerance in which they are often placed. They are the *sensitive forms* that are mobilised to move, in a transforming way, *sensitive affections,* where the question of *human dignity* is at the centre. In this, equally, it can decisively contribute and in a playful way *humanise, sensitise* and *emancipate,* in a way which the effort for its gradual task of consolidation, implementation and expansion is of indispensable value for the construction of a more just, free, plural, solidarity, diverse and non-violent society. *To register in spaces of culture,* in the *indignation, suffering, injustice* and *pain* of *characters* and *actors, artists* and *filmmakers,* and, above all, of *real people,* the spectrum of the image of a world overshadowed by the light-dark of images of the screen, is capable of disabling the darkness of the cinema rooms, and create light there where arises the field of possibilities of the common.[661]

References

Adorno S (1988) Os aprendizes do poder [The power apprentices]. Paz e Terra, Rio de Janeiro

Adorno TW, Horkheimer M (2006) In: de Almeida JMB (ed) A indústria cultural: o iluminismo como mistificação das massas. In Indústria cultural e sociedade [Society and Cultural Industry] (trans: Julia Elisabeth Levy), 3rd edn. Paz e Terra, São Paulo

Argan GC (2013) História da arte italiana [History of Italian art] (trans: Vilma de Katinsky). Cosac Naif, São Paulo

Banksy P (2014) The man, his work and the movement he inspired. Michael O'Mara Books Limited, London

Barbuy H (2017) As esculturas da Faculdade de Direito [The sculptures of the Faculty of Law]. Ateliê, São Paulo

Barros M d (2010) Poesia completa [Complete Poetry]. Leya, São Paulo

Benjamin W (1996a) A imagem de Proust. In: Magia e técnica, arte e política [Magic and techniques, art and politics] (trans: Sérgio Paulo Rouanet), 7th edn. Brasiliense, São Paulo

Benjamin W (1996b) Pequena história da fotografia. In: Magia e técnica, arte e política [Magic and techniques, art and politics] (trans: Sérgio Paulo Rouanet), 7th edn. Brasiliense, São Paulo

Benjamin W (1996c) A obra de arte na era de sua reprodutibilidade técnica. In: Magia e técnica, arte e política [Magic and techniques, art and politics] (trans: Sérgio Paulo Rouanet), 7th edn. Brasiliense, São Paulo

Benjamin W (1996d) Sobre o conceito de história. In: Magia e técnica, arte e política [Magic and techniques, art and politics] (trans: Sérgio Paulo Rouanet), 7th edn. Brasiliense, São Paulo

Benjamin W (2000a) Rua de mão única [One way street] (trans: Rubens Rodrigues Torres Filho, José Carlos Martins Barbosa), 7th edn. Brasiliense, São Paulo

[661] *Cf.* Rancière (1996), p. 137.

Benjamin W (2000b) Charles Baudelaire: um lírico no auge do capitalismo. In: Obras escolhidas [Selected works] (trans: José Carlos Martins Barbosa, Hemerson Alves Baptista), 3rd edn. Brasiliense, São Paulo
Benjamin W (2002) O conceito de crítica de arte no romantismo alemão [The concept of art critics in German romanticism] (trans: Márcio Seligmann-Silva), 3rd edn. Iluminuras, São Paulo
Bittar ECB (2011) Democracia, justiça e direitos humanos: estudos de teoria crítica e filosofia do direito [Democracy, justice and human rights: studies of critical theory and philosophy of law]. Saraiva, São Paulo
Bittar ECB (2015) Linguagem jurídica: semiótica, discurso e direito [Legal language: semiotics, discourse and law], 6th edn. Saraiva, São Paulo
Bittar ECB (2018) Introdução ao Estudo do Direito: humanismo, democracia e justiça [Introduction to Law: humanism, democracy and justice]. Saraiva, São Paulo
Boleslavski R (2015) A arte do ator [The art of the actor] (trans: J. Guinsburg). Perspectiva, São Paulo
Branco P (2015) Análise da arquitetura judiciária portuguesa: as dimensões de reconhecimento, funcionalidade e acesso à justiça [Analysis of Portugese judicial architecture]. E-Cadernos CES 23:01–24. http://eces.revues.org, Accessed 02 July 2017
Cabrera J (2006) O cinema pensa [The cinema thinks] (trans: Ryta Vinagre). Rocco, Rio de Janeiro
Calabrese O (2015) Como se lê uma obra de arte [How to read a work of art]. Edições 70, Lisboa
Callejón FB (2016) Verdad y certeza en el Dercho y en la Literatura. In: Marcílio FF, Leite GS, Filho RP (eds) AntiManual de Direito & Arte [Antimanual Law & Art], pp 333–351
Candeias MLL (2012) A fragmentação da personagem [The fragmentation of the character]. Perspectiva, São Paulo
Cardenuto R (2016) Antonio Benetazzo, permanências do sensível. In: Benetazzo A (ed) Reinaldo Cardenuto. Prefeitura de São Paulo, São Paulo, pp 09–30
Carlotti M (2010) Il bene di tutti. Fiorentina, Firenze
Carneiro MF (2002) Estética do direito e do conhecimento [Aesthetics of Law and the knowledge]. Rio Grande do Sul, Porto Alegre
Castelnuovo E, Peraya D (1979) O projeto semiótico. [The semiotic project] (trans: Alceu Dias Lima). Cultrix, USP, São Paulo
Caujolle C (2011) Sebastião Salgado (trans: André Telles). Cosac Naify, São Paulo
Chevalier J, Gheerbrant A (2005) Dicionário de símbolos [Dictionary of symbols] (trans: Vera da Costa e Silva, et al), 19th edn. José Olympio, Rio de Janeiro
Cananzi DM (2013) Formativitá e norma. Torino: G. Giappichelli Editore
Cornu G (1990) Linguistique juridique. Montchrestien, Paris
Courtés JC (1979) Introdução à semiótica narrativa e discursiva [Introduction to the narrative and discoursive semiotics] (trans: Norma Backes Tasca). Almedina, Coimbra
da Costa DB (2009) A crise do supereu [The crisis of the superego]. Juruá, Curitiba
da Cunha PF (2004) O Tímpano das Virtudes [The tympanum of the virtues]. Almedina, Coimbra
da Cunha PF (2010) Direito, poder e pró-vocação artística [Law, power and artistics provocation]. Boletim da Faculdade de Direito da Universidade de Coimbra 101:209–239
da Cunha PF (2013) Filosofia do Direito [Philosophy of law], 2nd edn. Almedina, Coimbra
Damatta R (1986) O que faz o brasil, Brasil? [What makes Brazil, Brazil?]. Rocco, Rio de Janeiro
de Barros DLP (1988) Teoria do discurso [Discourse theory]. Atual, São Paulo
de Oliveira AC (2009) A plástica sensível da expressão sincrética e enunciação global. In: de Oliveira AC, Teixeira L (eds) Linguagens na comunicação [Languages in communication]. Estação das Letras e das Cores, São Paulo, pp 79–140
de Oliveira MR (2011) Abuso de poder e violência não razoável; análise do filme Tropa de Elite. In: Adeodato JM, Bittar ECB (eds) Filosofia e Teoria Geral do Direito [Philosophy and general theory of law]. Quartier Latin, São Paulo, pp 815–850
de Oliveira AC (ed) (2014) Do sensível ao inteligível [From sensitive to intelligible]. Estação das Letras e Cores, São Paulo
de Oliveira AC, Teixeira L (eds) (2009) Linguagens na comunicação [Languages in communication]. Estação das Letras e das Cores, São Paulo

Deonna W (1950) La justice à l'Hôtel de Ville de Genève et la fresque des juges aux mains coupées. Revue Suisse d'art et d'archéologie 11:144–152. http://www.e-periodica.ch, Accessed 03 July 2017

Dewey J (2010) Arte como experiência [Art as experience] (trans: Vera Ribeiro). Martins Fontes, São Paulo

Dietrich AM, Machado R (eds) (2017) Artes, diversidades e afins [Arts, diversities and others]. UFABC, Santo André

Dondis DA (2007) Sintaxe da linguagem visual [Visual language syntax] (trans: Jefferson Luiz Camargo). Martins Fontes, São Paulo

Douzinas C (1999) Prosopon and antiprosopon: prolegomena for a legal iconology. In: Douzinas C, Nead L (eds) Law and the image. The Universtiy of Chicago Press, Chicago, pp 36–67

Douzinas C, Nead L (1999) Introduction. In: Douzinas C, Nead L (eds) Law and the image. The Universtiy of Chicago Press, Chicago

Dworkin R (1997) Direito, filosofia e interpretação [Law, philosophy and interpretation]. Cadernos da Escola do Legislativo 3(5):44–71

Eagleton T (2005) A idéia de cultura [The idea of culture]. Transl. Sandra Coelho Branco. Unesp, São Paulo

Eco U (1990) O signo [The sign] (trans: Maria Fátima Marinho), 4th edn. Presença, Lisboa

Eco U (1991) Semiótica e filosofia da linguagem [Semiotics and philosophy of language] (trans: Mariarosaria Fabris, José Luiz Fiorin). Ática, São Paulo

Eco U (1993) Opera aperta. Bompiani, Milano

Eco U (ed) (2007) História da feiúra [History of ugliness] (trans: Eliana Aguiar). Record, Rio de Janeiro

Eco U (2016) A definição da arte [The definition of art] (trans: Adriana Aguiar). Record, São Paulo

Elias N (1994) O processo civilizador [The civilizing process] (trans: Ruy Jugman). Jorge Zahar, Rio de Janeiro

Entretodos (2013) 6°. Festival de Curtas-Metragens em Direitos Humanos [6st Short-Films Festival in Human Rights]. DVD. FESPSP; Prefeitura de São Paulo; Estate, São Paulo

Entretodos (2014) 7°. Festival de Curtas-Metragens em Direitos Humanos [7th Short-Films Festival in Human Rights]. DVD. FESPSP; Prefeitura de São Paulo; Estate; SPCine, São Paulo

Entretodos (2015) 8°. Festival de Curtas-Metragens em Direitos Humanos [8th Short-Films Festival in Human Rights]. DVD 1, 2, 3, 4, 5 and 6. FESPSP; Prefeitura de São Paulo; Estate; SPCine, São Paulo

Felman S (2014) O inconsciente jurídico: julgamentos e traumas no século XX [The juridical unconscious] (trans: Ariani Bueno Sudatti. Prefácio Márcio Seligmann-Silva). Edipro, São Paulo

Ferracini R (2013) Ensaios de atuação [Performance tests]. Perspectiva/FAPESP, São Paulo

Fiorin JL (2009) Para uma definição das linguagens sincrética. In: de Oliveira AC, Teixeira L (eds) Linguagens na comunicação [Languages in communication]. Estação das Letras e das Cores, São Paulo, pp 15–40

Fiorin JL (2016) Argumentação [Argumentation]. Contexto, São Paulo

Flückiger A (2001) L'acteur et le droit: du comédien au stratège. Revue Européenne des Sciences Sociales 121:01–13. http://ress.revues.org/645, Accessed 26 June 2017

Fontanille J (2015a) La sémiotique face aux grands défis sociétaux du XXIe siècle. Actes Sémiotiques 118. https://www.unilim.fr/actes-semiotiques/5320. Accessed 26 Dec 2019

Fontanille J (2015b) Semiótica do discurso [Semiotics of discourse]. Contexto, São Paulo

Foucault M (1995) Vigir e punir [Watch and punish] (trans: Raquel Ramalhete), 12th edn. Vozes, Petrópolis

Franca Filho MT (2011) A cegueira da justiça [The blindness of justice]. Sergio Antonio Fabris, Porto Alegre

Franca Filho MT, Leite GS, Filho RP (2016) Antimanual de Direito & Arte [Anti-manual of law & art]. Saraiva, São Paulo

Fromm E (1987a) Ter ou ser? [To have or to be?] (trans: Nathanael C. Caixeiro), 4th edn. LTC, Rio de Janeiro

Fromm E (1987b) Anatomia da destrutividade humana [The anatomy of the human destructiveness] (trans: Marco Aurélio de Moura Matos), 2nd edn. Guanabara, Rio de Janeiro

Frugoni C (2005) Gli Affreschi Della Cappella Scrovegni A Padova. Einaudi, Torino
Galvão D (2009) Objetos. In: Bittar ECB, de Melo T (eds) Vidas à venda [Lives for sale]. Terceira Margem, São Paulo, p 69
Gandolfo F (2012) L'idea di giustizia nelle arti figurative del medioevo, in Arte e limiti. La misura del diritto [Art and limits] (Mangiameli, Agata C. Amato; Faralli, Carla; Mittica, Maria Paola, edits.), Aracneeditrice, Roma, pp 285–321
Garapon A (1998) O guardador de promessas [The promises keeper] (trans: Francisco Aragão). Instituto Piaget, Lisboa
Garapon A (1999) Bem julgar [Weel Judging] (trans: Pedro F. Henriques). Instutot Piaget, Lisboa
Goedert N, Maillard N (2015) Le Droit en représentation. Éditions Mare & Martins, Paris
González JC (2011) Derecho y literatura: la cultura literária del Derecho. Anais do I Simposio de Direito e Literatura, ed. Luis Carlos Cancellier de Olivo. FUNJAB, Boiteux, Florianópolis, pp 13–24
González JC (2016) Derecho y arquitectura. In: Marcílio FF, Leite GS, Filho RP (eds) AntiManual de Direito & Arte [Antimanual Law & Art], pp 59–82
Goodrich P (1999) The iconography of nothing: blank spaeces and the representation of law in Edward VI and The Pope. In: Douzinas C, Nead L (eds) Law and the image. The Universtiy of Chicago Press, Chicago, pp 89–114
Gorsdorf LF (2014) Direitos humanos e arte: diálogos possíveis para uma episteme. In: Silva EF, Gediel JAP, Trauczynski SC (eds) Direitos humanos e políticas públicas [Human rights and public polices]. Universidade Positivo, Curitiba, pp 51–66
Greimas AJ (1979) As aquisições e os projectos: prefácio. In: Courtés J (ed) Introdução à Semiótica narrativa e discursiva [Introduction to the narrative and discoursive semiotics] (trans: Norma Backes Tasca). Almedina, Coimbra, pp 07–34
Greimas AJ (1981) Semiótica e ciências sociais [Semiotics and Social Sciences] (trans: Álvaro Lorencini, Sandra Nitrini). Cultrix, São Paulo
Greimas AJ (1984) Sémiotique figurative et sémiotique plastique. Actes Sémiotiques 60:01–24
Greimas AJ (1987) De l'imperfection. Pierre Fanlac, Périgeux
Greimas AJ (2014) Sobre o sentido II: ensaios semióticos [About the meaning II: semiotic essays]. EDUSP, São Paulo
Greimas AJ, Courtés J (1993) Sémiotique: ditionnarire raisonné de la théorie du langage. Hachette, Paris
Guénoun D (2014) O teatro é necessário? [Is theater necessary?] (trans: Fátima Saadi). Perspectiva, São Paulo
Habermas J (2012) Teoria do agir comunicativo [Theory of communicative action] (trans: Paulo Astor Soethe). Martins Fontes, São Paulo
Haldar P (1999) The function of the ornament in Quintilian Alberti, and Court Architecture. In: Douzinas C, Nead L (eds) Law and the image. The Universtiy of Chicago Press, Chicago, pp 117–136
Han B-C (2015) A salvação do belo [The salvation of the beauty] (trans: Miguel Serras Pereira). Relógio d'Agua, Lisboa
Hayaert V, Garapon A (2014) Allégories de justice: la Grand'Chambre du Parlement de Flandre. F. Paillart, Flandre
Hermann N (2005) Ética e estética. EDIPUCRS, Porto Alegre
Jacob R (1994) Images de la Justice. Éditions Léopard d'Or, Paris
Janson HW (1992) História da arte [History of art] (trans: Ferreira de Almeida JA, Maria Manuela Rocheta Santos), 5th edn. Martins Fontes, São Paulo
Jay M (1999) Must justice be blind?: the challenge of images to the law. In: Douzinas C, Nead L (eds) Law and the image. The University of Chicago Press, Chicago, pp 19–35
Ket (2014) Planet Banksy. Michael O'Mara Books Limited, London
Lacerda BA (2012) Balança, espada e venda: a justiça e a imparcialidade do juiz. In: Trogo S, dos Santos Coelho NMM (eds) Direito, Filosofia e Arte [Law, philosophy and art]. RIDEEL, São Paulo
Lacoste J (1986) A filosofia da arte [The philosophy of art] (trans: Álvaro Cabral). Jorge Zahar, Rio de Janeiro

Landowski E (2014) Interações arriscadas [Risky interactions]. (trans: Luiza Helena O. da Silva). Estação das Letras e Cores, São Paulo

Lopes JRDL, Queiroz RMR, Acca TDS (2009) Curso de História do Direito [History of law], 2nd edn. GEN, São Paulo

Malland JS (2012) Tropical spray: viagem ao coração do grafite brasileiro (trans: Bruna Ary Laurent Régnier; Jovita Maria Greheim Noronha). Martins Fontes, São Paulo

Marcos RMDF (2016) A Faculdade de Direito de Coimbra em retrospectiva [The faculty of law of Coimbra in retrospect]. Imprensa da Universidade de Coimbra, Coimbra

Marcuse H (1998) Comentários para a redefinição do conceito de cultura. In: Cultura e Sociedade [Culture and society] (trans: Robespierre de Oliveira). Paz e Terra, São Paulo, pp 153–175

Marcuse H (2007) A dimensão estética [The aesthetic dimension] (trans: Maria Elisabete Costa). Edições 70, Lisboa

Martins J d S (2017) Sociologia da fotografia e da imagem, 2nd edn. São Paulo, Contexto

Mathias R (2016) Antropologia visual [Visual Anthropology]. Nova Alexandria, São Paulo

Martins AL, Barbuy H (1999) Arcadas: história da Faculdade de Direito do Largo de São Francisco [Arcades]. Melhoramentos, Alternativa, São Paulo

Meoni ML (2001) Utopia e realtà nel Buongoverno di Ambrogio Lorenzetti. Ifi, Firenze

Molinari D (2010) Victor Hugo: visions graphiques. Paris-Musées, Paris

Mounin G (1970) Introduction à la Sémiologie. Minuit, Paris

Nöth W (2005) A semiótica no século XX [Semiotics in the XX century], 3rd edn. Annablume, São Paulo

Nöth W (2012) Fundamentos semióticos do estudo das imagens [Semiotic foundations of the study of the images], in Tabuleiro das Letras: Revista do Programa de Pós-Graduação em Estudo de Linguagens. Universidade do Estado da Bahia 05:01–19

Oliveira APP (2016) Da ninguendade à humilhação social [Social humiliation]. Tese de Doutorado. USP, Faculdade de Direito, São Paulo

Ost F (2001) O tempo do Direito [The time of the law] (trans: Maria Fernanda Oliveira). Instituto Piaget, Lisboa

Panofsky E (2000) Idea (trans: Paulo Neves). Martins Fontes, São Paulo

Panofsky E (2009) Studi di Iconologia. Piccola Einaudi, Torino

Paolucci A (2013) Michelangelo e Raffaello in Vaticano. Giunti Editore, Roma

Perissé G (2004) Filosofia, ética e literatura [Philosophy, ethics and literature]. Manole, São Paulo

Pietroforte AV (2016) Análise do texto visual [Analysis of the visual text], 2nd edn. Contexto, São Paulo

Pignatari D (1987) Semiótica e literatura [Semiotics and literature], 3rd edn. Cultrix, São Paulo

Pignatari D (1995) Semiótica da arte e da arquitetura [Semiotics of art and of the architecture]. Cultrix, São Paulo

Pinto VC (2014) Direito urbanístico [Urbanistic law], 4th edn. Revista dos Tribunais, São Paulo

Pisani G (2015) I volti segreti di Giotto, 3rd edn. Programma, Bologna

Plaza J (2010) Tradução intersemiótica [Intersemiotics translation]. Perspectiva, São Paulo

Proença G (1990) História da arte [History of art]. Ática, São Paulo

Puls M (2006) Arquitetura e filosofia [Architecture and philosophy]. Annablume, São Paulo

Queirós LM (2018) Uma Universidade que mora em aposentos reais [A University that leaves in a royal place]. https://www.publico.pt/2013/06/22/jornal/uma-universidade-que-mora-em-aposentos-reais-26725680, Accessed 03 Sept 2018

Rancière J (2014) O espectador emancipado [The emancipated viewer] (trans: Ivone C. Benedetti.). Martins Fontes, São Paulo

Rastier F (1989) Sens et textualité. Hachette, Paris

Reale E (1996) A Faculdade de Direito do Largo de São Francisco [The faculty of law of the São Francisco Square]. Ac&M, Rio de Janeiro

Rendon PA (2014) Hacia uma semiótica del arte: implicaciones del pensamento peirceano en el estúdio del arte contemporâneo. Cuadernos de Filosofía Latinoamericana 11:127–145

Resnik J, Curtis D (1987) Images of Justice. Faculty Scholarship Series, Paper 917, http://digitalcommons.law.yale.edu/fss_papers/917. Accessed 07 Apr 2017

Resnik J, Curtris D (2011) Representing justice. Yale University Press, New Haven

Ricoeur P (2008a) O justo 1 [The just 1] (trans: Ivone C. Benedetti). Martins Fontes, São Paulo
Ricoeur P (2008b) O justo 2 [The just 2] (trans: Ivone C. Benedetti). Martins Fontes, São Paulo
Romano B (2013) Giudizio giuridico e giudizio estetico da Kant verso Schiller. G. Giappichelli Editore, Torino
Rossi EA (2007) Palazzo della Ragioe a Padova. Skira Editore, Milano
Salgado S (2014) Da minha terra à Terra [From my land to the Earth] (trans: Julia da Rosa Simões). Paralela, São Paulo
Santaella L (1992) A Assinatura das coisas [The signing of things]. Imago, Rio de Janeiro
Santaella L (2007) Linguagens líquidas na era da mobilidade [Liquid languages of the era of mobility]. Paulus, São Paulo
Santaella L (2016a) Memória e perspectivas da semiótica no Brasil [Memory and perspectives of Semiotics in Brazil]. Intexto 37:22–33
Santaella L (2016b) Temas e dilemas do pós-digital [Themes and dilemmas of the post-digital]. Paulus, São Paulo
Santaella L, Nöth W (1998) Imagem [Image]. Iluminuras, São Paulo, p 1998
Schwarcz LM (2017) Assombrados pela história. In: Bittar ECB (ed) História do Direito Brasileiro [History of Brazilian law]. Atlas, São Paulo, pp 587–599
Senna C (2012) Cordéis que educam e transformam [Poetry that teaches and transforms]. Global, São Paulo
Smith R (2013) Excelência no ensino da arte. In: Barbosa AM (ed) Arte-educação [Art-education]. Cortez, São Paulo, pp 131–147
Soulages F (2010) Estética da fotografia [The aesthetics of photography]. Tradução de Iraci D. Poleti e Regina Salgado Campos. SENAC, São Paulo
de Souza RT (2005) In: Guinsburg J, Barbosa AMB (eds) A filosofia e o pós-moderno. O pós-modernismo [The post-modernism]. Perspectiva, São Paulo, pp 85–100
Taylor KF (1999) The festival of justice, Paris, 1849. In: Douzinas C, Nead L (eds) Law and the image. The Universtiy of Chicago Press, Chicago, pp 137–177
Telles Junior G (1999) A folha dobrada [The folded sheet]. Nova Fronteira, Rio de Janeiro
Tore GM (2011) L'art comme création, ou la règle de nier la règle. Actes Sémiotiques (114):01–11. epublications.unifilm.fr. Accessed 06 June 2017
Tuzet G (2014) Contro le immagini. In: Carla F, Gigliotti V, Heritier P, Mittica MP (eds) Il Diritto tra testo e immagine. Mimesis, Milano, pp 175–188
Veras DT (2010) Homem-tração. In: Bittar ECB, de Melo T (eds) Cidades impossíveis [Impossible cities]. Portal Literatura, São Paulo, p 132
Vespaziani A (2010) Costituzionalità e narratività. In: Faralli C, Mittica MP (eds) Diritto e Letteratura. Aracne Editrice, Roma, pp 123–137
Vidigal A (2017) Faculdade de Direito do Largo de São Francisco: USP 190 Anos [The Faculty of Law of the São Francisco square: 190 years]. DBA Editora, São Paulo
Volli U (2015) Manual de semiótica [Manual of semiotics] (trans: Silva Debtto C. Reis), 3rd edn. Loyola, São Paulo
Von Martin A (1998) Sociología del Renacimiento (trans: Manuel Pedroso), 11th edn. Fondo de Cultura Económica, México
Wagner A, Sherwin RK (eds) (2014) Law, culture and visual studies. Springer, Dordrecht
Wagner A, Sherwin RK, Bhatia VK (2009) Diversity and tolerance in social-legal contexts: explorations in the Semiotics of Law. Ashgate, Burlington
Warat LA (1995) O direito e sua linguagem [Law and its language], 2nd edn. Sergio Antonio Fabris, Porto Alegre
Warat LA (2004a) Literasofia. In: Mezzaroba O, Rover AJ, Junior ADR, Monteiro CS (eds) Territórios desconhecidos [Unknown territories]. Fundação Boiteux, Florianópolis, pp 19–26
Warat LA (2004b) La cinesofia y su lado oscuro. In: Mezzaroba O, Rover AJ, Junior ADR, Monteiro CS (eds) Territórios desconhecidos. Fundação Boiteux, Florianópolis, pp 549–562
Werle MA (2011) A questão do fim da arte em Hegel. Hedra, São Paulo
Ziccardi MG (2014) Una giustizia senza benda e senza spada? In: Carla F, Gigliotti V, Heritier P, Mittica MP (eds) Il Diritto tra testo e immagine. Mimesis, Milano, pp 167–173

Chapter 5
Conclusions

"While art is the beauty salon of civilisation, neither art nor civilisation are safe".[1] This warning by John Dewey is resumed here, at the end of this work of research, precisely to point out the importance and meaning of *art*. It is at this precise level that we sought to resume, with the inter-disciplinary aid of numerous theoretical perspectives, the possibility of creating the link between *Law & Art*. And this to consider how fertile it can be this field of research and work of Law, so that one can reaffirm that Justice is found in its centre, and, also, to affirm that this relation cannot be strange to the jurist, and for this reason precisely, it should make itself present in the process of formation and discussion of legal concepts and classes. In this sense, the work ends up by giving a double meaning of contribution, on one hand, for the *Theory of Law*, and on the other hand, for the *Theory of Justice*.

In the approach that was sought to privilege, from the perspective of the relation between *Semiotics*, *Law* and *Art*, the investigation proved to be extremely challenging, but, in the end, fruitful and instigating. But, it is as fertile, as it is difficult to be constructed, hence the importance of the resource of approximation between the fields of knowledge of *Semiotics of Law* and of the *Semiotics of Art*. What one notices is that the relation between *Law & Art* is a complex relation, even in process of affirmation and construction, which spreads into diverse perspectives and fields of application, creating difficulties for the task of research.

If 15 years ago, this type of approximation could have been considered *vanguard,* currently there is a remarkable academic production, which has been establishing connections of numerous shades, favourable to approaches increasingly important for the analysis of Law. For no other reason, the relation between *Law & Art* is crossed by so many borders of work, like the *Philosophy of Art*, the *History of Art*, the *Anthropology of Art*, the *Sociology of Art*, which can, still, apply to various fields of knowledge within the universe of Law. It is precisely because of this, that it was possible to constitute a border of work in which the *Semiotics of Law* and the

[1]Dewey (2010), p. 577.

E. C. B. Bittar, *Semiotics, Law & Art*, Law and Visual Jurisprudence 2,
https://doi.org/10.1007/978-3-030-58880-9_5

Semiotics of Art are merged, to make interesting applications in the fields of *Semiotics of Painting*, *Semiotics of Architecture*, *Semiotics of Theatre*, *Semiotics of Literature*, *Semiotics of Culture*.

By analysing the whole symbolic load, and the various concrete works studied in this book, it is clear that Law needs Justice to justify itself, since the idea of Justice brings meaning to the daily practices of Law. But, the idea of Justice is in transformation in history, and it is this that also makes the *symbol of justice* go through modifications and variations, even if subtle. Therefore, the reading of *aesthetic texts* help the jurist understand the transformations experienced by the *idea of justice*. Consequently, many of the achievements contained (iconographic, analytical and reflective) in the exploratory nature of this research ends up guiding the reader towards the encounter of strength and importance that each historical period has attributed to the *symbol of justice*. Therefore, some important conclusions can then be developed: (1) the *symbol of justice* is a symbol that is stably present in culture, invoked in an ancestral way; (2) the *symbol of justice* is an aesthetic text in constant evocation in places of justice; (3) the *symbol of justice* has a strong appealing and inovocative nature of the duties in the area of Law; (4) the *symbol of justice* is explored to confer legitimacy to the exercise of power; (5) despite its stable nature, the *symbol of justice* is not invariable, suffering changes that accompany the transformations of history; (6) the *symbol of justice* receives aesthetic representations that apprehend the idea of justice in such a way as to always give it renewed meanings, echoing issues, values and contextual discussions. This is how this task gathers important evidence for the study semiotics of Justice, in the perception of its complex, problematic and changing relationship, in face of the tasks that circulate the symbolic universe of Law.

Reference

Dewey J (2010) Arte como experiência [Art as experience] (trans: Vera Ribeiro). Martins Fontes, São Paulo

References

Adeodato JM, Bittar ECB (2011) Filosofia e Teoria Geral do Direito: homenagem a Tercio Sampaio Ferraz Junior [Philosophy and general theory of law]. Quartier Latin, São Paulo

Adorno S (1988) Os aprendizes do poder [The power apprentices]. Paz e Terra, Rio de Janeiro

Adorno TW (1995) Educação após Auschwitz. In: Educação e emancipação [Education and emancipation] (trans: Maar WL). Paz e Terra, São Paulo

Adorno TW (2001) Minima moralia (trans: Morão A). Edições, Lisboa, p 70

Adorno TW, Horkheimer M (1985) Dialética do esclarecimento [Dialectics of the enlightenement] (trans: de Almeida GA). Jorge Zahar, Rio de Janeiro

Adorno TW, Horkheimer M (2006) A indústria cultural: o iluminismo como mistificação das massas. In: de Almeida JMB (ed) Indústria cultural e sociedade [Society and cultural industry] (trans: Levy JE), 3rd edn. Paz e Terra, São Paulo

Agrest D, Gandelsonas M (2013) Semiótica e Arquitetura. In: Nesbitt K (ed) Uma nova agenda para a arquitetura [A new agenda to the architecture]. CosacNaify, São Paulo, pp 129–141

Akamine Junior O (2012) Direito e estética [Law and aesthetics]. USP, Tese de Doutorado, São Paulo

Antich X (2012) Fármacos icónicos. Memoria y retórica en la fotografia de la guerra civil española. In: Cornelsen EL, Vieira EA, Seligman-Silva M (eds) Imagem e memória [Image and memory]. Rona; UFMG, Belo Horizonte, pp 191–227

Argan GC (2013) História da arte italiana [History of Italian art] (trans: de Katinsky V). Cosac Naif, São Paulo

Báez F (2006) História universal da destruição dos livros [Universal history of book destruction] (trans: Schlafman L). Ediouro, Rio de Janeiro

Banksy P (2014) The man, his work and the movement he inspired. Michael O'Mara Books Limited, London

Barbosa AM (2012) Arte-educação no Brasil [Art-education in Brazil], 7th edn. Perspectiva, São Paulo

Barbosa AM (org) (2013) Arte-educação [Art-education], 9th edn. Cortez, São Paulo

Barbuy H (2017) As esculturas da Faculdade de Direito [The sculptures of the faculty of law]. Ateliê, São Paulo

Barelli E, Pennacchietti S (2001) Dicionário das citações [Dictionary of quotations] (trans: Jannini K). Martins Fontes, São Paulo

Barthes R (1997) Elementos de semiologia [Elements of semiology] (trans: Blikstein I), 10th edn. Cultrix, São Paulo

Baudrillard J (1972) Pour une critique de l'économie politique du signe. Gallimard, Paris

E. C. B. Bittar, *Semiotics, Law & Art*, Law and Visual Jurisprudence 2,
https://doi.org/10.1007/978-3-030-58880-9

Beividas W, Lopes IC (2007) Veridicção persuasão, argumentação. Todas as Letras [All letters] 09 (1):32–41
Benedetti G (2013) Oggettività esistenziale dell'interpretazione. Rivista Internazionale di Filosofia del Diritto 3:339–364
Benjamin W (1996a) A imagem de Proust. In: Magia e técnica, arte e política [Magic and techniques, art and politics] (trans: Rouanet SP), 7th edn. Brasiliense, São Paulo
Benjamin W (1996b) Pequena história da fotografia. In: Magia e técnica, arte e política [Magic and techniques, art and politics], 7th edn. Brasiliense, São Paulo
Benjamin W (1996c) A obra de arte na era de sua reprodutibilidade técnica. In: Magia e técnica, arte e política [Magic and techniques, art and politics] (trans: Rouanet SP), 7th edn. Brasiliense, São Paulo
Benjamin W (1996d) Sobre o conceito de história. In: Magia e técnica, arte e política [Magic and techniques, art and politics] (trans: Rouanet SP), 7th edn. Brasiliense, São Paulo
Benjamin W (2000a) Rua de mão única [One way street] (trans: Filho RRT, Barbosa JCM), 7th edn. Brasiliense, São Paulo
Benjamin W (2000b) Charles Baudelaire: um lírico no auge do capitalismo. In: Obras escolhidas [Selected works] (trans: Barbosa JCM, Baptista HA), 3rd edn. Brasiliense, São Paulo
Benjamin W (2002) O conceito de crítica de arte no romantismo alemão [The concept of art critics in German romanticism] (trans: Seligmann-Silva M), 3rd edn. Iluminuras, São Paulo
Bittar ECB (2010) Os direitos humanos e a sensibilidade estética: educação em direitos humanos, resistência e transformação social. In: de Fátima Guerra Ferreira L, de Nazaré Tavares Zenaide M, Pequeno M (eds) Direitos humanos na educação superior [Human rights in the superior education]. UFPB, João Pessoa, pp 169–188
Bittar ECB (2011) Democracia, justiça e direitos humanos: estudos de teoria crítica e filosofia do direito [Democracy, justice and human rights: studies of critical theory and philosophy of law]. Saraiva, São Paulo
Bittar ECB (2012) Crise econômica, desglobalização e direitos humanos. Revista Mestrado em Direito [Journal Master in Law] 01:259–294
Bittar ECB (2013a) Diálogo, consciência cosmopolita e direitos humanos. Direitos fundamentais e justiça [Human rights and justice] 22:98–123
Bittar ECB (2013b) Democracia, justiça e emancipação social: reflexões jusfilosóficas a partir do pensamento de Jürgen Habermas [Democracy, justice and social emancipation: philosophical reflections on Habermas thought]. Quartier Latin, São Paulo
Bittar CA (2015a) Direito de Autor [Copyright], 6th edn. GEN; Forense, Rio de Janeiro
Bittar ECB (2015b) Linguagem jurídica: semiótica, discurso e direito [Legal language: semiotics, discourse and law], 6th edn. Saraiva, São Paulo
Bittar ECB (2018) Introdução ao Estudo do Direito: humanismo, democracia e justiça [Introduction to law: humanism, democracy and justice]. Saraiva, São Paulo
Boas F (2015) Arte primitiva [Primitive art] (trans: Pereira JC). Mauad, Rio de Janeiro
Boff L (2012) Sustentabilidade [Sustainability]. Vozes, Rio de Janeiro
Boleslavski R (2015) A arte do ator [The art of the actor] (trans: Guinsburg J). Perspectiva, São Paulo
Branco P (2015) Análise da arquitetura judiciária portuguesa: as dimensões de reconhecimento, funcionalidade e acesso à justiça [Analysis of Portugese judicial architecture], E-Cadernos CES 23:01–24. http://eces.revues.org. Accessed 02/07/2017
Brandi C (1986) Segno e immagine. Aesthetica, Palermo
Bucci E (2015) O Estado de narciso [Narcissus state]. Companhia das Letras, São Paulo
Bucci E (2016) A forma bruta dos protestos [The crude form of the protests]. Companhia das Letras, São Paulo
Buyssens E. Semiologia e comunicação linguística [Semiology and linguistic communication] (trans: Blikstein I), 3rd edn. Cultrix, São Paulo
Cabrera J (2006) O cinema pensa [The cinema thinks] (trans: Vinagre R). Rocco, Rio de Janeiro
Calabrese O (2015) Como se lê uma obra de arte [How to read a work of art]. Edições, Lisboa, p 70

Cananzi DM (2013) Formatività e norma: elementi di Teoria Estetica dell'interpretazione giuridica. G. Giappichelli Editore, Torino
Candé R (1994) História universal da música [Universal history of music] (trans: Brandão E). Martins Fontes, São Paulo
Candeias MLL (2012) A fragmentação da personagem [The fragmentation of the character]. Perspectiva, São Paulo
Cardenuto R (2016) Antonio Benetazzo, permanências do sensível. In: Benetazzo A (ed) Reinaldo Cardenuto. Prefeitura de São Paulo, São Paulo, pp 09–30
Carlotti M (2010) Il bene di tutti. Fiorentina, Firenze
Carneiro MF (2002) Estética do direito e do conhecimento [Aesthetics of law and the knowledge]. Rio Grande do Sul, Porto Alegre
Carontini E, Peraya D (1979) O projeto semiótico [The semiotics project] (trans: Lima AD). Cultrix, USP, São Paulo
Castelnuovo E (2006) Retrato e sociedade na arte italiana [Portrait and society in Italian art] (trans: de Mattos F). Companhia das Letras, São Paulo
Caujolle C (2011) Sebastião Salgado (trans: Telles A). Cosac Naify, São Paulo
Cervelli P (2018) La communicazione politica populista: corpo, liguaggio e pratiche d interazione. Actes Sémiotiques 121:118. https://www.unilim.fr/actes-semiotiques/6021. Accessed 14.01.2020
Chevalier J, Gheerbrant A (2005) Dicionário de símbolos [Dictionary of symbols] (trans: da Costa e Silva V et al), 19th edn. José Olympio, Rio de Janeiro
Comitê Nacional de Educação em Direitos Humanos (2013) Plano Nacional de educação em direitos humanos [National plan on human rights education]. Brasília: SDH; MEC; MJ; UNESCO. SMDHC, São Paulo
Conanzi DM (2013) Formatività e norma. G. Giappichelli, Torino
Congdon KG (1993) Art and teaching for peace and justice. J Soc Theory Art Educ 13:13–36
Cornu G (1990) Linguistique juridique. Montchrestien, Paris
Courtés JC (1979) Introdução à semiótica narrativa e discursiva [Introduction to the narrative and discoursive semiotics] (trans: Tasca NB). Almedina, Coimbra
da Costa DB (2009) A crise do supereu [The crisis of the superego]. Juruá, Curitiba
da Cunha PF (2004) O Tímpano das Virtudes [The tympanum of the virtues]. Almedina, Coimbra
da Cunha PF (2010) Direito, poder e pró vocação artística [Law, power and artistics provocation]. Boletim da Faculdade de Direito da Universidade de Coimbra 101:209–239
da Cunha PF (2013) Filosofia do Direito [Philosophy of law], 2nd edn. Almedina, Coimbra
Damatta R (1986) O que faz o brasil, Brasil? [What makes Brazil, Brazil?] Rocco, Rio de Janeiro
Danto AC (2015) O abuso da beleza [Beauty abuse] (trans: Süssekind P). Martins Fontes, São Paulo
Davis M (2007) Cidades mortas [Dead cities] (trans: Calado A). Record, Rio de Janeiro
de Aquino SRF (2014) O direito em busca de sua humanidade [Law in search for its humanity]. CRV, Curitiba
de Araújo CO (2005) Semiótica do Direito [Semiotics of law]. Quartier Latin, São Paulo
de Azambuja DC, Neto GG (2009) Representação, expressão, arte e psicanálise. In: Ciência e Cultura [Science and culture]. SBPC/FAPESP, São Paulo, pp 32–33
de Barros DLP (1988) Teoria do discurso [Discourse theory]. Atual, São Paulo
de Barros M (2010) Poesia completa [Complete poetry]. Leya, São Paulo
de Campos Barros VS (2016) A civilização chutou as portas do *Saloon*. In: Filho MF, Leite GS, Filho RP (eds) Antimanual de Direito & Arte [Anti-manual of law and art]. Saraiva, São Paulo, pp 200–242
de Figueiredo Marcos RM (2016) A Faculdade de Direito de Coimbra em retrospectiva [The faculty of law of Coimbra in retrospect]. Imprensa da Universidade de Coimbra, Coimbra
de Lima Lopes JR, Queiroz RMR, dos Santos Acca T (2009) Curso de História do Direito [History of law], 2nd edn. GEN, São Paulo

de Oliveira AC (org) (2009) A plástica sensível da expressão sincrética e enunciação global. In: Linguagens na comunicação [Languages in communication], eds. AC de Oliveira, L Teixeira, 79–140. Estação das Letras e das Cores, São Paulo

de Oliveira MR (2011) Abuso de poder e violência não razoável; análise do filme Tropa de Elite. In: Adeodato JM, Bittar ECB (eds) Filosofia e Teoria Geral do Direito [Philosophy and general theory of law]. Quartier Latin, São Paulo, pp 815–850

de Oliveira AC (org) (2014) Do sensível ao inteligível [From sensitive to intelligible]. Estação das Letras e Cores, São Paulo

de Oliveira AC, Teixeira L (orgs) (2009) Linguagens na comunicação [Languages in communication]. Estação das Letras e das Cores, São Paulo

de Sant'Anna DB (2014) História da beleza no Brasil [History of beauty in Brazil]. Contexto, São Paulo

de Souza RT (2005) A filosofia e o pós-moderno. In: Guinsburg J, Barbosa AM (eds) O pós-modernismo [The post-modernism]. Perspectiva, São Paulo, pp 85–100

de Souza Martins J (2017) Sociologia da fotografia e da imagem [Sociology of the photograph and the image], 2nd edn. Contexto, São Paulo

Deely J (1990) Semiótica básica [Basic semiotics] (trans: Pinto JCM). Ática, São Paulo

Deonna W (1950) La justice à l'Hôtel de Ville de Genève et la fresque des juges aux mains coupées. Revue Suisse d'art et d'archéologie 11:144–152. http://www.e-periodica.ch. Accessed 03/07/2017

Dewey J (2010) Arte como experiência [Art as experience] (trans: Ribeiro V). Martins Fontes, São Paulo

Didi-Huberman G (1999) The molding image: genealogy and the truth of resemblance in Pliny's natural history. In: Douzinas C, Nead L (eds) Law and the image. The Universtiy of Chicago Press, Chicago, pp 36–67

Dietrich AM, Machado R (orgs) (2017) Artes, diversidades e afins [Arts, diversities and others]. UFABC, Santo André

Dondis DA (2007) Sintaxe da linguagem visual [Visual language syntax] (trans: Camargo JL). Martins Fontes, São Paulo

dos Santos Coelho NMM (2012) Direito, arte e formação do jurista. In: Trogo S, dos Santos Coelho NMM (eds) Direito, Filosofia e Arte [Law, philosophy and art]. RIDEEL, São Paulo

Douzinas C (1999) Prosopon and antiprosopon: prolegomena for a legal iconology. In: Douzinas C, Nead L (eds) Law and the image. The Universtiy of Chicago Press, Chicago, pp 36–67

Douzinas C, Nead L (1999) Introduction. In: Douzinas C, Nead L (eds) Law and the image. The Universtiy of Chicago Press, Chicago

Dworkin R (1997) Direito, filosofia e interpretação [Law, philosophy and interpretation]. Cadernos da Escola do Legislativo 3(5):44–71

Eco U (org) (1990) O signo [The sign] (trans: Marinho MF), 4ª. ed. Presença, Lisboa

Eco U (org) (1991) Semiótica e filosofia da linguagem [Semiotics and philosophy of language] (trans: Fabris M, Fiorin JL). Ática, São Paulo

Eco U (org) (1993) Opera aperta. Bompiani, Milano

Eco U (org) (2007) História da feiúra [History of ugliness] (trans: Aguiar E). Record, Rio de Janeiro

Eco U (org) (2016) A definição da arte [The definition of art] (trans: Aguiar A). Record, São Paulo

Edelman B (1976) O direito captado pela fotografia [Law captured by the photograph] (trans: Martins S, de Carvalho P). Centelha, Coimbra

Elias N (1994) O processo civilizador [The civilizing process] (trans: Jugman R). Jorge Zahar, Rio de Janeiro

Elliott D, Silverman M, Bowman W (2017) Artistic citizenship: artistry, social responsibility and ethical praxis. Oxford University Press, Oxford

Entretodos (2013) 6°. Festival de Curtas-Metragens em Direitos Humanos [6st Short-Films Festival in Human Rights]. DVD. FESPSP; Prefeitura de São Paulo; Estate, São Paulo

Entretodos (2014) 7°. Festival de Curtas-Metragens em Direitos Humanos [7th Short-Films Festival in Human Rights]. DVD. FESPSP; Prefeitura de São Paulo; Estate; SPCine, São Paulo

Entretodos (2015) 8°. Festival de Curtas-Metragens em Direitos Humanos [8th Short-Films Festival in Human Rights]. DVD 1, 2, 3, 4, 5 and 6. FESPSP; Prefeitura de São Paulo; Estate; SPCine, São Paulo

Faralli C, Gigliotti V, Heritier P, Mittica MP (2014) Il Diritto tra testo e immagine. Mimesis, Milano

Felman S (2014) O inconsciente jurídico: julgamentos e traumas no século XX [The juridical unconscious] (trans: Sudatti AB, Seligmann-Silva PM). Edipro, São Paulo

Ferracini R (2013) Ensaios de atuação [Performance tests]. Perspectiva/FAPESP, São Paulo

Ferry L (2010) Diante da crise [In the face of the crisis] (trans: Jannini K). Difel, Rio de Janeiro

Fiorin JL (2009) Para uma definição das linguagens sincrética. In: de Oliveira AC, Teixeira L (eds) Linguagens na comunicação [Languages in communication]. Estação das Letras e das Cores, São Paulo, pp 15–40

Fiorin JL (2016) Argumentação [Argumentation]. Contexto, São Paulo

Flückiger A (2001) L'acteur et le droit: du comédien au stratège. Revue Européenne des Sciences Sociales 121:01–13. http://ress.revues.org/645. Accessed 26.06.2017

Fontanille J (2015a) La sémiotique face aux grands défis sociétaux du XXI [e] siècle. Actes Sémiotiques 118. https://www.unilim.fr/actes-semiotiques/5320. Accessed 26.12.2019

Fontanille J (2015b) Semiótica do discurso [Semiotics of discourse]. Contexto, São Paulo

Foucault M (1995) Vigir e punir [Watch and punish] (trans: Ramalhete R), 12th edn. Vozes, Petrópolis

Franca Filho MT (2011) A cegueira da justiça [The blindness of justice]. Sergio Antonio Fabris, Porto Alegre

Franca Filho MT, Leite GS, Filho RP (Coords) (2016) Antimanual de Direito & Arte [Anti-manual of law & art]. Saraiva, São Paulo

Fromm E (1987a) Ter ou ser? [To have or to be?] (trans: Caixeiro NC), 4th edn. LTC, Rio de Janeiro

Fromm E (1987b) Anatomia da destrutividade humana [The anatomy of the human destructiveness] (trans: de Moura Matos MA), 2nd edn. Guanabara, Rio de Janeiro

Frugoni C (2005) Gli Affreschi Della Cappella Scrovegni A Padova. Einaudi, Torino

Galeffi R (1979) Novos ensaios de estética [New essays in aesthetics]. UFBA, Bahia

Galvão D (2009) Objetos. In: Bittar ECB, de Melo T (eds) Vidas à venda [Lives for sale]. Terceira Margem, São Paulo, p 69

Gandolfo F (2012) L'idea di giustizia nelle arti figurative del medioevo. In: Mangiameli ACA, Faralli C, Mittica MP (eds) Arte e limiti. Aracneeditrice, Roma, pp 285–321

Garapon A (1998) O guardador de promessas [The guardian of the promises] (trans: Aragão F). Instituto Piaget, Lisboa

Garapon A (1999) Bem julgar [Well judge] (trans: Henriques PF). Instituto Piaget, Lisboa

Geertz C (2014) O saber local [The local knowledge] (trans: Joscelyne V), 14th edn. Vozes, Rio de Janeiro

Gémar J-C (1990) Pour une méthode générale de traduction: traduire par l'interprétation du texte. Meta: Journal des traducteurs 35(4):657–668

Goedert N, Maillard N (2015) Le Droit en représentation. Éditions Mare & Martins, Paris

Gomes ÁC (1985) A estética simbolista [The symbolist aesthetics]. Cultrix, São Paulo

González JC (2011) Derecho y literatura: la cultura literária del Derecho. In: de Olivo LCC (ed) Anais do I Simposio de Direito e Literatura. FUNJAB, Boiteux, Florianópolis, pp 13–24

Goodrich P (1999) The iconography of nothing: blank spaeces and the representation of law in Edward VI and The Pope. In: Douzinas C, Nead L (eds) Law and the image. The Universtiy of Chicago Press, Chicago, pp 89–114

Gorsdorf LF (2014) Direitos humanos e arte: diálogos possíveis para uma episteme. In: Silva EF, Gediel JAP, Trauczynski SC (eds) Direitos humanos e políticas públicas [Human rights and public polices]. Universidade Positivo, Curitiba, pp 51–66

Greimas AJ (1979) As aquisições e os projectos: prefácio. In: Courtés J (ed) Introdução à Semiótica narrativa e discursiva [Introduction to the narrative and discoursive semiotics] (trans: Tasca NB). Almedina, Coimbra, pp 07–34

Greimas AJ (1981) Semiótica e ciências sociais [Semiotics and social sciences] (trans: Lorencini Á, Nitrini S). Cultrix, São Paulo

Greimas AJ (1984) Sémiotique figurative et sémiotique plastique. Actes Sémiotiques 60:01–24

Greimas AJ (1987) De l'imperfection. Pierre Fanlac, Périgeux

Greimas AJ (2014) Sobre o sentido II: ensaios semióticos [About the meaning II: semiotic essays]. EDUSP, São Paulo

Greimas AJ, Courtés J (1993) Sémiotique: ditionnarire raisonné de la théorie du langage. Hachette, Paris

Guénoun D (2014) O teatro é necessário? [Is theater necessary?] (trans: Saadi F). Perspectiva, São Paulo

Guinsburg J, Barbosa AM (2005) O pós-modernismo [The post-modernism]. Perspectiva, São Paulo

Habermas J (1979) Communication and the evolution society (trans: McCarthy T). Beacon Press, Boston

Habermas J (1984) Mudança estrutural da esfera pública [Structural change in the public sphere] (trans: Kothe FR). Tempo Brasileiro, Rio de Janeiro

Habermas J (1989) Consciência moral e agir comunicativo [Moral conscience and communicative action] (trans: de Almeida GA). Tempo Brasileiro, Rio de Janeiro

Habermas J (1995) Theorie des kommunikativen Handelns: Zur Kritik der funktionalistischen Vernunft. Band 2. Suhrkamp, Frankfurt am Main

Habermas J (2003) Direito e democracia [Between facts and norms]. vs. I. e II. (trans: Siebeneichler FB), 2nd edn. Tempo Brasileiro, Rio de Janeiro

Habermas J (2004) Verdade e justificação [Truth and justification] (trans: Mota MC). Loyola, São Paulo

Habermas J (2012) Teoria do agir comunicativo [Theory of communicative action] (trans: Soethe PA). Martins Fontes, São Paulo

Haldar P (1999) The function of the ornament in Quintilian Alberti, and Court Architecture. In: Douzinas C, Nead L (eds) Law and the image. The Universtiy of Chicago Press, Chicago, pp 117–136

Han B-C (2015) A salvação do belo [The salvation of the beauty] (trans: Pereira MS). Relógio d'Agua, Lisboa

Hayaert V, Garapon A (2014) Allégories de Justice. F. Paillart, Flandre

Hermann N (2005) Ética e estética. EDIPUCRS, Porto Alegre

Hjelmslev LT (1975a) A estratificação da linguagem [Language stratification]. Os pensadores, 157 a 182 (trans: Netto JTC). Abril Cultural, São Paulo

Hjelmslev LT (1975b) Prolegômenos a uma teoria da linguagem [Prolegomena to a theory of language] (trans: Netto JTC). Os pensadores, 183–219. Abril Cultural, São Paulo

Hobsbawn EJ (2008) História social do jazz [Social history of jazz] (trans: Noronha A), 6th edn. Paz e Terra, São Paulo

Honneth A (2015) O direito da liberdade [The right of freedom] (trans: Krieger S). Martins Fontes, São Paulo

Ibdfam (2017) Direito e arte [Law and art]. Revista do IBDFAM, 34

Jackson B (1988) Sémiotique et études critiques du droit. Droit et Société 8:61–71

Jackson B (2017) A journey into Legal Semiotics. Actes Sémiotiques 120:01–25. epublications. unilim.fr. Accessed 27/06/2017

Jacob R (1994) Images de la Justice. Éditions Léopard d'Or, Paris

Janson HW (1992) História da arte [History of art] (trans: de Almeida JAF, Santos MMR), 5th edn. Martins Fontes, São Paulo

Jay M (1999) Must justice be blind?: the challenge of images to the law. In: Douzinas C, Nead L (eds) Law and the image. The University of Chicago Press, Chicago, pp 19–35

Junqueira JFF (2014) Jazz. Via Impressa, São Paulo

Ket (2014) Planet Banksy. Michael O'Mara Books Limited, London

Kevelson R (1986) Semiotics and methods of legal inquiry. Indiana Law J 61(3):355–371

Kharbouch A (2018) Manipulation et contagion: le discours ambivalent du populisme politique. Actes Sémiotiques 121:118. https://www.unilim.fr/actes-semiotiques/6021. Accessed 27.12.2019
Kristeva J (1981) Semiotica [Semiotics] (trans: Arancibia JM). Fundamentos, Madrid
Lacerda BA (2012) Balança, espada e venda: a justiça e a imparcialidade do juiz. In: Trogo S, dos Santos Coelho NMM (eds) Direito, Filosofia e Arte [Law, philosophy and art]. RIDEEL, São Paulo
Lacoste J (1986) A filosofia da arte [The philosophy of art] (trans: Cabral Á). Jorge Zahar, Rio de Janeiro
Landowski E (org) (1986) Pour une approche sémiotique et narrative du droit. Droit Prospectif, 11: 39–70
Landowski E (1988) Vérité et véridiction en droit. Droit et Société: Revue Internationale de Théorie du Droit et de Sociologie Juridique 8:45–59
Landowski E (1993a) La sociedade figurada (trans: Aguilar GH et alii). Universidad Autónoma de Puebla; Fondo de Cultura Económica, México
Landowski E (1993b) La sociedad figurada: ensayos de sociosemiótica (trans: Hernández G et al). Fondo de Cultura Económica, México
Landowski E (2005) Para uma semiótica sensível. Educação & Realidade [Education and reality] 30:93–106
Landowski E (2014) Interações arriscadas [Risky interactions]. Estação das Letras e Cores, São Paulo
Landowski E (2017) Interactions (socio) sémiotiques. Actes Sémiotiques 120:01–20. epublications. unilim.fr. Accessed 06/06/2017
Landowski E (2018) Populisme et esthésie. Actes Sémiotiques 121:118. https://www.unilim.fr/actes-semiotiques/6021. Accessed 27.12.2019
Lauthère-Vigneau C (Direct) (2008) Mai 68. Denoël, Paris
Leonardi Filho LS (2006) Descrição semiótica do Direito [A semiotics description of law]. Editora Scortecci
Linhares JMA (2017) O binómio casos fáceis/casos difíceis e a categoria da inteligibilidade sistema jurídico [The binomial easy cases/hard cases and the category of legal system intelligibility]. Universidade de Coimbra, Coimbra
Lipovetsky G (2003) L'ère du vide. Gallimard, Paris
Lipovetsky G, Charles S (2004) Os tempos hipermodernos [The hypermodern times] (trans: Vilela M). Barcarolla, São Paulo
Lipovetsky G, Serroy J (2014) O capitalismo estético na era da globalização [The aesthetic capitalism in the age of globalization]. Edições, Lisboa, p 70
Lombardo G (2003) A estética da antiguidade clássica [The aesthetics of the classic antiguity] (trans: Santos IP). Estampa, Lisboa
Malland JS (2012) Tropical spray: viagem ao coração do grafite brasileiro (trans: Régnier BAL, Noronha JMG). Martins Fontes, São Paulo
Mangiameli ACA, Faralli C, Mittica MP (2012) Arte e limiti. La misura del diritto. Aracneeditrice, Roma
Marci T (2012) Prospettiva pittorica e costruzione giuridica. Tangram, Trento
Marcuse H (1998) Comentários para a redefinição do conceito de cultura. In: Cultura e Sociedade [Culture and society] (trans: de Oliveira R). Paz e Terra, São Paulo, pp 153–175
Marcuse H (2007) A dimensão estética [The aesthetic dimension] (trans: Costa ME). Edições, Lisboa, p 70
Martins AL, Barbuy H (1999) Arcadas [Arcades]. Melhoramentos/Alternativa, São Paulo
Mathias R (2016) Antropologia visual [Visual anthropology]. Nova Alexandria, São Paulo
Matos M (Org) Lírica do direito [Liric of law]. Millenium, Migalhas, Campinas
Mazzucco E (2017) Il crimine e l'arte. Tippi, Roma
Melo ER (2004) Nietzsche e a justiça [Nietzsche and justice]. Perspectiva/FAPESP, São Paulo
Meoni ML (2001) Utopia e realtà nel Buongoverno di Ambrogio Lorenzetti. Ifi, Firenze

Molinari D (2010) Victor Hugo: visions graphiques. Paris-Musées, Paris
Moor P (2010) Dynamique du système juridique: une théorie générale du droit. Genève; Bruxelles; Paris: Schulthess; Bruylant; LGDJ
Mounin G (1970) Introduction à la Sémiologie. Minuit, Paris
Nazario L (2005) Quadro histórico do pós-modernismo. In: Guinsburg J, Barbosa AM (eds) O pós-modernismo [Post-modernism]. Perspectiva, São Paulo, pp 23–70
Nesbitt K (org) (2013) Uma nova agenda para a arquitetura: antologia teórica [A new agend to architecture] (trans: Pereira V), 2nd edn. CosacNaify, São Paulo
Netto JTC (1980) Semiótica, informação e comunicação [Semiotics, information and communication]. Perspectiva, São Paulo
Nöth W (2005) A semiótica no século XX [Semiotics in the XX century], 3rd edn. Annablume, São Paulo
Nöth W (2012) Fundamentos semióticos do estudo das imagens [The semiotic fundamentals of the study of images]. Tabuleiro das Letras 05:01–19
Novaes A (org) (2003) O homem-máquina [The man-machine]. Companhia das Letras, São Paulo
Oliveira APP (2016) Da ninguendade à humilhação social [Social humiliation]. Tese de Doutorado. USP, Faculdade de Direito, São Paulo
Ost F (2001) O tempo do Direito [The time of the law] (trans: Oliveira MF). Instituto Piaget, Lisboa
Pais CT. Conceptualisation, information, signification, production du sujet. Acta Semiotica et Linguistica 5:41–60
Panofsky E (2000) Idea (trans: Neves P). Martins Fontes, São Paulo
Panofsky E (2009) Studi di Iconologia. Piccola Einaudi, Torino
Paolucci A (2013) Michelangelo e Raffaello in Vaticano. Giunti Editore, Roma
Pastore JAD (2009) A arte do inconsciente. In: Ciência e Cultura [Science and culture]. SBPC/ FAPESP, São Paulo, pp 20–24
Perissé G (2004) Filosofia, ética e literatura [Philosophy, ethics and literature]. Manole, São Paulo
Pietroforte AV (2016) Análise do texto visual [Analysis of the visual text], 2nd edn. Contexto, São Paulo
Pignatari D (1987) Semiótica e literatura [Semiotics and literature], 3rd edn. Cultrix, São Paulo
Pignatari D (1995) Semiótica da arte e da arquitetura [Semiotics of art and of the architecture]. Cultrix, São Paulo
Pinto VC (2014) Direito urbanístico [Urbanistic law], 4ª. edn. Revista dos Tribunais, São Paulo
Pisani G (2015) I volti segreti di Giotto, 3rd edn. Programma, Bologna
Plaza J (2010) Tradução intersemiótica [Intersemiotics translation]. Perspectiva, São Paulo
Proença G (1990) História da arte [History of art]. Ática, São Paulo
Puls M (2006) Arquitetura e filosofia [Architecture and philosophy]. Annablume, São Paulo
Queirós LM (2018) Uma Universidade que mora em aposentos reais [A university that leaves in a royal place]. https://www.publico.pt/2013/06/22/jornal/uma-universidade-que-mora-em-aposentos-reais-26725680. Accessed 03/09/2018
Radbruch G (1997) Filosofia do Direito [Philosophy of law] (trans: de Moncada LC), 6th edn. Arménio Amado, Coimbra
Rancière J (2009a) O inconsciente estético [The aesthetic unconscious] (trans: Netto MC). Editora, São Paulo, p 34
Rancière J (2009b) A partilha do sensível [Sharing the sensitive] (trans: Netto MC). Eixo Experimental; Editora, São Paulo, p 34
Rancière J (2011) El malestar en la estética (trans: Petrecca MÁ, Vogelfandg L, Burello MG). Buenos Aires, Capital Intelectual
Rancière J (2014) O espectador emancipado [The emancipated viewer] (trans: Benedetti IC). Martins Fontes, São Paulo
Rapoport NB (2013) Analysis and the arts. In: Bankowski Z, Mar MD, Maharg P (eds) The arts and the legal academy. Ashgate, England, pp 101–118
Rastier F (1989) Sens et textualité. Hachette, Paris

Rastier F (2017) De la sémantique structurale à la sémiotique des cultures. Actes Sémiotiques 120:01–13. epublications.unilim.fr. Accessed 06/06/2017

Reale E (1996) A Faculdade de Direito do Largo de São Francisco [The faculty of law of the São Francisco Square]. Ac&M, Rio de Janeiro

Rendon PA (2014) Hacia uma semiótica del arte: implicaciones del pensamento peirceano en el estúdio del arte contemporâneo. Cuadernos de Filosofía Latinoamericana 11:127–145

Resnik J, Curtis D (1987) Images of Justice. Faculty Scholarship Series, Paper 917. http://digitalcommons.law.yale.edu/fss_papers/917. Accessed 07/04/2017

Resnik J, Curtis D (2011) Representing Justice. Yale, New Haven

Ribeiro RJ (org) (2001) Humanidades [Humanities]. EDUSP, São Paulo

Ricoeur P (2008a) O justo 1 [The just 1] (trans: Benedetti IC). Martins Fontes, São Paulo

Ricoeur P (2008b) O justo 2 [The just 2] (trans: Benedetti IC). Martins Fontes, São Paulo

Romano B (2013) Giudizio giuridico e giudizio estetico da Kant verso Schiller. G. Giappichelli Editore, Torino

Rosa H (2015) Social acceleration (trans: Trejo-Mathys J). Columbia, New York

Rossi EA (2007) Palazzo della Ragione a Padova. Skira Editore, Milano

Rouanet SP (1987) As razões do iluminismo [The reasons of enlightenment]. Companhia das Letras, São Paulo

Salazar A (1961) Que é arte? [What is art?], 3rd edn. Arménio Amado, Coimbra

Salgado S (2014) Da minha terra à Terra [From my land to the Earth] (trans: da Rosa Simões J). Paralela, São Paulo

Santaella L (1992) A Assinatura das coisas [The signing of things]. Imago, Rio de Janeiro

Santaella L (2007) Linguagens líquidas na era da mobilidade [Liquid languages of the era of mobility]. Paulus, São Paulo

Santaella L (2016a) Memória e perspectivas da semiótica no Brasil [Memory and perspectives of semiotics in Brazil]. Intexto 37:22–33

Santaella L (2016b) Temas e dilemas do pós-digital [Themes and dilemmas of the post-digital]. Paulus, São Paulo

Santaella L, Nöth W (1998) Imagem [Image]. Iluminuras, São Paulo

Schwarcz LM (2017) Assombrados pela história. In: Bittar ECB (ed) História do Direito Brasileiro [History of Brazilian Law]. Atlas, São Paulo, pp 587–599

Sebeok TA (2001) Signs: an introduction to semiotics, 2nd edn. University of Toronto Press, Toronto

Seligman-Silva M (2012) Imagens do trauma e sobrevivência das imagens: sobre as hiperimagens. In: Cornelsen EL, Vieira EA, Seligman-Silva M (eds) Imagem e memória [Image and memory]. Rona Editora, FALE-Faculdade de Letras da UFMG, Belo Horizonte, pp 63–79

Seligman-Silva M, Cornelsen EL, Vieira EA (orgs) (2012) Imagem e memória [Image and memory]. Rona; FALE-UFMG, Belo Horizonte

Senna C (2012) Cordéis que educam e transformam [Poetry that teaches and transforms]. Global, São Paulo

Smith R (2013) Excelência no ensino da arte. In: Barbosa AM (ed) Arte-educação [Art-education]. Cortez, São Paulo, pp 131–147

Soulages F (2010) Estética da fotografia [The aesthetics of photography]. Tradução de Iraci D. Poleti e Regina Salgado Campos. SENAC, São Paulo

Streck LL, Trindade AK (2013) Direito e literatura [Law and literature]. Atlas, São Paulo

Tanner LE (2006) The jazz images. Abrams, New York

Taylor KF (1999) The Festival of Justice, Paris, (1849). In: Douzinas C, Nead L (eds) Law and the image. The Universtiy of Chicago Press, Chicago, pp 137–177

Teixeira L (2009) Para uma metodologia de análise de textos verbovisuais. In: de Oliveira Lucia Teixeira AC (ed) Linguagens na comunicação [Language in communication]. Estação das Letras e das Cores, São Paulo, pp 41–77

Telles Junior G (1999) A folha dobrada [The folded sheet]. Nova Fronteira, Rio de Janeiro

Terré F (2015) Introduction générale au droit, 10th edn. Dalloz, Paris

Tibbitts F (2002) Understanding what we do: emerging models for human rights education. Int Rev Educ 48:159–171

Tore GM (2011) L'art comme création, ou la règle de nier la règle. Actes Sémiotiques 114:01–11. epublications.unifilm.fr. Accessed 06/06/2017

Tranter K (2017) Seeing law: the comic, icon and the image in law and justice. Int J Semiot Law 2017:01–04. http://link.springer.com/journal. Accessed 03/07/2017

Tuzet G (2014) Contro le immagini. In: Faralli C, Gigliotti V, Heritier P, Mittica MP (eds) Il Diritto tra testo e immagine. Mimesis, Milano, pp 175–188

Veras DT (2010) Homem-tração. In: Bittar ECB, de Melo T (eds) Cidades impossíveis [Impossible cities]. Portal Literatura, São Paulo, p 132

Vespaziani A (2010) Costituzionalità e narratività. In: Faralli C, Mittica MP (eds) Diritto e Letteratura. Aracne Editrice, Roma, pp 123–137

Vidigal A (2017) Faculdade de Direito do Largo de São Francisco: USP 190 Anos [The faculty of law of the São Francisco Square: 190 years]. DBA Editora, São Paulo

Volli U (2015) Manual de Semiótica [Semiotics manual] (trans: Reis SDC), 3rd edn. Loyola, São Paulo

Von Martin A (1998) Sociología del Renacimiento (trans: Pedroso M), 11th edn. Fondo de Cultura Económica, México

Wagner A, Bhatia VK (2009) Diversity and tolerance in social-legal contexts: explorations in the semiotics of law. Ashgate, Burlington

Wagner A, Sherwin RK (eds) (2014) Law, culture and visual studies. Springer, Netherlands

Warat LA (1995) O direito e sua linguagem [Law and its language], 2nd edn. Sergio Antonio Fabris, Porto Alegre

Warat LA (2004a) Literasofia. In: Mezzaroba O, Rover AJ, Junior ADR, Monteiro CS (eds) Territórios desconhecidos [Unknown territories]. Fundação Boiteux, Florianópolis, pp 19–26

Warat LA (2004b) La cinesofia y su lado oscuro. In: Mezzaroba O, Rover AJ, Junior ADR, Monteiro CS (eds) Territórios desconhecidos. Fundação Boiteux, Florianópolis, pp 549–562

Werle MA (2011) A questão do fim da arte em Hegel [The question of the purpose of the art in Hegel]. Hedra, São Paulo

Ziccardi MG (2014) Una giustizia senza benda e senza spada? In: Faralli C, Gigliotti V, Heritier P, Mittica MP (eds) Il Diritto tra testo e immagine. Mimesis, Milano, pp 167–173